New Politics of Decisionism

New Politics of Decisionism

Violeta Beširević (Ed.)

eleven
international publishing

Published, sold and distributed by Eleven International Publishing
P.O. Box 85576
2508 CG The Hague
The Netherlands
Tel.: +31 70 33 070 33
Fax: +31 70 33 070 30
email: sales@elevenpub.nl
www.elevenpub.com

Sold and distributed in USA and Canada
Independent Publishers Group
814 N. Franklin Street
Chicago, IL 60610, USA
Order Placement: +1 800 888 4741
Fax: +1 312 337 5985
orders@ipgbook.com
www.ipgbook.com

Eleven International Publishing is an imprint of Boom uitgevers Den Haag.

ISBN 978-94-6236-897-2
ISBN 978-94-6274-984-9 (e-book)

Table of Contents

1 Introduction

Violeta Beširević[*]

When the President does it, that means that it is not illegal – *Richard Nixon*

If man were angels, no government would be necessary – *James Madison*

1.1 What Brings Schmitt to the Title of the Book

The famous Chantal Mouffe's question "Why should we read Carl Schmitt today?"[1] could be answered in different ways, but the most usual answers would be: (a) to challenge anti-liberalism or discredit liberalism; (b) to oppose/give some content to his claim that the distinction between a friend and an enemy forms the essence of every political idea. Following Mouffe's question, it will be useful to explain why this publication got the Schmittian sort of title.

First, whether one belongs to those who believe that Schmitt's teaching is overrated, or those who never saluted the growing revival of interest in Schmitt, or those who identify with his ideas, one cannot deny that in main details the contemporary politics across the globe all too much reassemble Schmitt's anti-liberalism.

Second, people have always been searching for security. In recent times, global demands for security resulted from several crises in a row, exemplified mostly in the international terrorism on the aggravated scale, the global economic disaster and the 'migration' crisis. In debating crisis management, a clear political split over the issue of how to deal with the crisis, inside or outside the law, soon emerged. In constitutional democracies, possible responses could have been grounded in the rule of law and adherence to 'friendship and hospitality to balance the acts of hostility.'[2] However, the recent political events revived the idea of unlimited power 'to save the existence of the state'.

Arguments of this kind may be found in Carl Schmitt's scholarship in which he closely connected unlimited power with the decision-making (decisionism) in a time of an

* Professor of Law at Union University Law School Belgrade and member of the Board of Directors of the European Public Law Organization.

1 *See* C. Mouffe, 'Introduction: Schmitt's Challenge', *in* C. Mouffe (Ed.), *The Challenge of Carl Schmitt*, Verso, London, New York, 1999, p. 1.

2 N. Ben-Asher, 'Legalism and Decisionism in Crisis', *Ohio State Law Journal*, Vol. 71, No. 4, 2010, p. 757.

exceptional crisis.[3] To a large extent, Schmitt's points on decisionism enlighten the title of this volume, although its central, underlying idea runs afoul of populism and available strategies to respond to it.

To explain the new politics of decisionism one should illuminate the idea of decisionism in the first place.

1.1.1 *Schmitt's Decisionism (the Theory of Sovereignty)*

What Schmitt had argued during the Weimar crisis could be, in a nutshell, reduced to the following: the responses to the crisis endangering the very existence of a (liberal) state had to be based on democracy but not on the rule of law. Consider the following.

According to Schmitt, the state of emergency required suspension of the general legal order because of its exceptional nature that could not be dealt with in general legal norms, since law could not anticipate in advance all situations in which it would be required to preserve the state:

> [b]ecause a general norm, as represented by an ordinary legal prescription, can never encompass a total exception, the decision that a real exception exists cannot therefore be entirely derived from this norm.[4]

As the state of the exception must be governed and the general legal order is suspended, who then decides that 'real exception exists'? Here, Schmitt replaces the law with the authority of competence and famously argued that "[s]overeign is he who decides on the exception".[5]

If the sovereignty derives from the authority, and not from a general norm, someone has to decide how to apply the legal norm. According to Schmitt, crisis management and the preservation of state require personal judgment:

> The most guidance the constitution can provide is to indicate who can act in such a case. If such action is not subject to controls, if it is not hampered in some way by checks and balances, as is the case in a liberal constitution, then it is clear who the sovereign is. He decides whether there is an extreme emergency as well as what must be done to eliminate it. Although he stands outside

3 Schmitt developed his theory of decisionism in C. Schmitt, *Political Theology: Four Chapters on the Concept of Sovereignty* [1922], trans. G. Schwab, The MIT Press, Cambridge/MA, 1985.

4 *Id.*, p. 6.

5 *Id.*, p. 5.

> the normally valid legal system, he nevertheless belongs to it, for it is he who must decide whether the constitution needs to be suspended in its entirety.[6]

In other words, when the survival of a state is at stake, the constitution based on the limited government is of little help because a liberal constitution, with its system of checks and balances can limit a manoeuvring place to adopt the necessary measures to preserve the state. Instead, the decision which measures to adopt requires unlimited power.[7]

Accordingly, Schmitt's decisionism (the theory of sovereignty) "implies a subject who makes the decision and content of a decision".[8] For Schmitt, these two components are not of equal weight, however. The main question in the state of the exception is who is to decide ("[w]hat matters for the reality of legal life is who decides"[9]) and not whether the content of that decision corresponds to the legal norm, because "whether the extreme exception can be banished from the world is not a juristic question".[10] Simply put, everything depends on who decides. Schmitt had articulated decision-making power, made a connection with the representation and vested the power at the executive:

> The President, by contrast [to the parliament] has the confidence of entire people not mediated by the medium of a parliament splintered into parties. This confidence, rather, is directly united in his person.[11]

Now, Schmitt links decisionism with his definition of the political. According to him, "the concept of the state presupposes the concept of the political".[12] Because the sovereignty implies a decision on whether the extreme situation exists and whether exceptional state action is required, a state of emergency involves also making a basic decision on who is an enemy and who is a friend of the state. Therefore, every political idea "can be reduced to the distinction between friend and [public] enemy".[13] In the absence of the public enemy,

---

6 *Id.*, p. 7.

7 For a detailed explanation on this point, *see* R. Howse, 'From Legitimacy to Dictatorship – and Back Again: Leo Strauss's Critique of the Anti-Liberalism of Carl Schmitt', *Canadian Journal of Law & Jurisprudence*, Vol. 10, No. 1, 1999, p. 1.

8 M. Hoelzl, 'Ethics of Decisionism: Carl Schmitt's Theological Blind Spot', *Journal for Cultural Research*, Vol. 20, No. 3, 2016, p. 238.

9 Schmitt, 1922 (trans. Schwab, 1985), p. 34.

10 *Id.*, p. 7.

11 C. Schmitt, *Constitutional Theory* [1928], trans. J. Seitzer, Duke University Press, Durham and London, 2008, p. 370.

12 C. Schmitt, *The Concept of Political* [1932], trans. G. Schwab, University of Chicago Press, Chicago, 2007, p. 19.

13 *Id.*, p. 26. Note that Schmitt made a distinction between private and public enemies on religious grounds, and did not consider private enemies to be a treat for the state.

the political and the state would cease to exist. Consequently, Schmitt welcomes a state action against the political–public enemy.

Finally, in the sphere of politics, Schmitt makes no room for parliamentarism because a distinction between a friend and an enemy requires decisionism based on personal judgment, not a deliberation. For Schmitt, decisionism is based on democracy which he does not equate with parliamentarism: "The belief in parliamentarism, in government by discussion, belongs to the intellectual world of liberalism. It does not belong to democracy."[14] What is, then, democracy according to Schmitt?

> Every actual democracy rests on the principle that not only are equals equal but unequals will not be treated equally. Democracy requires, therefore, first *homogeneity* and second – if the need arises – *elimination or eradication of heterogeneity* [...] A democracy demonstrates its political power by knowing how to refuse or keep at bay something foreign and unequal that threatens its homogeneity.[15]

In Schmitt's version of illiberal democracy, the most important political decision to be made is that of who is an enemy of the state. Consequently, no room for cherishing individual freedoms and the liberal equality exists.[16] This does not follow only from his belief that when a state is in a great peril, individuals and institutions protecting them are to be set aside because the most significant threat is the threat to nation and its way of life.[17] It also follows from the fact that he does not consider the equality of all persons to be grounded in democracy but in liberalism,[18] against whose principles he advocated passionately.

If the state of peril requires a sovereign who will decide what national interest is and what measures are necessary to protect it, then, at this point, democracy comes closer to dictatorship.[19] However, in Schmitt's view, "[...]dictatorship is not antithetical to democracy".[20] What justifies dictatorship in the time of crisis still appeals to democracy and the will of people: "Even during a transitional period dominated by the dictator, a democratic identity can still exist and the will of the people can still be the exclusive criterion."[21] As Tom Sorell explained:

14 C. Schmitt, *The Crisis of Parliamentary Democracy* [1923], trans. E. Kennedy, The MIT Press, Cambridge/MA, 2000, p. 8.
15 *Id.*, p. 9. (emphasis added).
16 For more details, on Schmittian equality *see* Schmitt, 1928 (trans. J. Seitzer, 2008), pp. 257-264.
17 For more details, *see* Tom Sorell, 'Schmitt, Hobbes and the Politics of Emergency', *Filozofski vestnik*, Vol. 24, No. 2, 2003, p. 228.
18 Schmitt, 1923 (trans. Kennedy, 2000), p. 13.
19 For his view on dictatorship *see* C. Schmitt, *Dictatorship. From the Origin of the Modern Concept of Sovereignty to the Proletarian Class Struggle*, trans. M. Hoelzl and G. Ward, Polity Press, Cambridge, 2014.
20 Schmitt, 1923 (trans. Kennedy, 2000), p. 28.
21 *Id.*

> There is no organizing the state so as to eliminate completely any need for a dictator, and a national democracy may not have much chance of survival if its head of state cannot in some circumstances take on the role of dictator – the role of someone who declares an emergency and then uses personal judgment to eliminate it. A state with no potential to be led by a dictator, with no potential for an authoritative identification of the enemy would be, in Schmitt's terms, radically depoliticized [...].[22]

Many have explained why Schmitt was wrong.[23] However, to deal with Schmitt's substantial flaws is not within the purpose of this Introduction.[24] Instead, his teaching here serves to enlighten the present politics of decisionism.

1.1.2 New Politics of Decisionism

Before I transpose Schmitt's argumentation in the contemporary politics, it is worth repeating the basic tenets of his theory on decisionism: in the time of extreme crisis, where the existence of a (liberal) state is in peril, decision-making on whether a state of crisis exists, who is an enemy and how to preserve the state and its way of living, cannot be based on deliberation and the rule of law but on a personal judgment made by one who decides that the state of exception exists; a power to decide on these issues should be vested in the executive and should be unlimited because what matters in the time of crisis is a decision in favour of people as a whole, not individual freedom; therefore, only upon personal judgment of the head of the executive necessary measures to defend the interest of people can save the state and restore legal order.[25]

Schmitt's points on decisionism have considerable advantage in understanding the attacks on constitutional democracies today. Looked at in this way, it is easy to document

22 Sorell, 2003, p. 229. For a different reading of Schmitt's concept of dictatorship, *see* A. Kalyvas, *Democracy and the Politics of the Extraordinary. Max Weber, Carl Schmitt, and Hannah Arendt*, Cambridge University Press, Cambridge, 2008.

23 *See, e.g.*, S. Holmes, *The Anatomy of Antiliberalism*, Harvard University Press, Cambridge/MA, 1996, pp. 37-60; L. Vinx (Ed.), *The Guardian of the Constitution. Hans Kelsen and Carl Schmitt on the Limits of Constitutional Law*, Cambridge University Press, Cambridge, 2015; W. Scheuerman, *Carl Schmitt. The End of Law*, Rowman & Littlefield, Lanham, 1999; D. Dyzenhaus (Ed.), *Law as Politics. Carl Schmitt's Critique of Liberalism*, Duke University Press, Durham, 1998; a special issue on Carl Schmitt in *Cardozo Law Review*, Vol. 21, No. 5-6, 2000.

24 For an extended discussion on Schmitt *see, e.g.*, Holmes, 1996; Mouffe, 1998; D. Dyzenhaus, *Legality and Legitimacy. Carl Schmitt, Hans Kelsen and Hermann Heller in Weimar*, Oxford University Press, Oxford, 1997; J. W. Müller, *A Dangerous Mind. Carl Schmitt in Post-War European Thought*, Yale University Press, New Haven, 2003; D. Dyzenhaus (Ed.), 1998; S. Legg (Ed.), *Spatiality, Sovereignty and Carl Schmitt. Geographies of the Nomos*, Routledge, Abingdon, 2011; J. Tralau (Ed.), *Thomas Hobbes and Carl Schmitt. The Politics of Order and Myth*, Routledge, Abingdon, 2011.

25 For the summary of Schmitt's decisionism *see also* Hoelzl, 2016, pp. 236-238.

that everything in the politics undertaken 'to protect state and our way of living' in 'war against terrorism', financial meltdown across the globe and specifically in 'migration' crisis 'depended on who decided'.

First, in a growing number of states there is a claim "that politics should follow general will of the people"[26] or, better said, 'real/ordinary/authentic people', who should be defended from the enemy, discernible not anymore along traditional historical lines that divided different nations, but along present threats to 'silent majority' in a giving country, being that immigrants, Islam, the European Union, the corrupted politicians, the feminists, George Soros, migrant workers, LGBT population or all of them together.

Second, we have been witnessing the perception that in the presence of the enemy (terrorists, immigrants, *etc.*), constitutional democracy – based on a limited government – no longer suffices because it does not favour homogeneity but diversity, not national interests but rights, not exclusion but inclusion, not unlimited executive term in office but executive term limits,[27] all that prevents successful defence against an enemy. Moreover, the technology revolution that went global significantly contributed to the production of imaginary threats/enemies and made the attacks on liberalism/constitutionalism hostile than ever before. The principles of constitutionalism are often declared unsustainable because they deprive authentic people of security, while the idea of identity politics, which insists on the unity of the nation to defeat the enemy, is on the rise.

Third, this new politics of decisionism, exemplified, for example, in the ruling power of Trump, Orbán, Erdoğan, Polish PiS or the Brexitians, do not discard democracy as a rule of majority – it discards representative/parliamentary democracy and party politics (pluralism) and, as best captured by Nadia Urbinati, "makes democracy an extreme majoritarianism" in order to justify "a discriminatory use of the state power against the minority".[28] In many jurisdictions across the globe, in traditional and new democracies alike, the growing personification of everyday politics, justified by a different 'state of exception', forced a liberal representative politics to retreat.[29] Accordingly, there is an ongoing trend to exclude the rule of law component from democracy and reduce it to the plebiscite elections, which was Schmitt's discourse, as well.

26 C. Mudde, 'Populism: An Ideational Approach', *in* C. R. Kaltwasser *et al.* (Eds.), *The Oxford Handbook of Populism*, Oxford University Press, Oxford, 2017, p. 33.

27 For term limits manipulation, *see* D. Landau, 'Term Limits Manipulation across Latin America – and what Constitutional Design Could Do about It', *Consitutionnet*, 21 July 2015, www.constitutionnet.org/news/term-limits-manipulation-across-latin-america-and-what-constitutional-design-could-do-about-it.

28 N. Urbinati, 'Populism and the Majority Principle', *in* Kaltwasser *et al.* (Eds.), *The Oxford Handbook of Populism*, Oxford University Press, Oxford, 2017, p. 585.

29 For a development in Eastern Europe, *see* I. Krastev & S. Holmes, 'Explaining Eastern Europe', *Journal of Democracy*, Vol. 39, No. 3, 2018, pp. 117-128. For developments in other regions, *see* Kaltwasser *et al.*, 2017, pp. 101-263.

There is a vivid tendency to name this new wave of politics – *populism* – and the populist politics undertaken to discredit constitutionalism and entrench "a new set of rules for the political game" (Müller) – *populist constitutionalism*.[30] Nevertheless, Isaiah Berlin's claim that the concept of populism suffers from Cinderella complex – "there is a shoe [the word 'populism'] but not a foot"[31] [a definition] – continues to be on the table. Questions like *what is populism* – ideology, movement, political discourse to mobilize 'the people' demagoguery or something else, *whether populism actually exists* and *how to respond to populist politics* still beg for 'true answers'.

This volume joins an opened, but not yet closed discussion on the current global political phenomena commonly termed 'populism'.

1.2 Outline of the Volume

The volume came as a follow-up to the conference organized in November 2017 under the same title at the University of Belgrade, School of Political Science and School of Law. The volume is organized into three parts.

Since the scholarship on populism is still maturing, many contributions in this volume begin with the definitional and conceptual approach with an aim to resolve the 'Cinderella' issue. However, Part I – *The Current Rise of Populism: Deconstructing Issu*es – specifically focuses on definitional and conceptual issues and sheds some new light on the causes that brought contemporary democracy in crisis. This part is opened by Samuel Issacharoff's contribution *Democracy's Deficits* in which he considers four central institutional challenges to democracy: the accelerated decline of political parties and other institutional forms of popular engagement; the paralysis of the legislative branches; the loss of the sense of social cohesion; and the decline in state competence. Although he offers a sombre picture, Issacharoff finishes his chapter in an optimistic tone, built equally on the trust in internal democratic resources, including civil society, the courts and the rule of law principles, and the manifested inability of populist regimes to achieve deliverance.

The next two chapters aim at deconstructing the notion and the concept of populism. In his chapter *Populism – A Notion Rising above Its Content*, Tibor Várady traces the notion of populism through court jurisprudence and public discourse. While he believes that there is a rational reason to be afraid of present politics labelled as populist, Várady, at the same time, warns that it is still debatable whether the present use and overuse of the notion

30 For an influential definition on populism *see* Mudde, 2017, and J. W. Müller, *What is Populism?*, University of Pennsylvania Press, Philadelphia, 2016. Müller also explains the concept of populist constitutionalism in J. W. Müller, '*Populist Constitutions – A Contradiction in Terms?*', *VerfBlog*, 23 April 2017, https://verfassungsblog.de/populist-constitutions-a-contradiction-in-terms.

31 I. Berlin, 'To Define Populism', *The Isaiah Berlin Virtual Library*, 14 October 2013, http://berlin.wolf.ox.ac.uk/lists/bibliography/bib111bLSE.pdf, p. 6, para. 139.

'populism' describe the core of the problem, whether an opposite concept has been made clearly distinguishable and whether the notion of populism reflects a clear content that could serve as a starting point in seeking remedy.

David Rasmussen in the chapter entitled *Reflections on the Nature of Populism and the Fragility of Democracy: Democracy in Crisis* opens discussion on populism by considering the concept of the political defined by John Rawls. In the rest of the chapter Rasmussen offers a historical and a normative perspective of populism and joins the ongoing discussion on the relationship between populism and democracy, aware of the fact that even though the populist form is pre-democratic, it is a part of the current political paradigm that still needs an adequate response.

Nenad Miščević closes Part I with his contribution *Populism and Nationalism*, in which he explores the relationship between populism and nationalism, closely tied, both conceptually and empirically. The first part of the chapter is dedicated to forms of interaction between populism and nationalism, both at the level of concepts (what kind of nationalism is compatible with what kind of populism) and at the level of actual historical causal interaction. To illustrate a discussion, in the second part Miščević offers a case study devoted to Croatia and shows why the actual government in Croatia is not a loud national populist one, although it has all preconditions to satisfy the elements of the populist rule.

The second part of the volume, *Comparative Populism: Case Studies*, considers populism in comparative perspective, on the basis of several jurisdictions including Hungary, Israel and Serbia.

András Bozóki opens Part II with his discussion on Hungary, often quoted as an example of textbook populism. In the chapter *Beyond Illiberal Democracy: The Case of Hungary*, Bozóki demystifies the notion of illiberal democracy, the label frequently used by Victor Orbán (not without pride) to describe the nature of his rule. Bozóki shows why illiberal democracy is not a democracy, but fluid and relatively less authoritarian and less violent regime type among the hybrid regimes. By describing the Orbán regime as a hybrid regime with mafia state structure, unorthodox economic policy that serves social inequality, ethno-nationalism and re-feudalization, Bozóki demonstrates that populism and illiberalism slide towards authoritarianism, but that in the case of Hungary, the international embeddedness of the regime (the membership in the EU) hinders or makes the slide slower.

In his focus on the populist impulse in Israel, Adam Sinhar, in the chapter *Populism, Free Speech, and Anti-Entrenchment Principle*, develops the anti-entrenchment principle as a possible response to populist tendency to silence a critical minority. To limit the policy of so-called 'freedom of finance', used by the Israeli government to censor opinions and activities not compatible with its views, Sinhar suggests borrowing the anti-entrenchment principle from election law. He argues that this strategy will make government under a constitutional duty to support the very messages that resist the policies it wishes to promote.

Part III continues by focusing on Serbia, less often debated in the scholarship of populism. This gap is filled by the contribution of Dušan Spasojević. In the chapter entitled *Transforming Populism – From Protest Vote to Ruling Ideology: The Case of Serbia*, he captures the preconditions for populism to grow from a set of ideas (Mudde) to an ideology, by presenting ideological transformation of the ruling SNS party from radical, populist and nationalistic party without any governing potential towards the ruling, predominant, pro-EU, centre-right populist party. Spasojević shows that the ideological shift of SNS can also be understood as a departure from the old-style populism that was ideologically more defined and 'thicker', towards the contemporary, more acceptable and adaptable 'thinner' version.

Case studies from Poland, Turkey, Romania and Serbia, offered in Part III, *Courts under the Populist Challenge*, serve to discuss a general issue of the relationship between the courts and populism. Attacks on the judiciary in Poland, which have amounted to a paradigmatic case of the populist challenge to constitutional democracy, are briefed and explained by Marcin Matczak in his contribution *Poland: From Paradigm to Pariah? Facts and Interpretations of Polish Constitutional Crisis*. Matczak explores historical, legal and sociological causes of the populist attacks on the Constitutional Tribunal, the National Council of Judiciary and the Supreme Court. Looked at in this way, he argues that the neglected social frustrations in transition, a formalistic approach to the rule of law and emerging social narratives on liberal values, contributed to a backsliding of Poland into authoritarianism.

In her contribution *Populism and the Turkish Constitutional Court: From a Game Broker to a Strategic Compromiser*, Bertil Emrah Oder explains an ambivalent approach of the Constitutional Court towards the strong populist rule in today's Turkey. Although it was once known as a decisive defender of the secularist Turkey, in the context of a strong presidency and the populist pressure, the Court took a rather strategist approach. Relying on the Court's recent case law, Oder shows that under the populist pressure, the Court has preferred not to clash with presidential preferences and the parliament in exercising an abstract or a concrete constitutional review, but, at the same time it refrained from supporting these institutions in a constitutional complaint procedure.

The central issue addressed by Simona Tanasescu in her contribution *Romania: From Constitutional Democracy to Constitutional Decay?* is judicial populism, exemplified in the case of the Romanian Constitutional Court. After providing general points on constitutional democracy under stress, she scrutinizes the politics of the Constitutional Court in cases involving fundamental freedoms and the separation of powers principle. Tanasescu concludes that through a constant validation of a systematic weakening of checks and balances, the Constitutional Court is contributing to the ongoing decay of constitutional democracy in Romania.

A similar conclusion, but for different reasons, reaches Violeta Beširević in her contribution that closes Part III and the volume. In the chapter *If Schmitt Were Alive…Adjusting Constitutional Review to the Populist Rule in Serbia*, Beširević aims to advance a general question of whether the courts, in particular, constitutional courts, can confront the politics of populism. She shows that the management of the state of emergency, reflected mostly in Kosovo's unilateral declaration of independence, the financial crisis and high-profile corruption cases, amounted to the reaffirmation of 'primacy of the Political' in the Serbian sense of Schmitt. Beširević argues that in transitional Serbia, a constitutional review had been discouragingly irrelevant in the struggle for consolidation of democracy. By focusing attention on the Court's decisions delivered within the mandate of the ruling populists, she concludes that a constitutional review is not an available strategy in Serbia to confront the populist regime, either.

Part I
The Current Rise of Populism: Deconstructing Issues

2 Democracy's Deficits

*Samuel Issacharoff**

2.1 Introduction

History confounds certainty. Barely a quarter century after the collapse of the Soviet empire, it is democracy that has entered an intense period of public scrutiny. The election of President Trump and the Brexit vote are dramatic moments in a populist uprising against the post-war political consensus of liberal rule. But they are also signposts in a process long in the making, yet perhaps not fully appreciated until the intense electoral upheavals of recent years. A percentage or two change in the Brexit vote, or a few tens of thousands of votes cast differently in a few key states in the United States, would certainly have postponed the confrontation but would not have altered the fundamental concerns. With the realignment of the Dutch and French elections, the emergence of a hard-right populism in Hungary and Poland, and the mushrooming of anti-governance alliances in Italy and Spain, deeper questions must be asked about the state of democracy. Italy may have had 44 governments in a 50-year span, but power rotated among a familiar array of parties, personalities and policies – until now.

At issue across the nuances of the national settings is a deep challenge to the core claim of democracy to be the superior form of political organization of civilized peoples. It is odd, and highly dispiriting, to have to engage this question so soon after democracy seemed ascendant as never before. With the collapse of the Soviet Union and its empire, the twentieth century concluded with democracy having defeated its two great authoritarian rivals, and the popular election of governments spread across a greater swath of the Earth than ever before. Francis Fukuyama's embellished claim that the end of history was upon us[1] accurately captured the sense that electoral democracy alone seemed to lay claim to political legitimacy.[2] Further, the opening to democracy invited economic liberalization,

---

* Bonnie and Richard Reiss Professor of Constitutional Law, New York University School of Law. This chapter was previously published in *The University of Chicago Law Review*, Vol. 85, No. 2, 2018, pp. 485-519. My deep appreciation to Gregory Crane and Stephen Levandowski for their research assistance.

1 *See* F. Fukuyama, 'The End of History?', *The National Interest*, Summer 1989, pp. 3-4. ("What we may be witnessing is not just the end of the Cold War, [...] but the end of history as such: that is, the end point of mankind's ideological evolution and the universalization of Western liberal democracy as the final form of human government.")

2 At the peak of the democratic wave, in 2000, Freedom House listed 120 countries, 63% of all nations, as meeting the baseline criteria for democratic governance. Freedom House, *Freedom in the World 2000*,

and the resulting market exchanges were allowing huge masses to rise from poverty, even in hold-out autocratic states like China or Vietnam.

Clearly the era of democratic euphoria has ended. The rise of Islamic terrorism and the failure of the Arab Spring were certainly warning shots, but grave as these might be, they did not challenge the core of democratic government. The inevitable trade-off between security and liberty that accompanies external threats to democratic regimes is a serious challenge and can itself compromise core legitimacy. But democracies that withstood what Philip Bobbitt terms the long wars of the twentieth century[3] were unlikely to come undone in the face of enemies who sought to target civilians, but were in no position to pose a sustained military threat of any kind. Even the problematic military engagements in Afghanistan or Iraq bitterly divided democratic societies but did not threaten an epochal confrontation with democracy itself.

Instead, the current moment of democratic uncertainty draws from four central institutional challenges, each one a compromise of how democracy was consolidated over the past few centuries. The four I wish to address are: first, the accelerated decline of political parties and other institutional forms of popular engagement; second, the paralysis of the legislative branches; third, the loss of a sense of social cohesion; and fourth, the decline in state competence. While there are no doubt other candidates for inducing anxiety over the state of democracy, these four have a particular salience in theories of democratic superiority that make their decline or loss a matter of grave concern. Among the great defences of democracy stand the claims that democracies offer the superior form of participation, of deliberation, of solidarity and of the capacity to get the job done. We need not arbitrate among the theories of participatory democracy, deliberative democracy, solidaristic democracy or epistemic democratic superiority. Rather, we should note with concern that each of these theories states a claim for the advantages of democracy, and each faces worrisome disrepair.

https://freedomhouse.org/report/freedom-world/freedom-world-2000. ("[E]lectoral democracies constitute 120 of the 192 internationally recognized independent polities.")

3 P. Bobbitt, *The Shield of Achilles: War, Peace, and the Course of History*, Anchor Books, New York, 2003, pp. xxi-xxii. ("This war [...] began in 1914 and only ended in 1990. The Long War, like previous epochal wars, brought into being a new form of the State – the market-state.").

2.2 PARTICIPATION: FAILING POLITICAL PARTIES

Political parties created democracy and modern democracy is unthinkable save in terms of the parties.[4]

Parties [are] the distinctive, defining voluntary associations of representative democracy.[5]

One indicator of the age of the American constitution is the absence of any role for political parties, by contrast to Article 21 of the German Constitution, for example. The Framers of the Constitution equated parties with factions and aimed for a form of democratic politics that would rise above sectional concerns, immediate gratification of wants and the risk of succumbing to the passions of greed and envy. Until the twentieth century, political parties were not granted constitutional recognition – indeed, the first nineteenth-century constitution that addressed the status of political parties was that of Colombia in 1886, and there in order to ban parties. By contrast, the constitutions of the twentieth century privilege political parties as the galvanizing force of democratic politics.[6]

As experience in electoral self-government grew, democrats throughout the world learned that parties provide a forum for the integration of the different interests that must coalesce for successful policy making, more so in first-past-the-post elections than in proportional representation systems. Even in parliamentary systems, some aggregation is necessary to draw sufficient attention to the party platform and to make the party a desirable suitor in forming a governing coalition. But mostly parties were the institutional mechanism for translating interests and ideology into governance. Politics is the art of the possible, even if what is possible and necessary at any particular moment fails to inspire. Without parties, responsible and productive governance rested on the happenstance of enlightened leaders, rather than an institutionalized mechanism for taking hard decisions, cutting deals, accepting short-term costs for longer-term gain and all the mechanisms that define wise stewardship.

In the United States, parties served as the political expression of the spirit of voluntary associations critical to the young Republic. As Alexis de Tocqueville noted,

---

4 E. E. Schattschneider, *Party Government*, Farrar & Rinehart, New York, 1942, p. 1.

5 N. Rosenblum, *On the Side of the Angels: An Appreciation of Parties and Partisanship*, Princeton University Press, Princeton, 2008, p. 459.

6 *See* T. Ginsburg, 'Constitutions as Political Institutions', *in* J. Gandhi & R. Ruiz-Rufino (Eds.), *Routledge Handbook of Comparative Political Institutions*, Routledge, London and New York, 2015, p. 101, p. 106. ("In our work on the Comparative Constitutions Project, [Zachary] Elkins, [James] Melton, and I identify certain core provisions to written constitutions [...] In the nineteenth century [...] few constitutions mentioned political parties, while most written in the twentieth century do so.").

> Americans of all ages, all conditions, and all dispositions, constantly form associations [...]. Wherever, at the head of some new undertaking, you see the government in France, or a man of rank in England, in the United States you will be sure to find an association.[7]

By the time Tocqueville came to America, political parties were emerging as among the most salient of these associations. They provided the organizational resources for political campaigns, selected candidates, coordinated platforms and disseminated information about politics.[8] In exchange, parties dispensed patronage and access to power, the glue that held the activist wings of the party in check and that allowed a coordinating discipline to be imposed on the party's elected representatives. As I have written elsewhere, the organizational fabric of parties came undone in the United States in the late twentieth century, partially as a result of legal reforms that left significant aspects of party governance outside the control of party leaders[9] and partially through external factors such as the rise of low-cost social media and the mechanisms of direct access to funding and the party constituency.

Examined globally, the American experience of tottering political parties appears emblematic rather than exceptional. The result in country after country is the dissolution of the discipline of political parties in favour of a politics of free agency formed largely around the persona of individuals or momentary issues, devoid of a sustaining institutional presence. In the American context, Richard Pildes describes this central feature of contemporary politics as the process of political fragmentation:

> the external diffusion of political power away from the political parties as a whole and the internal diffusion of power away from the party leadership to individual party members and officeholders.[10]

But the breaking-up of central institutions extends far beyond the domain of politics – the economic conglomerates of yesteryear such as ITT and Gulf & Western were long since dismantled in favour of independent specialized units. In the political domain, fragmentation is a fact of life in all democratic countries, meaning that attempts to find the causal roots at the national level will necessarily be incomplete. The process of what is termed

---

7 A. Tocqueville, *Democracy in America* [1840], trans. Henry Reeve, The Floating Press, Auckland, 2009, p. 979.

8 V. O. Key, Jr., *Politics, Parties and Pressure Groups*, Thomas Y. Crowell Company, New York, 1942.

9 S. Issacharoff, 'Outsourcing Politics: The Hostile Takeover of Our Hollowed-Out Political Parties', *Houston Law Review*, Vol. 54, No. 4, 2017, pp. 845-880.

10 *See* R. H. Pildes, 'Romanticizing Democracy, Political Fragmentation, and the Decline of American Government', *Yale Law Journal*, Vol. 124, No. 3, 2014, p. 809.

'fissuring' in labour economics[11] reflects the broad destabilization of large integrated organizations in the face of technological change, ease of communication, globalization and other pressures on previous advantages of scale. Whether across supply markets or in the domain of politics, ease of communication and transportation puts pressure on broad horizontal organizations whose prime advantage was access to markets, economic or political.

As parties fragment, a spiral ensues. Targeting specific groups of voters, activists and donors requires more focused and generally more extreme messages. Broad-tent parties become an impediment to a new form of politics that channels passion rather than rewarding the necessarily limited returns from governance. More broadly, the disengagement from the parties leads to what Emanuel Towfigh terms the 'party paradox' in which parties, though necessary to democratic functioning, become a contributing source of disenchantment with the political process: "This paradox of representation may reduce the acceptance of political decisions by the electorate and contribute to the overall disillusion with democracy."[12]

Weakened political parties do not have the institutional fortitude to withstand hostile challenges from outsiders, as evident in the United States where Donald Trump and Bernie Sanders (the former a marginal affiliate of the Republicans; the latter not even a member of the Democratic Party) were able to displace established party figures and, in the case of President Trump, walk away with the party endorsement and ultimately the presidency. In place of programs and governance, candidacies are now centred on individuals and elections are framed as a referendum on the leadership of that individual. Even in Germany, the country that has best resisted the assault on democratic institutions, there is a noted increase in the personalization of the campaigns of Chancellor Angela Merkel.[13] Candidate-driven elections are increasingly the norm in Europe as parties that emerged from the capacity to gain parliamentary representation are no longer needed as an electoral platform.[14] Even the desultory elections for the European Parliament witnessed an effort to

---

11 D. Weil, *The Fissured Workplace: Why Work Became So Bad for So Many and What Can Be Done to Improve It*, Harvard University Press, Cambridge/MA, 2014.

12 E. Towfigh *et al.*, 'Do direct-democratic procedures lead to higher acceptance than political representation?: Experimental survey evidence from Germany', *Public Choice*, Vol. 167, No. 1-2, 2016, p. 47.

13 H. Schoen & R. Greszki, 'Third Term for a Popular Chancellor: An Analysis of Voting Behavior in the 2013 German Federal Election', *German Politics*, Vol. 23, No. 4, 2014, pp. 251-267. ("In the 2013 German federal election, the trend towards increased electoral volatility and fragmentation continued. [...] [I]n the 2009 election the conservative CDU/CSU fought a personalized campaign in which it aimed successfully to capitalize on Merkel's increased popularity. In the 2013 election, the CDU/CSU campaign was, once again, focused on Chancellor Merkel, who was now the unchallenged leader of her party.")

14 C. J. Bickerton & C. I. Accetti, 'Democracy Without Parties? Italy After Berlusconi', *The Political Quarterly*, Vol. 85, No. 1, 2014, pp. 23-28 (describing fragmentation across the spectrum of Italian politics); M. Buhlmann, D. Zumbach & M. Gerber, 'Campaign Strategies in the 2015 Swiss National Elections: Nationalization, Coordination, and Personalization', *Swiss Political Science Review*, Vol. 22, No. 1, pp. 15-

attract personalities to the candidate roster in a vain attempt to boost voter turnout.[15] Direct candidate appeal to voters goes hand-in-hand with the documented fragmentation of political parties in, among other places, Bolivia, Bulgaria, Denmark, Ecuador, Finland, France, Guatemala, India, Israel, Italy, Netherlands and Thailand.[16]

In this sense, the desperate gambit of Prime Minister David Cameron to seek to solidify his political base by appealing to plebiscitary alternatives to parliament emerges from the failure of political discipline in the legislative setting. It well follows the pattern in the Europe Union of seeking to alter its perceived democratic deficit through greater use of referenda and other tools of direct democracy.[17] Put less delicately, Nigel Farage, the leader of the UK Independence Party (UKIP), touted the Brexit vote as the story of the British people telling the political elite to stick it.

> It is, after all, rather extraordinary that over half the voting population defied a large majority of its own elected parliament, all of the traditional political parties, and virtually every important institution in the country – from the Central Bank, to the leaders of industry, to the trade unions.[18]

Nor did the Brexit fiasco prevent embattled Italian Prime Minister Matteo Renzi from turning to a constitutional referendum to shore up his government in 2016, with the same disastrous results.[19] Just as critical is the disenchantment with political parties and parliamentary weakness that gave rise to Brexit in the first place: "[T]ensions have grown in most Western nations between the existing processes of representative democracy and calls by reformists for a more participatory style of democratic government."[20]

---

28. ("[A]lthough national campaign coordination exists, Swiss elections are to a considerable extent still cantonal and personal affairs.").

15 *See, e.g.*, H. Schmitt, S. Hobolt & S. A. Popa, 'Does Personalization Increase Turnout? Spitzenkandidaten in the 2014 European Parliament Elections', *European Union Politics*, Vol. 16, No. 3, 2015, pp. 347-368 ("The 2014 European Parliament elections were the first elections where the major political groups each nominated a lead candidate (Spitzenkandidat) for the Commission presidency in the hope that this would increase the visibility of the elections and mobilize more citizens to turn out [...].")

16 P. Melo, 'How Many Political Parties Should Brazil Have? A Data-Driven Method to Assess and Reduce Fragmentation in Multi-Party Political Systems', *PLOS ONE*, Vol. 10, No. 10, 2015, p. 2 citing C. Anckar, 'Size and Party System Fragmentation', *Party Politics*, Vol. 6., No. 3, 2000, pp. 305-328.

17 A. Auer, 'European Citizens' Initiative: Article I-46.4 Draft Convention', *European Constitutional Law Review*, Vol. 1, No. 1, 2005, pp. 79-86.

18 J. Shapiro, 'Brexit was a rejection of Britain's governing elite. Too bad the elites were right', *Vox*, 25 June 2016, www.vox.com/2016/6/25/12023532/brexit-rejection-britains-governing-elite.

19 *See* J. Horowitz, 'Italy's Premier, Matteo Renzi, Says He'll Resign After Reform is Rejected', *The New York Times*, 4 December 2016, https://nyti.ms/2k5yVgh ("Prime Minister Matteo Renzi said he would resign after voters decisively rejected constitutional changes.").

20 R. J. Dalton, W. Bürklin & A. Drummond, 'Public Opinion and Direct Democracy', *Journal of Democracy*, Vol. 12, No. 4, 2001, p. 141.

If Brexit highlights the perceived weakness of political parties as coordinators of democratic politics, it begs the question of the root cause of that weakness. In substantial part, the weakness follows from the simple fact that the parties cannot claim to speak for much of a constituency. In other words, they have significantly lost their participatory quality.

In the 1950s, 20% of Britons were members of political parties; today that figure is about 1%.[21] According to the yearly Pew Foundation studies of American political behaviour, party identification in the United States is at an observed all-time low. Currently, 39% of Americans identify as independents, 32% as Democrats and 23% as Republicans: "This is the highest percentage of independents in more than 75 years of public opinion polling."[22]

Party failures are intrinsically connected to the demise of the institutional supports of those parties. Throughout the twentieth century, parties relied heavily on other forms of organization to provide their active constituency. For the Democratic Party in the United States, or for the Labour Party in Britain, or for the Social Democratic parties of Western Europe, that organizational backing came heavily from the labour unions. For the Republicans in the United States, or the Tories in Britain, or the Christian Democrats and conservative parties in Europe, the organizational ties were to the chambers of commerce or other locally based representatives of small businesses and agricultural interests.

Taking the United States as an example, the decline of underlying institutions is as precipitous as the decline of parties. Union density today is at an all-time low since the New Deal created federally mandated rights of collective bargaining. Union decline captures only a part of the picture. Significant as well is the shift in composition of the unionized workforce reflected in the domination of unionization in the public sector. While about 11% of the American workforce is unionized, the figure for the private sector has fallen below 7%, while public sector unionization remains about 35%.[23] Not only have unions declined outright but, perhaps more significantly, they cease to be an independent source of support for political parties outside the state realm. To the extent that unions centrally become the expression of public employees, they no longer organize a constituency independent of the political realm. Instead labour unions are largely an expression of the political party to which they are affiliated and become another political actor whose fortunes

21 'What's Gone Wrong with Democracy', *Economist*, 1 March 2014, www.economist.com/news/essays/21596796-democracy-was-most-successful-political-idea-20th-century-why-has-it-run-trouble-and-what-can-be-do.

22 Pew Research Center, 'Trends in Party Identification, 1939-2014', 7 April 2015, www.people-press.org/interactives/party-id-trend.

23 M. Dunn & J. Walker. U.S. Bureau of Labor Statistics, 'Union Membership in the United States', September 2016, www.bls.gov/spotlight/2016/union-membership-in-the-united-states/pdf/union-membership-in-the-united-states.pdf.

are tied to that party's electoral capabilities.[24] Not surprisingly, efforts to consolidate Republican political power at the state level, as exemplified by Governor Scott Walker in Wisconsin, seek to undermine the power of public sector unions as a proxy for the Democratic Party. These are not battles reflective of participatory engagement by diverse sectors of the society, but power struggles within the state itself.

On the other side of the ledger, we find a corresponding erosion of broad-scale institutional engagement. In the United States the best example comes from the evolution of the Chamber of Commerce from the organizational representative of local enterprise to the exponent of the interests of concentrated capital:

> Mention the Chamber of Commerce, and most people think of a benign organization comprised mostly of small business owners who meet for networking and mutual support in local chapters across the United States. But today's Chamber is anything but that [...].[25]

The Chamber's interests are now highly focused around a small number of industries and interests, including "tobacco, banking, and fossil fuels".[26] According to one article, 64 donors were responsible for 50% of all donations, while 94% of all donations came from a pool of just 1,500 top donors.[27]

Across the political spectrum, parties become tied not to broad-based constituency organizations, but to much narrower sectional interests, already well-entrenched in the corridors of power. The claim of parties as a special arena of participatory engagement in the democratic project wanes accordingly. The parties emerge hollowed out, just as do their organizational bases of support.

---

24 The concern over the legal implications of the distinct role of public sector unionism in the United States go back at least to H. H. Wellington & R. K. Winter, Jr., 'The Limits of Collective Bargaining in Public Employment', *Yale Law Journal*, Vol. 78, No. 7, 1969, pp. 1124-1125.

25 D. Brodwin, 'The Chamber's Secrets: A Closer Look at the U.S. Chamber of Commerce Reveals It May Not Be as Pro-business as It Claims', *U.S. News*, 22 October 2015, www.usnews.com/opinion/economic-intelligence/2015/10/22/who-does-the-us-chamber-of-commerce-really-represent; *see generally* A. Katz, *The Influence Machine: The U.S. Chamber of Commerce and the Corporate Capture of American Life*, Spiegel & Grau, New York, 2015.

26 *Id.* ("Founded in 1912, the U.S. Chamber of Commerce has been shaped by its CEO Tom Donohue into a powerful lobbying and campaigning machine that pursues a fairly narrow special-interest agenda. It's now the largest lobbying organization in the United States (ranked by budget). It mostly represents the interests of a handful of so-called 'legacy industries' – industries like tobacco, banking and fossil fuels which have been around for generations and learned how to parley their earnings into political influence. The Chamber seeks favorable treatment for them, for example, through trade negotiations, tax treatment, regulations and judicial rulings.").

27 Brodwin (2015).

2.3 DELIBERATION: THE WEAKNESS OF LEGISLATIVE BRANCHES

> *[Deliberative] collective decision-making ought to be different from bargaining, contracting and other market-type interactions, both in its explicit attention to considerations of the common advantage and in the ways that that attention helps to form the aims of the participants.*[28]

> *[T]he democratic method is that institutional arrangement for arriving at political decisions which realizes the common good by making the people itself decide issues through the election of individuals who are to assemble in order to carry out its will.*[29]

Rarely would Joshua Cohen and Joseph Schumpeter be lumped together in theories of democratic legitimacy. Yet they both look to a discursive element to raise the capacity of democratic governance to reach the common good, and to reach beyond mere sectional claims on spoils. For Cohen and the deliberativist tradition, the domain of discourse is in public participation and direct engagement. For Schumpeter and those in his tradition, myself included, elite competition in the electoral arena provides the foundations for citizen engagement and education, and the ensuing retrospective accountability for the exercise of governmental power.

For present purposes, however, we limit our discussion to the institutionalization of deliberation in the legislative arena. Democracies are conceived around legislative power, from the Magna Carta's parliamentary check on the crown, to the expansive role of Congress as Article I of the Constitution, to the revolutionary emergence of parliamentary power throughout the nineteenth century. Colloquially, we used to speak of the Senate as the 'world's greatest deliberative body'. It is no overstatement to say that this is the world's ennobling democratic inheritance. Or, put another way, the hallmark moments of twentieth-century authoritarian rule are intertwined with plebiscitary triumphs of a Hitler or Mussolini.

Yet, in the modern era, the words 'Congress' and 'dysfunction' seem to go together like a horse and carriage, with some apology to Frank Sinatra. Consider that the total enacted legislation annually by the US Congress has declined considerably from the 1970s, in which as many as 804 bills were passed, to the present, in which only 296 bills were passed.[30] But focusing on the United States misses much of the picture. Across a number

---

28 J. Cohen, 'Deliberation and Democratic Legitimacy', *in* A. Hamlin & P. Petit (Eds.), *The Good Polity: Normative Analysis of the State*, Basil Blackwell, Oxford, 1989.

29 J. A. Schumpeter, *Capitalism, Socialism and Democracy*, Routledge, London, 2010, p. 225 (ebook).

30 GovTrack, 'Statistics and Historical Comparison', www.govtrack.us/congress/bills/statistics (showing that the 95th Congress passed 804 bills while the 113th Congress passed 296).

of markers, the legislative branches of mature democracies have declined as centres of policy debate and formation. In their place, executives have adopted more muscular policy-making roles, checked primarily by courts.

This is a large topic to which I have devoted an entire monograph. But for the current presentation, consider just one partial indicator of the trend over time in the United States. Since Franklin Roosevelt's fabled first 100 days in office ushered in the transformative New Deal, presidents have routinely devoted themselves to hitting the ground running, using the initial period of pride among the partisans and disorganization among the vanquished to show muscular leadership. The effort to blaze through the first 100 days has not changed, but the form has. The number of legislative initiatives of the first 100 days has dropped steadily, from 76 new statutes under Roosevelt, to 7 and 11 under George W. Bush and Barack Obama, respectively.[31] Even though, of course, presidents do not pass legislation, and even though they might often confront a Congress or a Chamber with an opposition majority, the drop-off does not mean presidential inaction. While legislation has dropped, executive decrees have increased throughout the modern period. Consistent with this trend, President Trump has no significant legislative activity at all during his first 100 days of the Trump administration and the number of legislative initiatives stands at zero.[32] The result is rising executive unilateralism,[33] the increased dependence on administrative law to set policy and the central checking role of the courts as restraints on presidentialism – even in formally parliamentary systems. Doctrinally, the absence of congressional action not only removes the central democratic branch from the reins of government, but also makes more difficult judicial constraint. Following Justice Jackson's famous *Steel Seizure* typology,[34] the power of the executive is at its lowest ebb when the president seeks to countermand the actions of Congress. The unstated flip side of Jackson's observation is that the pathway for judicial repudiation of executive action is correspondingly easier when Congress has blazed the trail. When Congress fails to act, the mechanisms of democratic constraint are compromised.

For Justice Jackson, congressional inaction posed the most difficult issues for democratic governance and, by extension, for the judiciary. As Justice Jackson framed the problem,

31 J. Azari, 'A President's First 100 Days Really Do Matter: But Don't Hold Trump to FDR's Standard', *FiveThirtyEight*, 17 January 2017, https://fivethirtyeight.com/features/a-presidents-first-100-days-really-do-matter/.

32 The major congressional action was an expedited procedure to withdraw regulatory decrees within a fast-track window. There were no new legislative initiatives.

33 *See* S. Issacharoff & R. H. Pildes, 'Between Civil Libertarianism and Executive Unilateralism: An Institutional Approach to Rights during Wartime', *Theoretical Inquiries in Law*, Vol. 5, No. 1, 2004, pp. 1-45 (surveying the response of American courts in periods of crisis where the executive asserts a need for unilateral action).

34 *Youngstown Sheet & Tube Co. v. Sawyer* (*Steel Seizure*), 343 U.S. 579, 637 (1952) (Jackson, J., concurring).

> When the President acts in absence of either a congressional grant or denial of authority, he can only rely upon his own independent powers, but there is a zone of twilight in which he and Congress may have concurrent authority, or in which its distribution is uncertain. Therefore, congressional inertia, indifference or quiescence may sometimes, at least as a practical matter, enable, if not invite, measures on independent presidential responsibility. In this area, any actual test of power is likely to depend on the imperatives of events and contemporary imponderables rather than on abstract theories of law.[35]

In the absence of legislative initiative, executive power naturally rushes to fill the void, whether through governance by direct decree or by indirect administrative command. Without the legislative branch offsetting the powers of the executive, the job of defining the boundaries of prerogative power and regulatory authority falls to the judiciary. As Justice Jackson cautions, the lines of judicial engagement are least clear – the 'zone of twilight' – when there is institutional failure in the legislature, and the 'least dangerous branch' finds itself at risk of open conflict with the executive.[36]

There is nothing distinctly American about hypertrophic executive power in the modern era. Even before the UK Supreme Court had to engage the authority of the prime minister to implement Brexit, a topic to which I shall return in concluding, the British government confronted the military consequences of executive unilateralism in the disastrous Iraqi campaign. One proposal, from the House of Lords Select Committee on the Constitution, would have implemented limitations similar to those of the American War Powers Act, obligating parliamentary approval for any long-term military engagement.[37] As Prime Minister Brown observed at the time,

> Now that there has been a vote on these issues so clearly and in such controversial circumstances, I think it is unlikely that except in the most exceptional

35 *Id.*

36 How this conflict plays out is the subject of R. Dixon & S. Issacharoff, 'Living to Fight Another Day: Judicial Deferral in Defense of Democracy', *Wisconsin Law Review*, Vol. 2016, No. 4, 2016, pp. 683-731.

37 House of Lords, Select Committee on the Constitution, 'Waging War: Parliament's Role and Responsibility', 15th Report of Session 2005–06, 27 July 2006, para. 3. ("The purpose of our inquiry has been to consider what alternatives there are to the use of Royal prerogative power in the deployment of the armed force … and in particular whether Parliamentary approval should be required for any deployment of British forces outside the United Kingdom […].") In the following years, the interplay between the prime minister and Parliament developed informally, until the point in 2014 "the prime minister acknowledged that a convention of Commons approval now existed". P. Lagassé, 'Parliament and the War Prerogative in the United Kingdom and Canada: Explaining Variations in Institutional Change and Legislative Control', *Parliamentary Affairs*, Vol. 70, No. 2, 2017, p. 289.

> circumstances a government would choose not to have a vote in Parliament [before deploying troops].[38]

The lack of accountability and the absence of parliamentary engagement was confirmed by the 2016 Chilcot Report, whose many condemnations of Prime Minister Blair included unilateral decision-making by the executive.[39]

It is not possible in this one exposition to engage the extensive discussions at the level of national democracies on parliamentary failure to check the executive. A review of the literature shows a persistent theme among both academic commentators and pundits to be the collapse of responsible government at the parliamentary level.[40] The causes for that collapse in the academic literature include concerns about thresholds of representation, party fragmentation, increasing presidentialism and semi-presidentialism, and the displacement of parliamentary authority by international accords or, in the case of Europe, the overreach of Brussels.[41] Pundits are more inclined to point to the venality or corruption of parliamentary officials, though in some countries, such as Brazil, the two come together.[42]

---

38 'Backing for Brown Plan for MPs to Decide War', *Daily Mail*, 30 April 2015, www.dailymail.co.uk/news/article-346890/Backing-Brown-plan-MPs-decide-war.html.

39 Committee of Privy Counsellors –The Report of the Iraq Inquiry, adopted on 6 July 2016, HC 264, para. 409. (Critiquing Blair's actions, the report noted that "there should have been a collective discussion by a Cabinet Committee or small group of Ministers on the basis of inter-departmental advice agreed at a senior level between officials at a number of decision points which had a major impact on the development of UK policy before the invasion of Iraq".)

40 *See, e.g.*, M. Foley, *The British Presidency*, Manchester University Press, Manchester 2000, p. 108 (noting "that Blair and his followers operated on the assumption that parliament was no longer a central force of political significance [...]"); Z. Karabell, How the GOP Made Obama One of America's Most Powerful Presidents, *Politico*, 14 April 2016, www.politico.com/magazine/story/2016/04/barack-obama-gop-most powerful-213814 (positing that Republicans in Congress as "the so-called Party of No only provoked the Obama administration into finding innovative ways to exercise [greater unilateral] power [...]. Rather than containing the White House, congressional Republicans liberated it").

41 *See, e.g.*, A. Bradford, 'The Brussels Effect', *Northwestern University Law Review*, Vol. 107, No. 1, 2012, pp. 1-68 (describing how regulations passed in Brussels can result in globalization of standards); C.R. Farina, 'Congressional Polarization: Terminal Constitutional Dysfunction?', *Columbia Law Review*, Vol. 115, No. 7, 2015, pp. 1689-1738 (synthesizing political science literature about congressional polarization); M. Kumm, 'The Legitimacy of International Law: A Constitutional Framework of Analysis', *The European Journal of International Law*, Vol. 15, No. 5, 2004, pp. 907-931 (discussing conflicts between international law and national domestic self-government); J. J. Linz, 'The Perils of Presidentialism', *Journal of Democracy*, Vol. 1 No. 1, 1990, p. 51 (arguing that presidentialism is less conducive to democracy than parliamentarism); Pildes, 2014, p. 809 (positing that political fragmentation is the cause of recent government dysfunction, such as "the inability of party leaders to bring along recalcitrant minority factions of their parties"); M. Amann *et al.*, 'Is Germany's Parliamentary Hurdle Obsolete?', *Der Spiegel*, 4 October 2013, www.spiegel.de/international/germany/experts-5-percent-parliamentary-hurdle-in-germany-should-be-lowered-a-925817.html (surveying political scientists' critiques of the Bundestag's 5% hurdle to seat parties).

42 An astonishing number of Brazil's Congress members have faced indictment in recent years. *See, e.g.*, A. Boadle & A. Soto, 'Brazil's Indicted Senate Head Removed by Supreme Court', *Reuters*, 6 December 2016, www.reuters.com/article/us-brazil-politics-renan-idUSKBN13U2RR (reporting the removal of the Senate President following an indictment); P. Kiernan, 'Brazil's Former House Speaker Eduardo Cunha

Parliamentary democracies are centred on the parties. Candidates run as part of a slate and the demand for a larger share of seats in parliament is what offers the prospect of national stewardship. The collapse of the parliaments compounds the effect of the collapse of parties and the two are both the cause and effect of each other. Invariably, the locus of political activity shifts to the executive and the defining feature of democratic politics turns to the triumphalist claims of the victorious head of state. Consider this account of contemporary politics:

> What we are seeing in the presidential campaigns [...] is that the more chance the candidates have of winning – or the more chance they think they have of winning – the more they are prepared to play the game that I call "national presidentialism." They go in for speeches that amount to saying: "If I'm elected, then everything [...] is going to be different because I'm the only one able to lead this country" [...]. All that matters is how the candidate is going to be able to restore [the nation's] image once he or she has been given supreme power.

This account of contemporary politics would ring true in many democracies around the world, the United States clearly included. In my native Argentina, such 'caudillo politics' have generally been the mark of the demise of democracy rather than its fulfilment. That this particular statement happens to be about France and that the speaker is Daniel Cohn-Bendit, the leader of the 1968 student uprising, only makes it a bit more piquant.[43]

2.4 Solidarity: The Threats to Social Cohesion

A central theme of my work on *Fragile Democracies*[44] concerns the inherent difficulty in democratic governance in the absence of a democratic polity. Strikingly, and perhaps paradoxically, elections are seen in post-World War II state formation as the means towards the creation of a democratic state rather than a system of choice among those already committed to a common enterprise of collective governance. In countries emerging from colonial rule or despotic regimes, elections were the confirmation of a democratic transformation, even as they often served as the marker of who would hold state authority in a world of unfinished 'us-versus-them' business. Our era of diversity may applaud the ben-

Sentenced to Prison for Corruption', *Wall Street Journal*, 30 March 2017, www.wsj.com/articles/brazils-former-house-speaker-eduardo-cunha-sentenced-to-prison-for-corruption-1490893914 (reporting the sentencing of the former House Speaker "in a case that has landed scores of politicians and businessmen behind bars").

43 D. Cohn-Bendit, 'Presidentialism: The French Disease', *Esprit*, Vol. February, No. 2, 2012, p. 75.

44 S. Issacharoff, *Fragile Democracies: Contested Power in the Era of Constitutional Courts*, Cambridge University Press, Cambridge, 2015.

efits of such broad democratic aspirations, but citizens of Burundi or Bosnia-Herzegovina or Iraq would well understand the frailties of democracy without a solidaristic commitment to a collective future.

The role of communitarian solidarity suffers from the traumas of the twentieth century, from Nazism to the ethnic slaughter in the Balkans. One reads back with horror at Carl Schmitt proclaiming that, "Democracy requires [...] first homogeneity and second [...] elimination or eradication of heterogeneity." The unmistakable message is that "[a] democracy demonstrates its political power by knowing how to refuse or keep at bay something foreign and unequal that threatens its homogeneity".[45]

Yet, a look back at our democratic inheritance shows how central earlier generations thought about the sense of shared identity, and that the ties between social cohesion and self-government is not an invention of twentieth-century reaction. In the background of the founding documents of constitutionalism in the United States is the claim, no doubt jarring from a slave society, that the American blessings of liberty could be traced to the conception of homogeneity of the population that echoes in Schmitt. In the words of John Jay, in Federalist 2:

> [...] Providence has been pleased to give this one connected country to one united people – a people descended from the same ancestors, speaking the same language, professing the same religion, attached to the same principles of government, very similar in their manners and customs, and who, by their joint counsels, arms, and efforts, fighting side by side throughout a long and bloody war, have nobly established general liberty and independence.[46]

Jay may today be the least celebrated of the Federalist authors, but the sentiment was widely shared, with John Stuart Mill later extending the argument to make this not simply an observation about America but a prerequisite for democracy:

> Free institutions are next to impossible in a country made up of different nationalities. Among a people without fellow-feeling, especially if they read and speak different languages, the united public opinion necessary to the working of representative government can not exist.[47]

---

45 C. Schmitt, *The Crisis of Parliamentary Democracy* [1923], trans. E. Kennedy, The MIT Press, Cambridge/MA, 1988, p. 9.

46 J. Jay, 'Concerning Dangers from Foreign Force and Influence for the Independent Journal', The Federalist Papers No. 2, *Yale Law School*, http://avalon.law.yale.edu/18th_century/fed02.asp.

47 J. S. Mill, *Considerations on Representative Government* [1861], The Floating Press, Auckland, 2009, pp. 344-345.

Liberal theorists in the twentieth century, including notably John Rawls, continued the tradition of making claims for just treatment of citizens turn, at least in part, on a shared sense of "political traditions, institutions of law, property and class structure, with their sustaining religious and moral beliefs and underlying culture. It is these things that shape a society's political will [...]".[48] The arguments do not sound in the need for consanguinity so much as the continued importance of a sense of collective identity in order to sustain citizen self-government. Across democratic societies, political parties provided the organizational framework for sports leagues, adult education projects and newspapers – all of which served as intermediaries between citizens and the broader society. These agencies of civil society are weakened and leave citizens increasingly disengaged from political life, as reflected in declining voter participation rates across the democratic world. The problem of lack of collective identity is more acute at the higher levels of efforts at European governance being compromised by trying to craft a 'democracy without a demos'.

Among the contemporary challenges in advanced democratic societies are significant erosions in the sense of collective solidarity that provided the historic glue for the common project of democratic governance. For immediate purposes, I focus on two: the challenge of immigration and the challenge of declining living standards of the broad mass of the population – the toilers, soldiers and voters of democratic states. There are many manifestations of contemporary social dissolution. But the combination of economic insecurity and the presence of perceived outsiders seems invariably to lead to fear of the other as taking over and blame on the other for the corresponding loss in social standing and wealth. The point here is not the normative claim that this sense is or is not justified, or even the positive claim of a causal relation between immigration and economic malaise. Rather, the issue is the democratic challenge posed by widespread sentiments among the plebeian classes of being under siege. There is not a populist movement in a Western democracy at present that does not play to both xenophobia and economic insecurity. The immediate question is why these strains have such force at present and why they seem to operate in tandem.

While the answers are no doubt complex, they must begin with an assessment of the empirical realities of modern democratic societies, still reeling from the financial meltdown of 2008. The brute fact is that there is a loss of cohesion that accompanies high periods of immigration until the new immigrants are integrated into the national consensus. What Americans celebrate as the melting pot is undoubtedly a process of change and recreation of the national identity, but provides for mechanisms of integration of waves of immigrant populations. Even in the best of circumstances, the process of integration and the corresponding accommodation of prior governing values will take time. What hopefully ends

48 J. Rawls, *The Law of Peoples*, Harvard University Press, Cambridge/MA, 2001, p. 106.

up a richer cultural environment (oftentimes with side improvements from food to music) invariably begins as a project of social and linguistic strain.

Taking the United States as the key example, there is no escaping the fact that immigration has risen dramatically in the United States in the past quarter century and that the level of foreign-born Americans is at the highest level in a century – precisely the time of the last great burst of nativist populism in the United States.

Figure 1 The rise of immigration in the US

What is striking here, apart from any concerns about the distribution of immigrant labour skill levels, or even the number of legal versus illegal immigrants, is just the sheer number. The last immigration-fuelled nativist turn transformed American politics for a generation, including closed-border constraints on immigration, isolationist politics and even Prohibition directed at the drinking habits of recent immigrants.

The challenge of immigration emerges politically in tandem with the sense of loss in the economic sphere. In what is referred to as the 'elephant curve' produced by the World Bank, there is a graphic depiction of a global redirection of wealth over the 20-year period leading into the financial meltdown, perhaps as significant as any ever recorded. The graph shows a stunning rise in the real incomes of the great majority of the world's population, with huge numbers being lifted from poverty – primarily, though not exclusively, the result of the Chinese economic transformation.

Figure 2 Global redirection of wealth

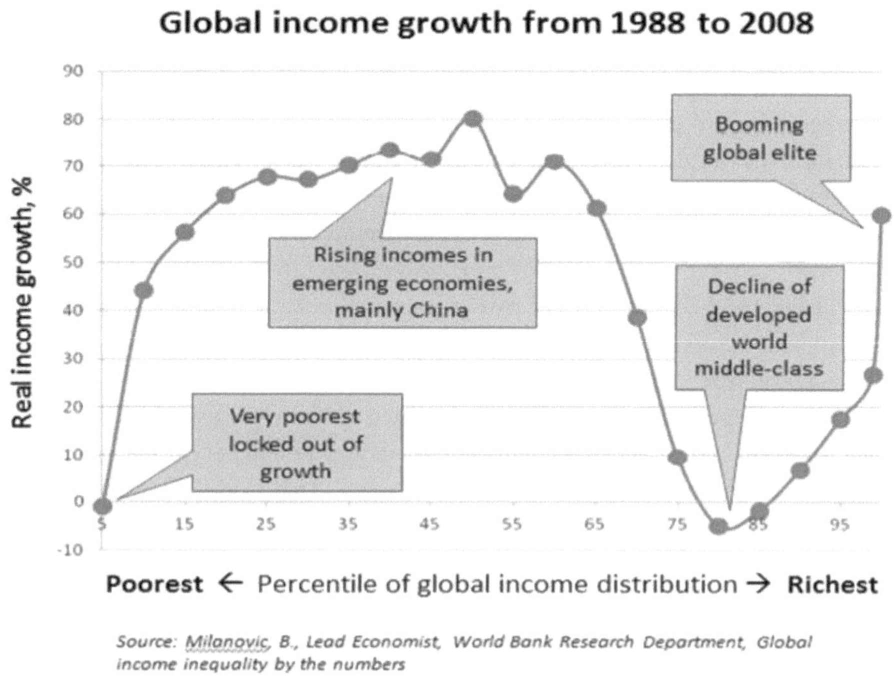

With the exception of the very poorest of the poor, the past 30 years has witnessed a transformation of lives around the world from extreme poverty to levels of income, health, material possessions and life prospects that begin to challenge those of the advanced industrial democracies. The graph further reflects the rise of finance and the dominance of the top 1%, a subject of democratic challenge for some form of equitable redistribution. But the most important part of this chart is the downward curve where real levels of income did not increase and in fact decreased over the same 20-year period. This is the two deciles of the world's population found at roughly the 65th to 85th percentiles of world income distribution. That group is roughly the working classes and lower middle classes of the advanced industrial countries that form the longest standing core of democratic societies.

As a normative matter, redistribution from wealthier nations to poorer ones in a period of rising wealth must be applauded. The economic dislocations in the advanced industrial countries translate on the ground into hundreds and hundreds of millions of people being lifted from truly destitute conditions. But the global processes that have done much to alleviate human suffering do not dampen the consequences of the inability of the advanced societies to cushion the domestic effects of international migration and global economic integration or to redistribute internally from the winners to the losers from globalization.

The democratic sense of solidarity comes under siege as the labouring backbones of the advanced industrial countries find themselves challenged by a lost sense of recognizing their country amid rapidly changing demographics. It also comes as the rest of the world is exerting downward pressures on their living standards and wealth shifts markedly to other parts of the world. As voters, these threatened groups in advanced societies were the backbone of the major parties of twentieth-century democracy, the labour and social democratic parties on the left, and the Christian Democratic and centre parties on the right.

Both labour and the centre-right parties were traditionally cautious to negative on immigration and cross-border trade. While their policies differed, each saw a central part of its political role as protecting the always vulnerable working class and small entrepreneurial class, including the highly subsidized agricultural classes in countries like France, from economic dislocation. Both immigrants and the entry of cheaper goods from abroad threatened the less dynamic sectors of the advanced world economies. This is especially true for the working classes. Private sector labour unions saw immigration as a source of downward pressure on wages, and resisted it as such. By contrast, public sector unions primarily attend to the level of government expenditures on employment and tend to be neither protectionist on trade nor cautious on immigration. When we look to the upper Midwest voting for Donald Trump or the decayed industrial north of England voting for Brexit, the message of governmental failure to provide for basic social security rings loudly. And, when coupled with the sense of the traditional institutions being disengaged from working-class concerns, the field is left open to populist anger, whether from the right or left.

Indeed, the message resonates in those communities feeling left behind. One simple measure in the United States is to break down the vote by county, the basic unit of local governance. Donald Trump won roughly five times as many counties as Hillary Clinton, but the counties that Clinton won included almost all the largest and most dynamic urban areas of the country – indeed, although a numerical minority, the counties won by Clinton generated 64% of the national gross domestic product.[49] In Britain, the same pattern was obtained in the Brexit vote. Leaving aside Scotland and the eastern precincts of Northern Ireland (where voters were probably more inclined to leave the United Kingdom than the

49 M. Muro & S. Liu, 'Another Clinton-Trump Divide: High-output America vs. Low-output America', *Brookings*, 29 November 2016, www.brookings.edu/blog/the-avenue/2016/11/29/another-clinton-trump-divide-high-output-america-vs-low-output-america; J. Tankersley, 'Donald Trump Lost Most of the American Economy in this Election', *Washington Post*, 22 November 2016, www.washington-post.com/news/wonk/wp/2016/11/22/donald-trump-lost-most-of-the-american-economy-in-this-election/?utm_term=.737cd052686f.

European Union), the Brexit vote matched the economic prospects of the local populations. Brexit lost in London and the relatively prosperous South, and carried most of the rest of the country, save for a few areas of economic resurrection in Manchester and Liverpool.[50] Put another way, Brexit was the dominant choice of those over 40, the generations that had felt declining wage prospects, but not the generation under 40.[51] Comparable distributions could be found in the French presidential elections as well.

The groups threatened by declining economic prospects, a sense of isolation in their own countries and the combined effects of foreign threat delivered Brexit and President Trump's victories in the upper Midwest. Now feeling vulnerable, these voters are increasingly deserting their former political affiliations in favour of angry populist reactions, frequently led by demagogic appeals to isolation and the sense of lost horizons. From Brexit to Five Star to President Trump to the Front National to Podemos, the trends are dramatic. The historic array of post-war political parties offered neither economic security nor the sense of political protection from outsiders and were displaced by those much closer to the sense of populist dismay.

In particular, the financial crisis of 2008 appears to have been the defining blow that exposed the frailty of democracies. The sudden economic dislocation stressed the already weak political institutions of governance and the ability of traditional political parties to offer prospects of remediation. For the labouring classes of the advanced democracies, for whom the decades leading to 2008 had offered a steady decline in real wages, confidence in any remnant of the political status quo to cushion the further post-crisis economic decline was exceedingly low. Without functioning politics, democracies are ill-prepared to offer security, redistribution or optimism about life prospects for their citizens. That huge numbers of the populations of the democratic countries no longer confided in the solidaristic commitment of the society or its capacity to protect them fuelled the current populist backlash.

50 'EU Referendum: The Result in Maps and Charts', *BBC*, 24 June 2016, www.bbc.com/news/uk-politics-36616028.

51 *Id.*

2.5 GETTING IT DONE

Democratically produced laws are legitimate and authoritative because they are produced by a procedure with a tendency to make correct decisions.[52]

Over the past two centuries, democracies have outfought, out-innovated and out-produced their rivals. With singular capacity, democracies raised the living standards of the broad masses of their population, raised education levels to permit citizen engagement and at the same time were able to trust powerful militaries to protect them from foreign assault without succumbing to military rule. History is obviously much more complicated and this is a somewhat tendentious reading, but it captures the ideological consensus that prevailed after the collapse of the Soviet empire and the brief era of presumed democratic universalism.

As the elephant curve chart on income distribution shows, however, the optimistic story is under serious challenge. The China/Singapore models of authoritarian rule coupled with high state competence challenge an emerging feature of democracies: the presence of multiple veto points blocking the creation of public goods and equitable policies. Mature democracies include mechanisms of transparency, 'due process', and participation that provide an entry point for private interests to block undesired governmental action. Under such circumstances, it is easier to block than to build and the result is to raise the costs of public endeavours dramatically. Fukuyama terms this the rise of 'vetocracy', defined as

> [...] a situation in which special interests can veto measures harmful to themselves, while collective action for the common good becomes exceedingly difficult to achieve. Vetocracy isn't fatal to American democracy, but it does produce poor governance.[53]

Easy confirmation can be found in the wobbly efforts of the Republicans in the US Congress to pass from a party of opposition to a party of governance on their signature demand for the repeal of the Affordable Care Act. After 7 years of campaigning on a promise to repeal Obamacare, a clear Republican majority in the House of Representatives had trouble even proposing legislation to be submitted to a congressional vote.

The central claim to superior competence of democracies is not the process of governance but the outputs that result; deliberation is necessarily slower and more complicated than decree. At some point, however, deliberation is not a process of citizen inputs but a

---

52 D. M. Estlund, *Democratic Authority: A Philosophical Framework*, Princeton University Press, Princeton, 2009, p. 8.

53 F. Fukuyama, 'America: The Failed State', *Prospect*, 13 December 2016, www.prospectmagazine.co.uk/magazine/america-the-failed-state-donald-trump.

public choice nightmare in which vested sectional interests can marshal resources to overwhelm the passive majority. The result is a failure of public policy leadership and a collapse into rewards for privileged access to the strongest forces in government, almost invariably the executive. As I have described the process elsewhere, "the 'three C's' of consolidated power take hold: clientelism, cronyism, and corruption".[54] The result is "weak democracies with autocratically minded leaders, who govern through informal, patronage networks ... [C]lientelism binds many citizens to ruling elites through cooptation and coercion".[55] Such failing democracies have no necessary organizational superiority to more decisive regimes, and indeed, the presence of numerous veto points to action may actually make democracies less capable.

Consider an example from airport construction, a massively complex undertaking that has not even been attempted in the United States since the opening of the Denver airport in 1995. An international traveller to Beijing cannot help but be awed by the majestic beauty of Terminal 3 international arrivals. Built for the opening of the Beijing Olympics, and designed by English architect Norman Foster, its dramatic arches evoke both the red lacquer motifs of Imperial China and the bird's nest design of the Olympic stadium. The new terminal was constructed, from design to completion, in 4 years, a massive effort that included three work crews a day, labouring on rotating 8-hour shifts.

By contrast, consider China's Terminal 3 with Heathrow's Terminal 5 in London. Like Terminal 3 in Beijing, Heathrow's Terminal 5 is designed by Norman Foster. Yet it is at best functional, a desperately needed additional space for an overcrowded airport. It has no grandeur, no inspiration, no sense of tribute to a rising power – and it took 20 years to complete.

When pressed about this in a BBC interview, Foster acknowledged the gains in completion time in China from more efficient labour use, from lower regulatory demands, from ease of siting and a host of other factors. But even on Foster's account, there were years of delay that could not be accounted for. Instead what emerges is the capacity of Chinese authorities to simply get the job done:

> [Y]ou've taken out the democratic process, you've taken out the plan, so that comes down to decision making, it comes down to having a very, very clear idea of objectives and getting on with it.[56]

54 Issacharoff, 2015, p. 158.

55 Balkans in Europe Policy Advisory Group, 'The Crisis of Democracy in the Western Balkans. Authoritarianism and EU Stabilitocracy', March 2017, p. 7, www.biepag.eu/wp-content/uploads/2017/03/BIEPAG-The-Crisis-of-Democracy-in-the-Western-Balkans.-Authoritarianism-and-EU-Stabilitocracy-web.pdf.

56 'BBC Dream Builders with Norman Foster', www.fosterandpartners.com/media/1028028/NF-BBC-Dream_Builders_transcript.pdf.

Of course, my home airport in New York is LaGuardia, which makes Terminal 5 look like paradise. Among New York's signature contributions to democratic dysfunction is the much ballyhooed opening of the Second Avenue subway extension in 2017, a mere 88 years after it was initially proposed. Even more striking than the delay were the extravagant costs, themselves a self-imposed problem of poor governance. Digging a subway in a dense urban environment necessitates disrupting delivery of gas, water, telecommunications, etc. Doing so efficiently in turn requires coordination so that service disruptions and alternative sources can be adjusted. The builder of the subway found coordination among the various utilities and regulatory agencies that covered each service so daunting that they decided the only solution was to dig deep into the bedrock of Manhattan so as to avoid having any contact with any other utilities or administrators.[57] The result is that more than 80 years after first proposed, the Second Avenue subway finally opened in 2017, encompassing a total of four subway stops, running a grand total of three kilometres, and pricing in at a whopping figure of over $1 billion per kilometre.[58]

The capacity to cushion the dislocations of the modern global economy and the press of immigration is another measure of state competence. Germany's capacity to integrate the former East Germany confirms the difficulty of the enterprise, even among people who already shared a language and a clear national identity. It is here that all the themes of democratic stress come together. The inability of institutional political actors to debate policy, to appeal to collective interest and to assure through competent leadership all drain the vitality of the democratic project. Populist anger is stoked by state incompetence and increased clientelism for those with privileged access to the executive. Weakened forms of participation and deliberation, in turn, compound the sense of democratic failure.

2.6 CONCLUSION

The picture of democracy presented here is certainly sombre, but it need not be funereal. The identified deficits in democratic governance are serious, no doubt. But the advanced industrial democracies are sophisticated societies with great internal resources. Three are worth noting here because they are significant sources of resilience. Undoubtedly there are many more, but these three flow immediately from the discussion above, and the last points back to the role of law, a topic thus far not addressed.

---

57 M. Yglesias, 'NYC's Brand New Subway is the Most Expensive in the World – That's a Problem', *Vox*, 1 January 2017, www.vox.com/policy-and-politics/2017/1/1/14112776/new-york-second-avenue-subway-phase-2.

58 A. Levy, 'U.S. Rail Construction Costs', *Pedestrian Observations*, 16 May 2011, https://pedestrianobservations.wordpress.com/2011/05/16/us-rail-construction-costs.

First, waves of populist anger tend to be conjunctural. The immediate spark for the latest political tide appears to be the consequences of the financial crisis of 2008. Economic recovery is the likeliest source of any easing of enraged politics. But populist reaction translates poorly into governance, as the US Republican Party has shown in its hesitating transition from opposition to ruling. The current populist wave began at least a decade earlier in Latin America than in Europe or the United States, and it is now sputtering out amid corruption scandals and the inability to achieve deliverance.

Second, democratic states abound in civil society institutions that resist the anti-liberalism of caudillo politics. One of the main failings of the founding constitutional vision in the United States was the lack of any space for intermediating institutions that stood between the state and the citizenry. Tocqueville's observations about the notable abundance of association in the young Republic may be generalized to all democratic countries, even in the more state-oriented politic orders of Europe. Even a strict Montesquieu-inspired division of government powers proved not to anticipate the manner in which democratic societies function. From the press to community associations to political parties to churches there is far more resilience than just a formal account of the separation of powers between the legislature and the executive.

Third, democratic societies develop thick legal institutions bounded by the rule of law. Moments of populist passion confront constitutional constraints and the restraining force of constitutional courts, as I addressed at length in *Fragile Democracies*. The Brexit vote provides a useful illustration. Although advocacy for popular initiatives in Britain has a long history, going back at least to A.V. Dicey more than a century ago,[59] the process is relatively unutilized and the relation between the subjects of referendum and ensuing governmental action remains unclear. As the House of Lords Select Committee concluded, "we regret the ad hoc manner in which referendums have been used, often as a tactical device, by the government of the day".[60]

In the aftermath of Brexit, Prime Minister Cameron departed the scene and a chastened Tory government formed under Prime Minister Theresa May. The government allowed the Brexit vote to stand as the will of the people and took the first steps towards unwinding Britain's participation in the European Union. This provoked a legal challenge leading to a remarkable discussion in the UK Supreme Court on the nature of British democratic governance. In an approach that hearkens back to Justice Jackson's careful dissection of the delicate balance of powers between the executive and the legislature, the Court framed the inquiry:

---

59 A. V. Dicey, 'Ought the Referendum to be Introduced into England?', *Contemporary Review*, Vol. 57, 1890.

60 House of Lords, Select Committee on the Constitution, Referendums in the United Kingdom: Report with Evidence, 12th Report of Session 2009-10, p. 20, https://publications.parliament.uk/pa/ld200910/ldselect/ldconst/99/99.pdf.

> [The] Act envisages domestic law, and therefore rights of UK citizens, changing as EU law varies, but it does not envisage those rights changing as a result of ministers unilaterally deciding that the United Kingdom should withdraw from the EU Treaties.[61]

That a weak government had appealed directly over the head of Parliament to enraged voters did not alter the institutional commitments to the democratic supremacy of Parliament. Nor could the prime minister invoke plebiscitary approval as a substitute for proper institutional process:

> The question is whether that domestic starting point, introduced by Parliament, can be set aside, or could have been intended to be set aside, by a decision of the UK executive without express Parliamentary authorization. We cannot accept that a major change to UK constitutional arrangements can be achieved by ministers alone; it must be effected in the only way that the UK constitution recognizes, namely by Parliamentary legislation. This conclusion appears to us to follow from the ordinary application of basic concepts of constitutional law to the present issue.[62]

Rule of law principles may serve to break the more worrisome manifestations of populist anger. In some countries, as in Hungary and increasingly Poland, the institutions may be overwhelmed by the concerted forces of politics. But they can provide a necessary challenge and an avenue of repair. In the words of the US court confronting the Trump Administration's proposed travel bans and the Administration's claims to unaccountable executive discretion:

> There is no precedent to support this claimed unreviewability, which runs contrary to the fundamental structure of our constitutional democracy … [T]he Government's 'authority and expertise in [such] matters do not automatically trump the Court's own obligation to secure the protection that the Constitution grants to individuals,' even in times of war […] [Our cases] make clear, courts can and do review constitutional challenges to the substance and implementation of immigration policy.[63]

61 *R v. Secretary of State for Exiting the European Union*, [2017] UKSC 5, Judgment of 24 January 2017, www.supremecourt.uk/cases/docs/uksc-2016-0196-judgment.pdf.

62 *Id.*

63 *Washington v. Trump*, No. 17-35105, 2017 WL 526497 (9th Cir. 9 February 2017) (*per curiam*).

3 Populism – A Notion Rising above Its Content

Tibor Várady[*]

3.1 Some Introductory Remarks Concerning the Use of the Term 'Populism'

The term 'populism' is becoming increasingly popular in public discourse. It is difficult to deny – and I have no intention to try to deny – that the designation tackles (or tries to tackle) a serious problem. But wide use has made it more and more difficult to discern what ground is actually covered by this term.

A couple of years ago I was noting various contexts in which the term 'populism' was used – particularly in the press. For instance, the Hungarian *Népszabadság* on 2 May 2009 cites the Slovak *SME* comparing the Czech and Hungarian government crisis and concludes that

> what is common to both countries is that both have a strong populist opposition that took advantage of the fact that people do not want to abandon the illusion to work the socialist way and to live the capitalist way.

(Endeavouring, I guess, to portray a desire to work as workers did under socialism and to live as capitalists – rather than workers – do under capitalism.) On 13 April 2009, the *Wall Street Journal* criticized the populism of Viktor Orbán, submitting that Orbán proposes to lower taxes for both the employers and the employees. Nowadays (in 2018) the populism of Orbán is still very much on the agenda – mostly in connection with his attitude towards migrants. Going back to 2009, on 9 April 2009, the Belgrade weekly *Vreme* wrote about Obama's 'populist vision' of a nuclear-free world.

It is quite clear that by labelling something as 'populism' or qualifying someone as 'populist', the speaker or writer tends to expose an attitude, to debunk something that may look appealing, but which is actually negative. It is also a fact that the term 'populism' has gained considerable attraction in our days. The way the use of this term is commonly

---

* Professor Emeritus, Central European University, Budapest; Professor Emeritus of Law, Emory University, Atlanta. This chapter relies in part on Tibor Várady's article 'Populism and Unmasking', published in the *Hungarian Review*, 1 December 2013.

perceived, it hints an intellectual flair, while it contains an elegant condemnation of a person (or party, or government, or phenomenon).

Returning to the *Népszabadság*, in an interview given on 9 April 2009, Mr Steinmeier, (then) German Minister for Foreign Affairs, stated that the disappointment with the economic situation "strengthens nationalist and populist sentiments, and the voice of the street gets stronger". Steinmeier adds that it is important to overcome the causes of the crisis and to create a more just society in which a top executive will not earn as much as 500 nurses. Two months earlier (5 February 2009), the *New York Times* also wrote about executive pay and commented that Obama "[n]eeds to deflect a populist outrage over sky-high pay"; on March 17, 2009, the *Washington Post* wrote about a "populist anger at executives".[1] So where do we stand now? Is Steinmeier's proposal to curtail skyrocketing executive pays (in order to create a more just society), actually an endeavour to impede populism, or is this just another expression of populism? Returning to the *New York Times*, I read on 8 September 2010 that President Obama opposes any extension of the Bush-era tax cuts for the wealthy 'adding a populist twist' to an election season economic package.

Among the examples of the use of the term 'populism' I noted some years ago, there is another article in the *New York Times* referring to populism in Russia. On 30 September 2010, Andrew A. Kramer writes about the departure of Mr Luzhkov, mayor of Moscow.[2] He notes that

> for developers, Mr Luzhkov was more of a dream. They made a fortune in the post-Soviet capital in what will surely be remembered as one of the world's great real estate gold rushes, fed in its final phase by capital from Arab sheiks and Wall Street investors.

The article adds that Ms Baturina, the wife of mayor Luzhkov who owns a large development company, amassed a personal fortune of $2.9 billion according to Forbes magazine. Then it is added that "as mayor of Moscow, Mr. Luzhkov blended populism and arm-twisting of business to contribute to pension funds, public works and church restorations". I suppose that in this context the term 'populism' refers to service to noble causes exercised parallel with amassing a fortune.

Or, to cite a fresher example, I am reading in the *New York Times* of 23 September 2017 a comment on the (than incoming) Alabama Senate Republican primary runoff:

---

1 S. Labaton & V. Bajaj, 'Obama Calls for 'Common Sense' on Executive Pay', *New York Times*, 5 February 2009; M. Shear & P. Kane, 'Anger Over Firm Depletes Obama's Political Capital', *The Washington Post*, 17 March 2009.

2 A. E. Kramer, 'Mayor's Departure Could Slow Moscow's Growth', *New York Times*, 30 September 2010.

> If Mr. Moore wins the runoff on Tuesday, Republican leaders fear he will further widen the split in the party between populists and the establishment. That could embolden more lawmakers to defy the party leadership and encourage other insurgents to challenge Republican incumbents, no matter Mr. Trump's preference.

President Trump supported Luther Strange, Moore's opponent. However, Moore won. This should mean that populism prevailed over Trump (?).

So what is populism? The question is not whether we do or do not have excessive demagogy in our times, and the question is not whether politicians do or do not tend to make popular but unrealistic promises – or whether they tend to construe issues artificially. The question is whether the understandable urge to use the term 'populism' did or did not prevail over its content; in other words, whether the label 'populism' is a matching one, which also provides sufficient explanation. It is clear that there are (and there have always been) slogans and attitudes prompting the need for de-masking. The question is whether the more and more frequently used term 'populism' is fit for the task.

The term 'populism' is being typically used as a political qualification aimed to (dis)qualify an opponent. The designations 'communist' or, say 'fascist', are nowadays also often used for the same purpose. One may note, however, that there are parties or movements that are not trying to escape the designation 'communist' (or even 'fascist'). Yet, while in the nineteenth century, there were parties openly bearing the tag 'populist', this is not the case anymore. Practically nobody is accepting to bear the designation 'populist', no party is nowadays ready to identify itself with this title. This makes it even more difficult to perceive to term 'populist' on a ground outside political altercations.

The question also arises, what could (and should) be perceived as the opposite of populism.

3.2 An Attempt to Find Some Foothold in Legal Practice

Populism is not a legal term, and there are social sciences (other than law) that have more proficiency in facing controversies over its content. Thus, it is not for the courts to tell what populism actually is, or which connotation is right and which is wrong. At the same time, it is interesting to take note of the use of the terms 'populism' and 'populist' within a formalized procedure and within a discourse which is – at least in principle – prudent and fastidious in bringing into scrutiny notions and labels. I found some particularly interesting examples in the American judicial practice.

I would first like to mention some cases in which populism has a predominantly positive connotation and in which the juxtaposition with some form of elitism is in the front.

In an interesting case, the Supreme Court of Washington faced the issue whether the Constitution of Washington State allows employment of convicts in private companies. In its statement of reasons, the Supreme Court of Washington devoted considerable space to 'historical context', including a scrutiny of populism.[3] The key issue was whether a statute authorizing contracts between the Department of Corrections and private companies, did or did not violate the constitutional provision which stated that starting from 1890, convicts "shall not be let out by contract to any person, partnership or corporation", but which added that legislation shall "provide for the working of convicts for the benefit of the state". Seeking an answer to the question as to whether working for private companies may be considered to be within the exception of working 'for the benefit of the state', the Court investigated the historical background and established that "[i]n the years preceding Washington's constitutional convention the political life of our emerging state was dominated by the populist movement, which strongly influenced Washington's constitution". The Court added that

> Populism sprang primarily from agrarian roots and emphasized a philosophy of protection for small business and the working citizen. Central among the populist ideas was the protection of the individual from unfair advantages created by coalitions between big government and politically connected big businesses.[4]

In the light of this historical background, the Supreme Court of Washington came to the conclusion that "[W]ashington populists must have meant 'for the benefit of the state' to mean that prison labor could not be used to benefit private industry".[5] Relying on this assumption the Court declared that the statute allowing contracts between the Department of Correction and private companies represented a violation of the Constitution of Washington State (and consequently, the contracts themselves were concluded in violation of the Constitution).

To mention another example, a 1985 decision of the Supreme Court of the United States is mentioning populism in connection with racial discrimination.[6] The issue is again, constitutionality. The US Supreme Court scrutinized the constitutionality of a provision of the 1901 Alabama Constitution, which disenfranchised a person convicted of crimes involving 'moral turpitude'. Section 182 of the Alabama Constitution gave a long list of grounds for disqualifying persons both from registering and from voting. Those who were

---

3 *Washington Water Jet Workers Association, et al. Appellants v. Howard Yarborough, et al. Respondents*, 151 Wash 2d. 470, 90 P 3d 42 – the judgment was rendered on 13 May 2004. It was modified on 27 May 2004.

4 *Id.*, p. 11.

5 *Id.*

6 *Nell Hunter et al v. Victor Underwood*, 471 U.S. 222 (16 April 1985).

deprived from voting right included 'all idiots and insane persons', those who were convicted of treason, murder, arson, but also of 'malfeasance in office', 'obtaining property or money under false pretenses, bigamists, persons guilty of miscegenation, or 'living in adultery'. 'Moral turpitude' gained a special weight after a 1916 judgment of the Alabama Supreme Court, which declared that this designation can be extended to an act that is not punishable by law, but which is *immoral in itself*.[7] Again, we find in the 1985 judgment a historical analysis that extends to populism as well. The US Supreme Court came to the conclusion that discriminating intent was a motivating factor behind Section 182 of the Alabama Constitution. An expert estimate was relied upon that showed that Section 182 disenfranchised approximately 10 times as many blacks as whites. The Supreme Court gave credit to the expert opinion of Dr J. Mills Thornton, who stated that Southern Democrats sought to stem the resurgence of populism which threatened their power. According to the Supreme Court, the aim of Section 182 was to prevent the resurgence of populism, by disenfranchising practically all blacks and a large number of whites. The decision was reached that Section 182 of the Alabama Constitution violates the (federal) constitutional principle of equal treatment.

In the above two cases populism appears in a more positive and – if this term still means anything – leftist connotation. Populists are perceived as those who are protecting the individual from unfair advantages created by coalitions between big government and politically connected big businesses; and as the opponents of those who want to disenfranchise black voters.

One can also find, however, US court decisions in which populism has a negative connotation. In a 27 February 2009 decision of the Supreme Court of Nebraska, populism is again contemplated in a historical context and in connection with racial discrimination. This time, however, populism is not perceived as an opponent, but as an ally of racism. The Court also added the qualification 'reactionary'. It is not quite clear from the context whether this is a qualification of populism in general, or whether this hints that there are various kinds of populism, including 'reactionary populism'. In this case, an action was brought to vacate an arbitral award which had held that the fact that a state trooper joined of a group affiliated with the Ku Klux Klan, was not a just cause for termination under the collective bargaining agreement. The Supreme Court of Nebraska vacated the arbitral award.[8] The case is about Mr Henderson, a Nebraska state trooper whose wife left him in favour of a Hispanic man. This led Mr Henderson to join the Knights Party, an affiliate of the Ku Klux Klan, 'working toward White Christian Renewal'. In his application form, he made the following attestation: "I am white and not of racially mixed descent. I am not married to a nonwhite, I do not date nonwhites, nor have I nonwhite dependents." After

7 *Pippin v. State*, 197 Ala. 613, 616, 73 So. 340, 342 (1916).

8 *State of Nebraska v. Robert Henderson*, Supreme Court of Nebraska, 277 Neb. 240 (27 February 2009).

Mr Henderson was fired, the case went to arbitration, and the arbitrators held that the firing was without sufficient ground. The Nebraska State Patrol sought vacation of the award on the ground of violation of public policy. The Nebraska Supreme Court held that the award did, indeed, violate public policy (which leads essentially to the conclusion that a member of the state police cannot join an organization affiliated with the Ku Klux Klan). In its historic analysis, the Court takes note that during its heyday in the 1920s, the rhetoric of the Ku Klux Klan "was fueled by fear of Catholic European immigrants". Later on, "[t]he Ku Klux Klan was vigorous in its campaign against blacks, Jews, foreigners, Catholics, and women suffragists".[9] This led to the observation about the 'reactionary populism' of the Ku Klux Klan; and in this context, populism (or, at least, 'reactionary populism') has a clearly negative connotation.

Again, a different context appears in the arguments advanced in another case, in which a flight attendant filed a suit against tobacco companies. The case was started in 1991 and it reached the District Court of Appeal of Florida in 2005.[10] The plaintiff, Ms French sued tobacco companies, and she was awarded 5.5 million US dollars in damages for injuries she incurred as a result of second-hand smoke. On appeal, one of the arguments of the tobacco companies was that "Ms French's counsel willfully and repeatedly injected quasi populist rhetoric and anti-business prejudice into this trial".[11] The Court rejected this argument, without scrutinizing what 'quasi-populist rhetoric' actually is. One may note that the linking of populism with anti-business attitude (and thus, positing the big business as the elite) is not rare or new. Polányi writes about the nineteenth-century quarrels between the populists and Wall Street.[12]

Staying with court cases, I would also like to mention two judgments which give emphasis to the term 'populism', but in the context of which it is difficult to discern any frame of reference. In a 1988 New York decision, we have the story of a child prodigy from Florida (Stephen Baccus), who was 14 when he graduated from the University of Miami, and started legal studies.[13] He got his JD when he was 17, and he also passed the Florida Bar. The problem emerged when he moved to New York and submitted an application for the February 1987 New York bar examination. The Board rejected his application, because Mr Baccus had not yet reached 21 years of age and had entered law school before reaching the age of 18. Mr Baccus argued that these requirements violate the constitutional

9 *Id.*, p. 15; in support of these conclusions, the Court cites M. W. Schuyler, 'The Ku Klux Klan in Nebraska 1920-1930', *Nebraska History* 66, 1985, pp. 234-256.

10 *Philip Morris Inc. et al v. Lynn French District Court of Appeal of Florida*, Third District. 897 So. 2d 480 (22 December 2004, rehearing was denied on 13 April 2005).

11 *Id.*, p. 490.

12 K. Polányi, *A nagy átalakulás – Korunk gazdasági és politikai gyökerei*, Napvilág kiadó, Budapest, 2004, p. 285. Polányi wrote this book originally in English in 1944, under the title *The Great Transformation: The Political and Economic Origins of Our Times*, Farrar & Rinehart, New York, 1944.

13 *Stephen Baccus v. Arthur Karger et al.*, 692 F. Supp. 290, S.D.N.Y. (17 August 1988).

principle of equal protection. Just as in the majority of the cases mentioned before, the Court undertook a historical analysis, focusing in particular on the circumstances of the enactment of the New York Constitution (in 1846), which set the age requirement. In the concluding paragraph of the judgment – referring to the origin of the 1846 rules – the New York District Court (Southern District) underlined: "Thus, in a marriage between populism and general disdain for the legal profession was the 21-year-old requirement born." (Let me add that as far as the main issue was concerned, the Court held that the requirement that one could only commence legal studies after one's 18th birthday violates the equal protection clause, and it is unconstitutional. The Court also held that the requirement that one has to be over 21 years of age before taking the bar exam was 'reasonably tailored'. Thus, Baccus was allowed to take the bar, but he had to wait until his 21st birthday.)

In a case decided in 2008, a Texas court considered a dispute between an entrepreneur called Lavon Evans and the Haliburton Energy Services Inc. (The Haliburton company is also known for its deals in Iraq and for its links with Secretary of Defense Cheney.) The subject-matter of the dispute was the interpretation of a guarantee agreement.[14] One of the arguments of Mr Evans was that the draft was submitted by Haliburton, and this circumstance supported an interpretation against, rather than in favour of Haliburton. This is actually, a principle of interpretation dating back to Roman law (the *contra proferentem* principle), which has a rather wide acceptance (particularly if the term of the contract was not individually negotiated).[15] The Court stated, however, that "[r]elying on who the draftsman was as a means of interpretation is populist nonsense".[16] In this case, the negative connotation of the term 'populist' is obvious, although the anchor point of this connotation is less than clear.

I would like to add to these American cases an Israeli decision – and a criticism of this decision by an Israeli author.[17] Speaking of the populist endeavour of 'public sentiment mirroring', Alon Harel refers to the *El Al Israeli Airlines Ltd v. Danilovich* case.[18] The High Court of Justice accepted the proposition that a same-sex partner of an air steward is entitled to the same benefits as a different-sex partner. Yet in her statement of reasons, Justice Dorner stated that the case was decided "on the basis of accepted social outlooks". The author calls this 'judicial populism'. In his words:

14 *Halliburton Energy Services v. Lavon Evans*, United States District Court, S.D. Texas, 2008 WL 5525602 (29 April 2008).

15 This principle was also adopted in Sect. 5:103 of the European Contract Principles stating that "[w]here there is doubt about the meaning of a contract not individually negotiated, an interpretation of the term against the party which supplied it is to be preferred".

16 *Haliburton Energy Services v. Lavon Evans*, p. 2.

17 A. Harel, 'Courts in a Populist World', *VerfBlog*, 27 April 2017, https://verfassungsblog.de/courts-in-a-populist-world/.

18 *El Al Israeli Airlines Ltd. v. Danilovich*, 48(5) PD 749 (30 November 1994).

> Ordinarily, we might presume that a person's entitlement to a legal remedy would be enhanced by their facing social, economic and/or political discrimination. Yet according to Dorner, this is not the case. Only those who already benefit from community understanding and recognition can invoke judicial action and gain legal protection.[19]

In this context, the populist approach appears to be supporting a just cause, but with an argumentation that might jeopardize other just causes that did not gain acceptance by public sentiment.

3.3 What Is the Opposite of Populism?

The court decisions cited above are hinting some interesting angles, they also explain links with history – but they do not lead us towards a consistent notion.

A possible anchor of a notion could be the identification of an opposite side. In a considerable number of studies, populism is juxtaposed with elitism – but some caveats also appear. It is common knowledge that the concept of populism has been a subject of controversies within the political sciences, and it has acquired various connotations. The identification of an opposite notion may contribute to the formation of a frame of reference and to the clarity of the concept populism. In a collection of studies about populism, the editors (Yves Mény & Yves Surel) introduce the question by referring to Isaiah Berlin's well-known *adage*: "There is a shoe – in the shape of populism – but no foot to fit in."[20] Mény and Surel are also pointing out that this 'Cinderella complex' has not yet been resolved. One may add that, the 'shoe' has been reshaped by the efforts of the craftsmen of political opinions and campaigns – and this only made it even more difficult to fit.

It is simply not possible to find an uncontroversial scholarly definition of populism. Juxtaposition between populism and elitism appears to be a point of reliance. This is often cited, but it is also a fact that this juxtaposition was more evident (and more relevant) in earlier times. Speaking about the history of populism, John Lukács states that there were populist leaders and populist uprisings before Protestantism. He adds that these populist movements left some mark on the whole history of Europe and were "almost always directed against the aristocracy, but were not always leftist".[21] Mény and Surel state that the juxtaposition of populism with elitism is common ground, and they submit that the rhetoric that permeates populist discourse is "[b]ased on the celebration of the good, wise,

19 Harel, 2017.

20 Y. Mény & Y. Surel, 'The Constitutive Ambiguity of Populism', *in* Y. Mény & Y. Surel (Eds.), *Democracies and the Populist Challenge*, Palgrave Macmillan, Basingstoke, 2002, p. 3.

21 J. Lukács, *Demokrácia és Populizmus*, Európa kiadó, Budapest, 2008, p. 59.

and simple people and the rejection of the corrupt, incompetent interlocking elites".[22] In his book on populism, Paul Taggart offers a long survey of various definitions of populism, which show that the juxtaposition with elitism is the most reliable characteristic.[23] Citing Edward Shils he adds that "[t]he key to understanding populism lies in the relationship between elites and masses".[24] I shall add to list of those who perceive elitism as the antipode of populism the article of Tamás Gáspár Miklós entitled *Populism and Elitism*.[25]

In our days, the general criticism addressed to populism often ignores the original juxtaposition. This may be to some extent due to the fact that it is getting more difficult to identify and distinguish the 'populus' and the elite. Social classes have become less distinct, although social differences are still huge and excruciating. The nobility versus plebs distinction was formalized. Today, the position of the elite is not the result of a formal royal deed. It is still possible, of course, to identify an elite whose position is comparable to that of the nobility in medieval times. In his article 'Machiavellian Democracy: Controlling Elites with Ferocious Populism', J. McCormick from Yale University lists as "agents who do the domination", the "[R]oman nobility in the past, corporate magnates, entrenched bureaucrats, and government officials [...]"[26] Yet, present-day assertions often do not view populism as an opponent of 'corporate magnates'. During the 2016 US presidential elections, populism was often juxtaposed with 'the establishment' – but the populist winner can hardly be described as an 'opponent of corporate magnates'. The same applies to the October 2017 Czech elections. According to the title of the 22 October 2017 *Financial Times* – 'Populist billionaire wins Czech elections'. The *Financial Times* cites Milan Nic of the German Council of Foreign Relations. In his words, "[t]his is an earthquake. It is a total revolt against the established parties and the mainstream". Commenting on the victory of the billionaire Babiš, it is stated on the BBC website on 22 October 2017 that he campaigned on an anti-establishment platform and asserted that he is standing up "against self-serving establishment". This is another example showing that the antipode of populism is volatile, corporate magnates may or may not belong there. The question also arises, whether the term 'populism' captures the actual nature and the roots of 'revolt against established parties and the mainstream'.

Within contemporary public discourse and perceptions, the antipode is typically not on the screen in a distinguished way. One of the possible reasons for this is that the identification of an antipode would establish a more circumscribed and confined frame of reference that might impede some patterns of use. Also, it would be more difficult to reduce

22 Mény & Surel, 2002, p. 12.
23 P. Taggart, *Populism*, Open University Press, Philadelphia, 2000, pp. 10-22.
24 *Id.*, p. 11.
25 T. G. Miklós, 'Populizmus és elitizmus', *Élet és Irodalom* (weekly), 23 December 2005.
26 J. P. McCormick, 'Machiavellian Democracy: Controlling Elites with Ferocious Populism', *American Political Science Review*, Vol. 95, 2001, p. 303.

the perception of politics to a simple juxtaposition of populists on one side and honest politicians on the other side. Nowadays, characterizing someone as a populist is not just an observation, it is usually a condemnation. Such a condemnation is not excluded by the original concept, but it does not necessarily follow from it either. In social sciences 'populism' used to have some content as well, it was not just a stigma. At this point, the rift has been widening between the original concept and perceptions in social sciences on the one hand and present-day public discourse on the other. In the social sciences, the negative connotation is present, but it does not have a monopolistic position. It has been stated, for example, that in line with its anti-elitist character, populism tends to combine representative-electoral control with more direct forms of elite control.[27] Different views have been expressed regarding the question whether populism or elitism is more helpful (or more damaging). To cite an opinion among those that give more credit to populism, Michael Kazin submits that the true enemy of democracy is not populism but elitism, the platonic idea that the experts should play the game and keep the incompetent citizens out.[28] This angle may, of course, be contested, but it should not be completely disregarded. Many authors have also pointed out that the rise of populism is a sign that there are problems with the functioning of democracy. The big question is, of course, what alternative could be yielded by populism. Hitler was labelled a populist – but so was De Gaulle; Peron and Senator McCarthy were called populists, but so was Jimmy Carter.[29] It appears that Obama has not escaped this label either. There are persuasive reasons to worry about an aggressive version of populism combined with nationalism, but this worry is not a clear guidance in itself. According to Margaret Canovan, the endeavour to mark populism as either rightist or leftist, is a "lost cause".[30]

Identifying an antipode may have some sobering effects. It is too easy to identify opponents of populism as 'good guys', if we only know that they are opposing something bad (populism) but we do not really know what these people stand for. If some opponent of populism is identified as an 'elitist', or member/supporter of the establishment (or of anything specific), his heroism would be less obvious. By the same vein, if the juxtaposition populist-elitist/establishment is on the screen, it would be more difficult for populists, ardent opponents of the establishment, to remain heroes, after they won the elections – and after they became the political establishment (and, at least in part, the business establishment as well). Examples have shown that it is not impossible to continue populist rhetoric on behalf of the establishment, by way of identifying (or construing) a new

27 According to J. McCormick such an observation can be led back to Machiavelli. *Id.*, p. 311.

28 M. Kazin, *The Populist Persuasion: An American History*, New York, 1995, cited in N. Urbinati, 'Democracy and Populism', *Constellations*, No. 1, 1988, p. 11.

29 *See, e.g.*, M. Canovan, *Populism*, Junction Books, London, 1981, pp. 289-301.

30 *Id.*, p. 294.

antipode. Yet this would be more difficult if we had a greater public awareness of the basic juxtaposition.

3.4 What Is Actually Getting Condemned by the Label 'Populism'?

In present public discourse – and political discourse in particular – the term 'populism' is essentially reduced to condemnation, and it represents a rather powerful denouncement. The question arises, however, what is actually being denounced?

I shall return shortly to the press and public discourse. In its weekend issue of 19–20 August 2017, the Belgrade daily *Danas* reports about a scuffle within the Serbian opposition. This opposition has been labelling the ruling Serbian leader (Vučić) as populist. But when it came to an internal debate within the opposition, Mr Ješić from the Democratic Party declared that Mr Janković (opposition candidate against Vučič in the presidential elections some months ago) "is driven by populist thinking", because (among other things) he is seeking solutions in NGOs rather than in political parties. The formula is a simple one: If I disagree with someone, and if I want to show that he is wrong, I shall say that he is a populist.

Trying to identify some common impulse behind various uses of the terms 'populism' and 'populist', one could get close to the mark by pointing out the drive for unmasking – yielding a condemnation. The typical (and justified) targets are politicians and political speech. And there is, indeed, a growing need for unmasking. Promises made by politicians are usually not guided by an urge to spell out what should be done, but rather by a wish to say what is desirable to be said. It is also not a revelation anymore if one points out that those who decide what it is opportune to say, are typically not politicians themselves, but communication experts. They are suggesting, of course, slogans with promises for a better life. But the responsibility of communication experts does not extend until the achievement of a better life – it ends when the election results are published. What they promised themselves to the party that hired them, is an election result. Advisors always existed, of course, but their role has dramatically increased in recent time. This may be in line with the phenomenon of 'outsourcing'. In the introduction to their book *Government by Contract: Outsourcing and American Democracy*, two Harvard Law School Professors, Jody Freeman and Martha Minow, are stating: "[...] we live in an era of pervasive government outsourcing – what we call government by contract."[31]

In this setting, one of the most common and most strong denouncements made – the allegation that populism it is driven by demagoguery – is somewhat losing ground. Not

31 J. Freeman & M. Minow, 'Introduction: Reframing the Outsourcing Debates', *in* J. Freeman & M. Minow (Eds.), *Government by Contract: Outsourcing and American Democracy*, Harvard University Press, Cambridge/MA, 2009, p. 1.

because populists are not demagogues, but because parties opposing populism are not exempt from demagoguery either. One can read time and again, that party X is populist and demagogue, because it is focusing on migrants rather than on creation of jobs. There is every reason to condemn slogans spreading prejudices and stating that party X will protect good people (or a good nation) from evil migrants. This is an appalling demagoguery. But what about slogans about creation of jobs? Are they immune from demagoguery? In an article published in the *Guardian* in April 2008, the author (Monbiot) starts with the following sentence: "There is no nonsense so gross that it cannot be justified by the creation of jobs."[32] The author submits – relying on a sampling exercise – that if one were to accept at face value announcements about the creation of jobs "there would be 218 million workers in the UK". (Quite an impressive number, considering a population of about 61 million.)

As a matter of fact, the creation of jobs is an obvious priority, but also a common rhetorical shield. The more often you mention the 'creation of jobs', the more protected you are. References to 'socialist democracy', the 'fight for peace' or 'worker's self-management' had about the same role several decades ago. Each time you utter "I will create more jobs", (or earlier, "I will fight for peace and socialist democracy"), you added a piece of garlic to the string around your neck, which protects you against the vampires in the opposition, or rivals within your own team or party. In other words, the question is not whether populism is linked with demagoguery, but whether demagoguery is a distinguishing feature of populism compared with other contemporary political movements.

An important characteristic feature of present-day public discourse is an inordinate extension of the usage of the term 'populism'. In this setting, the targets of condemnation are getting dispersed. There is hardly any (real or perceived) deficiency or blemish left that was not called 'populism' by the opponents. But if every promise that is pleasing to wide social strata is called 'populism', what remains as a basis for comparison? Can the term 'populism' maintain any distinct meaning if we qualify as 'populism' all demagoguery, and every promise with a questionable basis? The overuse of the term leads to a faltering of the frame of reference behind the notion – and of the notion itself as well. Our consumer society is also marked by consumption of notions. As a further development – just as on financial markets – derivatives have appeared. For example: "Hitler was a populist. Thus, if Mr X. is a populist, he is a Hitler-type politician." The point is that, although Hitler may have been a populist, this label does not really grasp and cover Hitler's monstrosity. De Gaulle was also a populist. Bernie Sanders has also been called a populist. Thus, the question is, whether we are really getting to the core of the problem when we are saying that a politician who is spreading venomous xenophobia is a populist, when at the same time,

32 G. Monbiot, 'Jobs are Used to Justify Anything, but the Numbers Don't Add Up', *The Guardian*, 1 April 2008.

someone using tough rhetoric in order to get damages from tobacco companies is also labelled populist – just as Obama when he talks about a nuclear-free world, or a Serbian politician who prefers to rely on NGOs.

Condemning populism because of its reliance on demagogy certainly makes sense. But it is not easy to identify demagoguery as the characteristic that distinguishes populism from other political orientations. In our time, it has become even more difficult to distinguish populist demagoguery from general demagogy, due to the fact that political slogans are getting more and more meaningless – hence we have less and less ground for a comparison of meanings. This may – at least partially – be one of the yields of outsourcing, and copy-paste production of political messages by experts belonging to the same guild. Before the elections for the European Parliament in May 2014, I noted on the website "Political hashtags – EU wide" several hundred mottos. Most of them follow the same pattern, and – with some exceptions – one cannot really identify different political agendas behind the slogans. Here are some examples:

- In Europa prima Italia (In Europe, Italy first) – New Right Center
- Meno Europa in Italy, piú Italia in Europa (Less Europe in Italy, more Italy in Europe) – Forza Italia
- Lo chiedamo all'Europa (We ask Europe) – Partito Democratico, Italy
- Erfahrung und Durchsetzungskraft (Experience and assertiveness) – ÖVP Austria
- Europa besser machen (Make Europe better) – ÖVP Austria
- Europa im Kopf, Österreich im Herzen (Europe in the mind, Austria in the heart) – SPÖ, Austria
- ДПС в Европа, Европа в България (DPS in Europe, Europe in Bulgaria) – DPS Bulgaria
- Imposons une nouvelle croissance (Let us impose a new growth) – Parti Socialiste, France
- Malta Ahjar (A better Malta) – Nationalist Party, Malta
- Parempi Eurooppa syntyy tvostä rauhaa rakastamalla ja ongemia ratkaisemalla (A better Europe is born through work, love of peace and solving problems) – Kokoomus Finland
- Gemeinsam erfolgreich in Europa (Sharing success in Europe) – CDU Germany
- Für ein Europa, das den Menschen dient (For a Europe that serves the people) – CDU Germany
- Wir brauchen ein besseres Europa (We need a better Europe) – CSU Germany

Most slogans of parties labelled as radical populist are not breaking really different ground. One of the slogans of the French Front National is: "Non a Bruxelles. Oui à la France" (No to Brussels, Yes to France); another Front National slogan reads: "Le 25 mai, votez patriote" (On 25 May, vote patriotically). The Austrian FPÖ declares. "Wir machen Österreich stark!

Für ein freies Europa" (We make Austria strong! For a free Europe.). According to a similar (although less tactful) FPÖ slogan: "Österreich denkt um. Zu viel EU ist dumm" (Austria think again. Too much Europe is dumb.).

One of the very few slogans that puts across some spirit prompted by recent actual developments, is the slogan of the French Parti Pirate Sud Ouest: "La NSA sait déjà que vous allez votez pour nous" (The NSA already knows that you will vote for us).

The question arises how to compete with approaches described as populist, when convenient platitudes and blandness have become one of the mainstream recipes for success. It is simply not possible to posit the slogans of mainstream parties cited above (like *e.g.*, "Make Europe better") as truth-telling juxtaposed with populist lying. What these posters actually mirror is a growing assumption that there is an entitlement to meaninglessness.

On 9 October 2010, the *New York Times* selected as quotation of the day the words of Christopher Lehane, a consultant of the Democratic Party, who describes a candidate who does not fit customary standards, because "[h]e is most definitely not the blow-dry-haired, antiseptic, focus-group-tested candidate that most are used to in this day and age in politics".

The reliance on 'antiseptic, focus-group-tested' politicians and ideas does not help in shaping an entitlement for condemnation, and it does not help either in creating a vantage point from which it would be more easy to observe – and to confront – populism. To the contrary, it makes the juxtaposition more volatile, and it also engenders a revolt, and a need 'for something real'. This need might create a drive and offer a chance to anything what is not a serial production – including Trump.

3.5 DISCOVERY OR SIMPLY DENOUNCEMENT

Focusing on present patterns of use of the term 'populism' the question arises whether it yields revelation, discovery of a phenomenon, or just denouncement, condemnation; and whether the notion is still determined and constrained by a discernible content.

There are several causes prompting the separation of the term 'populism' from a defined (or at least definable) content. One such cause is overuse of the term 'populism' (particularly in political discourse) with the aim to qualify, or rather disqualify, a wide range of targets. A second cause is the loss of a clear juxtaposition with an antipode. 'Elitism' is losing its position as an opposing value, 'establishment' is stepping in, but only in some contexts and some areas. This helps politicians who are positing themselves as opponents of populism in projecting themselves simply as 'good guys' – but this does not help those who want to see populism within a clear system of coordinates. It is not difficult – nor is it unfair – to denounce most populist messages as bad messages, but the actual origin of these messages could be perceived more clearly if more attention were devoted to the question what has created room for populism (noticing meaninglessness and emptiness of mainstream political communication among the possible causes). Furthermore, the most frequently offered elucidation (populism is an exercise of demagogy) is not incorrect, but it fails to distinguish populism from rhetoric attitudes of other political parties.

One cannot deny that we are, indeed, facing threatening political ideas and attitudes. It is important to see them clearly, to discover and lay things bare. But this is not easy. Both the economy and the political environment are getting less and less transparent, and more and more difficult to grasp. Good intentions are not always sufficient guidance to endeavours aiming to reveal the truth behind (or in spite of) slogans. In political discourse, it has always been an everyday practice to point out that the other side is making false promises – or is simply lying. The introduction of the term 'populism' in the political discourse, hinted a stand above such squabbles. Many observers used the term 'populism' in expressing criticism, suggesting that what they are saying is not just an assertion that someone is lying, it is an observation of an educated spectator. This is certainly an added value. But of course, the maintenance of this flair is only possible if the goal remains the explanation (or maybe exposure) of a phenomenon, rather than just the condemnation of a political party or of a political leader. This flair is getting lost in present-day political discourse. It is difficult to maintain an analytic distance with an anchor in social sciences, if populism is not juxtaposed to elitism (or to any other discernible phenomenon), but populist guys are simply juxtaposed to good guys. The question is whether the terms 'populism' and 'populist' sustained an analytical clarity within their present use, whether they bring a clear vision of the problem – and hence, a chance to confront it. We are facing the problem of overuse of the notion of 'populism' and its separation from a coherent content. The avalanche of references to populism guided by the desire to denounce, or by a desire to suit a fashion, has also tainted instances of adequate and purposeful use. In public discourse, the term 'populism' is becoming more and more reduced to a rhetoric weapon that can be used against all kinds of opponents for the purpose of denouncement.

There is a rational reason to be afraid from a number of political forces and attitudes that are nowadays labelled as populist. The question is whether the present use (and overuse) of the notion 'populism' takes us to the core of the problem, whether an opposite side (and value) has been made recognizable on the screen – and whether the notion reflects a clear content that could serve as a starting point in seeking remedy.

4 Reflections on the Nature of Populism and the Fragility of Democracy: Democracy in Crisis

*David M. Rasmussen**

4.1 Introduction

In a previous paper, '*Rawls, Religion, and the Crisis of Civilization*',[1] I presented two concepts of the political, one that entailed a clash of civilizations associated with the Schmittian critique of liberalism and a second notion of the political that envisioned the political as an emerging domain eventually grounded in overlapping consensus. I argued that Rawls, among other things, kept the liberal project alive through the construction of a model that was able to accommodate pluralism, in contrast to the more restrictive perspective of classical liberalism, a phenomenon that is very much alive today,[2] which from his perspective could be characterized as a comprehensive doctrine.

What Rawls discovered in the aftermath of writing his *A Theory of Justice*[3] was that the congruence between the right and the good, the model constructed in the third part of that book, could not accommodate the fact of pluralism that he came to recognize characterized the modern democratic condition. I argued that in contrast to the Schmittian narrative, which dramatically postulated the political that would be characterized as originating in a life-and-death struggle of friend versus enemy,[4] the Rawlsian narrative, beginning in a similar place, the stark confrontation suggested by a *modus vivendi*, would step by step ascend to an overlapping consensus. What we know now is that when Rawls departed from epistemology as he did in *Justice as Fairness: Political not Metaphysical*[5] he developed

* Professor, Boston College, Department of Philosophy.

1 D. Rasmussen, 'Rawls, Religion, and the Crisis of Civilization', *Telos*, Vol. 2014, No. 167, 2014, pp. 107-125.

2 Quong and Gauss have recently taken the position of classic as opposed to political liberalism arguing for a kind of liberalism that is to be practiced by liberals alone. *See* G. Gaus, *The Order of Public Reason: A Theory of Freedom and Morality in a Diverse and Bounded World*, Cambridge University Press, Cambridge, 2011; J. Quong, *Liberalism without Perfection*, Oxford University Press, Oxford, 2010.

3 J. Rawls, *A Theory of Justice*, Harvard University Press, Cambridge/MA, 1971.

4 C. Schmitt, *The Concept of the Political* [1932], trans. G. Schwab, The University of Chicago Press, Chicago, 2007.

5 J. Rawls, 'Justice as Fairness: Political not Metaphysical', *in* S. Freeman (Ed.), *J. Rawls, Collected Papers*, Harvard University Press, Cambridge/MA, 1999, pp. 388-414.

a more or less historical argument, a political sociology, regarding how it happened that democratic society was able to move beyond a mere *modus vivendi.* In order to frame the argument, he would develop a two-stage model where the question of stability would be deferred to the second stage where overlapping consensus would be addressed.

Although we see shades of a veil of ignorance here, a borrowing from the original position framework of the *Theory of Justice,* it is also an easy way to abandon the realm of conflict that has characterized the political ever since the dawn of axial civilizations, as Eisenstadt of the school of multiple modernities has claimed:

> From the ideology and premises of the political program of modernity and the core characteristics of modern political institutions, there emerged three central aspects of the modern political process: the restructuring of center-periphery relations as the principal focus of political dynamics of modern societies; a strong tendency toward politicizing the demands of various sectors of society, and the conflicts between them; and a continuing struggle over the definition of the realm of the political. Indeed, it is only with the coming of modernity that drawing the boundaries of the political becomes one of the major foci of open political contestation and struggle.[6]

Quite frankly in modernity, the political is a contested domain. In some ways, to turn to the historical while at the same time sheltering the political in the two-stage model as Rawls has done, points to the fragility of democracy and maybe gives the clue to why populism has been so successful. In what follows I will consider populism from two perspectives, one historical and one normative, and then conclude by returning to the problem I have just raised.

4.2 What Is Populism? An Historical Perspective

Populism strikes at the heart of democracy. Its power is to take over the claims of democracy. Some maintain that it masks itself as a moral theory and it does have moral claims regarding immigrants and immigration, nationalism and the state of the nation, the distribution of power, race and ethnicity and many other things. Populism claims to listen to the cries of the oppressed people, the forgotten man and woman, the silent majority and the unrepresented. At its heart populism is a claim about the *authority* of a people. Or to put it another way, populism is a claim about the *legitimacy* of politics seen to lie in the authority of a people.

6 S. N. Eisenstadt, 'Multiple Modernities', *Daedalus*, Vol. 129, No. 1, 2000, p. 6.

In order to frame my approach to populism, I want to use part of Margret Canovan's argument in her delightful book, *The People.*[7] Her reading of the history of the concept goes back to the Romans and their use of the term, 'populous', which has a double meaning. On the one hand, it could refer to the plebeian *populous* and on the other, given Cicero's use of the term, it could refer to Roman population as such.[8] *Lex Regia,* was the oldest form of Roman law, royal law that found its legitimacy in the people. The rather vague idea contained in this doctrine was that the people were the ground of legitimacy for any form of political action: an institutional idea that can be traced to the numinous past beginning with the reign of Romulus.

This vague idea of a people who existed as the passive source of legitimacy, designated the 'people in reserve' by Canovan, would reappear in the by the twelfth century to ground the legitimacy of monarchical rule, which became more substantial particularly as a consequence of the Protestant reformation. With the publication of Locke's *Second Treatise on Civil Government,* the idea of people in reserve came to be ever more radical as the source of legitimacy when it was formulated in the famous phrase 'consent of the governed'. However, according to Canovan, it was the American Revolution that transformed the idea of the people, "from people in reserve to constituent sovereign".[9] She writes:

> The Declaration of Independence can in a sense be read as the culmination of traditional resistance theory [...] In their state constitutions and in the US Constitution itself, a mobilized people apparently exercised sovereignty by establishing entirely new institutions, replacing the authority of antiquity with the authority of present popular consent.[10]

What was unique about the American experience was that it united the two types of sovereignty; what had been the passive source of legitimacy, the people as passive, and the authority that had been generally granted to actually govern, the people as active. In a

7 M. Canovan, *The People*, Polity Press, Cambridge, 2005.

8 This duality is worth noting. The first reference is to the 'people' who occupied the Roman forum. They participated in a way that was more or less restricted to affirmation of the programs politicians were presenting to them. Acclamation was perceived as a legitimate form of representation but not a democratic form of representation. What interests me about Urbinati's analysis, which I will discuss in a moment, is that while Canovan sees a redemptive side to the duality of political representation Urbinati sees the sinister side, the reduction of citizenship to mere acclamation. If we draw out the implication of this view, we see in populism a reversion to a pre-democratic form of the political. Cicero saw the other side of the people as representative, namely, as a form of justification for legal action. It is this element of Cicero's thought that Augustine picks up in *The City of God* when he had an argument against the legitimacy of the Roman government. Augustine focuses on Cicero's use of the term 'commonwealth' understood as the will of the people.

9 Canovan, 2005, p. 27.

10 *Id.*

sense this is the ambiguity that rests at the heart not only of populism but also of democracy itself because the gap between ruler and ruled was never entirely closed.

This left room for appeals to the people against the people's government; and while these happened routinely during elections, they could never be exhausted by the process of voting. The coexistence of popular government with the authority of the sovereign people in reserve was to set the stage for populism in the sense of a movement to 'give government back to the people'.[11]

Thus far we can say that populism is about legitimate representation, *i.e.*, about representation, which lies in the concept of a people. This claim is to be put in a critical way because it is generally about the misrepresentation of a people. Further it often picks up on the Ancient Roman form of that claim by referring to the *common* people. Populism claims that the very ground on which democracy stands, its claim to represent the people, both as standing reserve and active governing body, fails because democracy is essentially governed by elites. Hence, if we are to have legitimate government it will be necessary to restore what has been usurped to the people whom populism claims to represent. Thus, we can say that populism rests on a claim about misrepresentation with the implicit message that it can resolve that problem by defining the proper representatives.

4.3 What Is Populism? A Normative Perspective[12]

From a normative perspective, populism can be defined as a certain kind of parasitic pathology that can attack representative democracy. As much of the literature suggests, we do not have a clear concept of populism. Certainly, a reason for this is that populism is more or less defined by the context in which it occurs. A more substantial reason for the obscurity of the term is because populism functions more or less negatively as implied by my choice of the term 'parasite', which can be defined as an organism that lives in or on another organism (its host) and benefits by deriving nutrients at the host's expense.

There are more positive definitions of populism associated with various political movements, most notably movements like one of the original forms of so-called populism

11 *Id.*, p. 29. To anticipate my argument, I would not necessarily call this populism. Urbinati makes a distinction between social or political movements and actual governance. The populists who developed the populist party in 1892 that were absorbed into the democratic party in 1896 never really governed as such. I am not trying to argue that this movement was illegitimate, simply that we were never able to see the other side, the governing side of populism.

12 In writing this chapter, I was particularly influenced by the work of Nadia Urbinati's two essays on the subject of populism: N. Urbinati, 'The Populist Phenomenon', *Raisons Politiques*, Vol. 51, No. 3, 2013, pp. 137-154; N. Urbinati, 'The Principle of the Majority', in C. L. Kaltwasser *et al.* (Eds.), *The Oxford Handbook of Populism*, Oxford University Press, Oxford, 2017.

associated with the founding of the American populist party in 1892.[13] However, to be realized populism has to become a form of governing and not simply a social movement. In accord with this definition, although populism is claimed to be the product of people's sovereignty; rather it is derived from their sovereignty that has already been established. In other words, populism arrives after the revolution is over and democratic sovereignty of the people has been established. To understand populism therefore it is necessary to understand liberal democracy from which it is derived as a negative form.

Populism thrives on dividing the democratic population into a binary opposition, generally between elites and non-elites, the authentic and the inauthentic, the good and the bad. Populism believes that this is an original insight but its very ability to impose this duality presupposes the given diversity of a democratic culture. Clearly, politics is constituted by conflict although it is not necessarily binary, the conflict can be characterized by diversity. As we shall see for a normative understanding of representative democracy it will be necessary to accommodate all the participants in the process.

> In populism the people are not really what *prima facie* appear as the people in its empirical entirety; rather, as Claude Lefort put it, first 'the people must be extracted from within the people'.[14]

In order to generate this division between the authentic and the so-called inauthentic members of the democratic order, populism generates a legitimation crisis[15] continuing to delegitimize legitimate members of the democratic order as well as the institutions they represent. In order to do this populism depends on continuous acts of polarization.[16]

In this sense, populism raises the problem of the legitimacy in a new way by attempting to undercut in the name of its own ideology the various institutions that would constrain it. In order to reduce the political order to the elites vs. the authentic people, it will be

---

13 Emergent democracy examples are: A. Sieyès, *What is the Third Estate*, Pall Mall Press, London, 1963; T. Jefferson, *The Declaration of Independence* (USA 1776); American Populist Party (1892, 1896) and emergent democracies in South America as examined in the book by E. Laclau, *On Populist Reason*, Verso, New York, 2007.

14 *See* in J. W. Muller, '"The People Must Be Extracted from Within the People": Reflections on Populism', *Constellations*, Vol. 21, No. 4, 2014, p. 485.

15 I think Habermas' notion of 'legitimation crisis' fits rather well here. In some ways populism thrives on a crisis of legitimation brought on by among other things economic conditions, which I do not talk about here but should be fundamental to the analysis. It was Aristotle who pointed out that when the division between the classes becomes to great the possibility for demagoguery becomes greater. No doubt the recent work by Thomas Picketty, *Capital*, makes this point from a more contemporary point of view. *See* T. Piketty, *Capital in the Twenty-First Century*, trans. A. Goldhammer, Harvard University Press, Cambridge/MA, 2014.

16 This is where the type of legitimation crisis generated by populism differs from the one defined by Habermas in the sense that for populism by polarizing is not part of democratic progress but is fundamentally regressive.

necessary to simplify it. Hence, the richness associated with a diverse democratic order must be undercut in order to achieve the opposition between those who presumably represent the constituent democratic order and those whom it claims do not.[17] Here I disagree with those who would claim an affirmative perspective for populism by legitimating a group that heretofore had no legitimate representation.[18] Instead, by an act of simplification populism undercuts the legitimate diversity of democratic society by claiming to represent only those who fit within its narrow ideological perspective.

As such populism chooses unity over equality hence departing from a core ingredient of modern democracy. By granting membership rights only to the majority of the chosen, it undercuts a universal commitment to equality that must be the basis of any democratic order. As such it materializes the collective into a single actor much in the way Lefort thought about totalitarianism.[19] In a similar way, populism effectively undercuts public opinion by trying to reduce it to a single expression or voice and in our current media culture that means it can dismiss the best of public opinion as fake news. In the same vein populism sacrifices equality for unity collapsing the distinction between leader and subject. In this sense populism reverts to its historical origins reaffirming what some have called Caesarism, the citizen being reduced to the subject who participates by acclamation, as did the participants in the old Roma forum.

Finally, populism requires at its base in the words of Carl Schmitt, the friend/enemy distinction. What Schmitt has argued for in *The Concept of the Political* is the ontological priority of the friend/enemy distinction.

My argument sees that distinction as derivative, in the sense that populism is parasitical on liberal democracy, which has a certain normative foundation. In order to do a complete analysis from the point of view of political liberalism it would be necessary to make the following comparisons. First, it would be necessary to consider populism's desire for unity in relationship to overlapping consensus. Second populism's obsession with simplification would be examined in relationship to the recognition of diversity within a representative

17 Alessandro Ferrara makes a very important point in his paper when he notes that under populism the voting majority is identified as having *constituent* power in relation to the other minorities which do not. He states: "As the embodiment of 'the people,' the electorate is attributed constituent power." *See* A. Ferrara, 'Can Political Liberalism Help Us Rescue "The People" From Populism?', *Philosophy & Social Criticism*, Vol. 44, No. 4, 2018, pp. 463-477.

18 *See* Laclau, 2007.

19 "Lefort characterizes the totalitarian system by a double 'fence': Totalitarianism abolishes the separation between state and society: the political power permeates society, and all preexisting human relations – class solidarity, professional or religious cooperation – tend to be replaced with a one-dimensional hierarchy between those who order and those who obey. This is made possible especially through the association between state and the party hierarchy which is always very close, so that the party hierarchy becomes the effective power. Lefort, like other theorists, thus identifies the destruction of public space and its fusion with the political power as a key element of totalitarianism." *See* https://en.wikipedia.org/wiki/Claude_Lefort#Conception_of_totalitarianism.

democratic community. Third, it would be necessary to examine populism's strategy of polarization in relationship to the need for integration within a democratic populous. Fourth, it would be imperative to consider populism's concentration on the rights of the majority in relationship to the claims of rights for minorities and the notion of universality for human rights. Fifth, in relationship to populism's desire to reduce public opinion to a singular view dismissing all other opinion as false it would be necessary find ways to support the diversity of public opinion as well as the burdens of judgment. Finally, it would be necessary counter the claims of populism regarding its representative subject with the claims of democratic citizenship as affirmed by political liberalism. In the end, it would be necessary to have stability for the right reasons.

4.4 The Fragility of Democracy

I want to return to the original problem, namely, the appeal of Political Liberalism to the two-stage model and the claim that such a move would make the normative claims of democracy suspect. In my view, what stands between the immediacy of an appeal to populism and the abstraction of a normative theory of democracy is the fact of pluralism. It is this fact that in the shape of political liberalism normative theory has attempted to address, the fact that shaped the work of the later Rawls in particular and normative democratic theory generally. In the process, the face of normative theory itself has changed from being based on strict forms of epistemology to, in Rawls case, a kind of political sociology, which sought for the new normative political values in what he has called in one of his articles, and I have adopted as a kind of orienting position, namely, 'the emerging domain of the political'. I do believe that Rawls, although on the right track, can be seen to have certain limitations, a certain naiveté, in constructing this domain that needs to be expanded beyond the Western foundations that were claimed for it.

However, if appropriately de-Westernized and expanded, the model of political liberalism is most appropriate for our emerging pluralistic democratic world. But of course, to attempt to confront the fact of pluralism is in some ways to confront the future and yet the curious dilemma that populism a remnant from the past, is that it is part of our current future. The paradox of populism is that even though its form is pre-democratic, it is part of the current political paradigm.[20]

The model I propose has the following components: first, there must be an accommodation to pluralism even if the claims of the culture are comprehensive. By comprehensive here I mean that the culture has been shaped by a particular ethos that will inform the building of a democratic orientation. Second, there must be some account of the relationship

20 *See* D. Rasmussen, 'From the Moral to the Political: The Question of Political Legitimacy in Non-Western Societies', *Philosophy & Social Criticism*, Vol. 43, No. 4-5, 2017, pp. 430-441.

between the moral, the religious (if the culture claims to be religious as in the case of certain Islamic societies) and the political. Third, there must be an account of unity within a society that shares a democratic point of view, an account that, like Rawls' liberal principle of legitimacy, anchors public unity in belief in a constitution. Fourth, there must be some way to account for a public political discourse, which could be characterized as public reason.

5 Populism and Nationalism

Nenad Miščević[*]

5.1 Introduction

The topic of this chapter is nationalism ('nativism', as sometimes called in the United States) and its relation to populism.[1] Since my interest is in nationalism, most attention will be paid to the right-wing and centre-right populist movements. This corresponds to the situation in the biggest part of Europe, and in the United States, where nationalist topics are being put forward by the right-wing populist. The leftist nationalist populism is more typical for Latin America. It is an open question whether it should count as being seriously nationalistic. A lot has been written on the topic.[2] However, I will leave it open here and mostly talk about the right-wing populism.

Pierre-André Taguieff in his book about populism, with a telling title, *La revanche du nationalism*,[3] presents populism as a kind of nationalism. He invented the useful term 'national-populist', which will be used in this chapter. However, it has become quite clear that nationalism is only one of the political 'isms' attracting the right-wing populists. The migration crisis has brought to the forefront populist self-identification with linguistic-cultural communities ('we Christians') that goes way beyond nationalism.

The first part of the chapter is more theoretical, dedicated to forms of interaction between populism and nationalism, both at the level of concepts (what kind of nationalism is compatible with what kind of populism) and at the level of actual historical causal interaction. I will look at the wider neighbourhood of nationalism, starting with patriotism (of stronger and weaker variety) and then pass to three species of nationalism, the classical one, the moderate, the statist one (the rule of law) and liberal nationalism. I am not aware that various kinds have been explicitly systematically discussed with regard to populism, so I hope to be able to present yet unexplored area of connections around populism. I will

* Professor of Philosophy at University of Maribor, Department of Philosophy (Slovenia); Visiting professor at Central European University, Department of Philosophy.

1 I am thankful to Violeta Beširević, who engaged me in writing this paper, and to Lea Ypi, with whom I have discussed the general idea of 'a changed playground'.

2 *See, e.g.*, D. V. Kingsbury, 'From populism to protagonism (and Back?) in Bolivarian Venezuela: Rethinking Ernesto Laclau's on *Populist Reason*', *Journal of Latin American Cultural Studies*, Vol. 25, No. 4, 2016, pp. 495-514; P. J. Krischke, *Populism and the Catholic Church: Political Crisis in Brazil, 1964*, Nova Science Publishers, New York, 2010; R. S. Jansen, *Revolutionizing Repertoires: The Rise of Populist Mobilization in Peru*, Chicago University Press, Chicago, 2017.

3 P. A. Taguieff, *La revanche du nationalisme*, PUF, Paris, 2015.

focus then on the 'isms' wider than nationalism, based on cultural belonging (Christian vs. Muslim, etc.) that have become central for the right-wing populists in the last decade. The option opposite to nationalism, cosmopolitanism, will be briefly explored. It will be noted that it has been attracting some left-wing, internationalist populists. This will conclude the theoretical part.

In the second part, national populism in Croatia will be considered. I will start from the historical background marked by the Yugoslav war(s) and very strong nationalism and argue that the actual government of Croatia is far from being a loud national populist one, especially if one looks at the top state officials, the president and the prime minister. This fact has been put forward in the sociopolitical literature, relying on actual empirical investigations. The absence of strong national populism in the highest ranks of the establishment presents a riddle: Croatia has all the precondition for such politics. I will, therefore, look for the answer to the riddle, *i.e.*, an explanation of the absence. It is to be found in the tension between two forces within nationalist populism – anti-elitism on the one hand and nationalism on the other. In the Croatian situation, the two do not go well together, since the ruling party has proved its patriotic attitude and is not open to anti-elitist attacks from this side. On the other hand, it did not take strongly nationalistic line, like in some of the neighbouring countries, but has tried to tamper the needed nationalist attachment. When considering the present-day situation in Croatia, one should also have in mind the pressures from the EU and the system of international justice. The reader of this volume will have an opportunity to read analyses of the neighbouring countries and notice similarities (for instance, with the Serbian ruling party) and contrasts (*e.g.*, with Orbán's politics). I hope that the story about Croatia will vividly illustrate the need for the distinctions proposed in the first part of the chapter.

The chapter concludes with the brief suggestion that the rise of populism, together with the appearance of the new national or cultural 'enemies', above all the immigrants, has dramatically changed the political playground. Consequently, the theory of nationalism (and cosmopolitism) should primarily find its place in relation to this new situation.

5.2 Nationalists of All Countries Unite!

"Nationalistes de tous les pays unissez-vous!"
[Nationalists of all countries unite!] Jean-Marie Le Pen

5.2.1 *Introductory Remarks*

Here is a very simplified sketch of what populism is. Many authors, prominently among them Jan-Werner Müller and Cas Mudde, note that the form common to all sorts of populism is quite simple and describe it as 'thin'.[4] Mudde explains:

> Populism is understood as a thin-centered ideology that considers society to be ultimately separated into two homogeneous and antagonistic groups, 'the pure people' versus 'the corrupt elite,' and which argues that politics should be an expression of the *volonte generale* (general will) of the People.[5]

Populism, so defined, has two opposites: elitism and pluralism.[6] First, there is the elite versus people ('underdog') contrast. Second, it is possible to distinguish two ways of characterizing 'the people': either in terms of social status (class, income level, etc.) or in terms of ethnic and/or cultural belonging.[7]

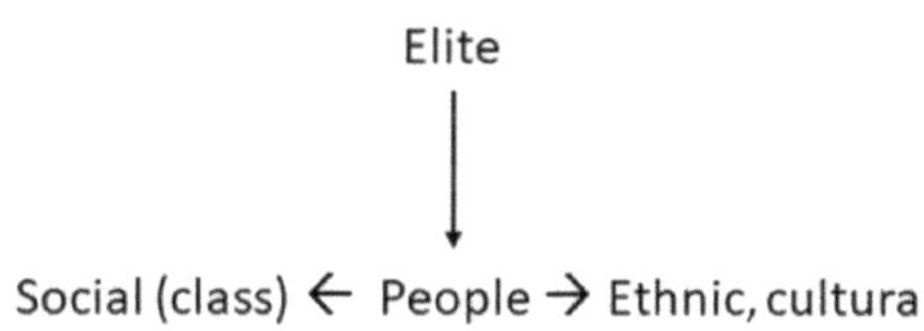

The second, horizontal dimension, distinguishes the predominantly left-wing from the predominantly right-wing populisms and leaves a place for a centrist populist option:

4 J. W. Müller, *What is populism?*, University of Pennsylvania Press, Philadelphia, 2016.
5 C. Mudde, *Populist Radical Right Parties in Europe*, Cambridge University Press, Cambridge, 2007, p. 23.
6 C. Mudde, 'The Populist Zeitgeist', *Government and Opposition*, Vol. 39, No. 4, 2004, p. 543.
7 De Cleen locates the 'articulation' of the two by specifying a dimension of populism distinct from the elite/underdog dimension and having to do with in-group/out-group contrast. *See* in B. De Cleen, 'Populism and Nationalism', *in* C. R. Kaltwasser *et al.* (Eds.), *The Oxford Handbook of Populism*, Oxford University Press, Oxford, 2017, pp. 342-362.

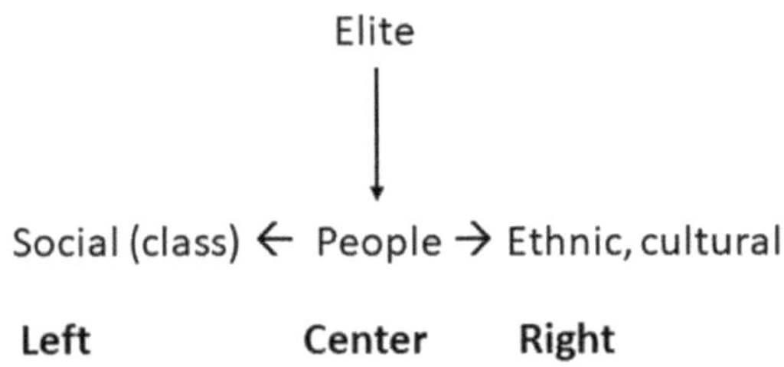

The leftist parties (the original SYRIZA, Podemos and the Latin American leftist parties) stress the social nature of the contrast: the poor versus the rich, the lower and the lowest classes versus the upper class and the like. Because the right-wing parties look at ethnic and cultural-linguistic characteristics of the 'demos', the topic of this chapter, populist nationalism, definitely belongs to the right-side of the picture. The centrist parties, like the Croatian 'Živi zid' party (Human Shield), borrow from both sides.[8]

Mudde has noted that 'populism' is an essentially contested concept.[9] Here is a methodological warning, not sufficiently voiced in the literature. When taking 'ideational' approach, one is often interested in conceptual relations (or relations in reality that correspond to the conceptual ones): is nationalism a kind of populism (does the extension of the concept 'nationalism' have a non-empty intersection with the one of the concept 'nationalism', and the like).[10] However, the issue of the relation between populism and its cognates can also be a historical, factual link and the account closer to a historical and sociological causal story.[11] To vary the example, one can be interested in the historical, nationalistic roots of Austrian populism and turn to the history of the *Freiheitlliche Partei*, its problematic causal-historical link with the Austrian Nazi forces (including the SS) and their ideology under the German occupation, etc. One thus has to distinguish conceptual from a causal link. In the sequel, the attention will be paid to both.

I will start a discussion by distinguishing a number of political ideas or ideologies in the wider field of national or national-like attachment.

First, a few words about a nation. The properties that a group has to have in order to be a nation are usually listed as kinship (or 'perception' of it), territorial contiguity, common culture, in particular, language, shared historical memories and a sense of common fate.[12]

8 'Živi zid' started in 2011 as NGO fighting eviction from occupying houses and forming a 'human shield'. Three years later, it became a party and entered into the Croatian parliament, where one of its leaders suddenly started advocated sending a war-ship to Slovenian sea-waters to fight for sea territory, a proposal normally not put forward even by the tough Croatian nationalists.

9 C. Mudde, 'Populism: An Ideational Approach', *in* C. R. Kaltwasser *et al.* (Eds.), p. 27.

10 *See*, for instance, the excellent chapter of A. Bozóki in this volume.

11 As a fine illustration, *see* the contribution of Dušan Spasojević in this volume.

12 *See* A. Gat & A. Yakobson, *Nations: The Long History and Deep Roots of Political Ethnicity and Nationalism*, Cambridge University Press, Cambridge, 2013.

A nation is seen as a political/state community giving the central place to this common affinity, identity and solidarity, the association of a people, usually defined by a certain culture and kin sentiments, with a particular state.

Second, the most famous modernist account of nationalism comes from Ernst Gellner.[13] Nationalism demands congruence between culture and state.[14] Classical nationalism is the political programme that sees creation and maintenance of a fully sovereign state owned by a given ethnonational group ('people' or 'nation') as a primary duty of each member of the group. Starting from the assumption that the appropriate (or 'natural') unit of culture is ethno-nation, it claims that a primary duty of each member is to abide in cultural matters by one's recognizably ethnonational culture. In the United States, this kind of attitude is called 'nativism'. Classical nationalists-nativists are usually vigilant about the kind of culture they protect and promote and about the kind of attitude people have towards their nation-state. This watchful attitude carries some potential dangers: many elements of a given culture that are simply not recognizably national, might and will sometimes, fall prey to such nationalist enthusiasms. Classical nationalism in everyday life puts various additional demands on individuals, from buying more expensive home-produced goods in preference to the cheaper imported ones to procreating as many future members of the nation as one can manage.

Besides classical nationalism (and its more radical extremist cousins), various moderate views are also nowadays classified as a nationalist. Indeed, the philosophical discussion has shifted to these moderate or even ultra-moderate forms, and most philosophers who describe themselves as nationalists, propose very moderate nationalist programmes. Let me characterize these briefly.

Nationalism in a wider sense is any complex of attitudes, claims and directives for action ascribing a fundamental political, moral and cultural value to nation and nationality and deriving obligations (for individual members of the nation and for any involved third parties, individual or collective) from this ascribed value. There are two versions (with some sub-versions) of this wider project. The first is moderate statist nationalism, where the nationalist programme is tempered by the set of minimal accepted human rights, in particular rights of minorities (*e.g.*, the country of Austria belongs primarily to Austrians, but its ethnically different members, Slovenes, Hungarians and others have minority rights), and also by the requirements of the parliamentary systems. The second version is even less traditionally nationalistic; it is the liberal nationalism, friendly to minorities, not just tolerant of them, possibly culminating in a multi-ethnic, multi-national state.

---

13 E. Gellner, *Nations and Nationalism*, Basil Blackwell, Oxford, 1983.

14 For Gellner, the nation goes together with industrial society. Industrial society demands homogeneity, so the kind of cultural homogeneity, demanded by nationalism, is a concomitant of industrial society, and we should accept it as unavoidable. A nation is thus a product of the age of nationalism, and can only be defined in terms of it.

In the rest of this section, a category close to nationalism, but often treated as distinct from it – patriotism will be discussed. Then, I will address the varieties of nationalism-nativism, the central topic of the chapter. A discussion on a wider populist alternative – communitarian non-national belonging, will follow: for instance, being Christian (in some very wide sense) as opposed to being Muslim. This is the crucial populist alternative to the ethnonational identity that shows that populism is not identical to nationalism. In the final part of the section, a few words about the alternative, traditionally opposed to nationalism, cosmopolitanism, and its possible relations to populism, will be offered.

5.2.2 *Patriotism*

The term 'patriotism' is used in many senses. It is sometimes taken to be centred around one's 'Patria': patriotism is the attachment to one's country in contrast to the attachment to one's people and its traditions (nationalism). Sometimes, it is taken to be much less aggressive than nationalism. Almost three-quarters of a century ago, George Orwell wrote that "patriotism is of its nature defensive, both militarily and culturally. Nationalism, on the other hand, is inseparable from the desire for power".[15] Together, the two pairs of characteristic (land vs. ethnic community and moderate vs. extreme) are often taken as the defining features of patriotism. Of course, the actual use of the term in political discourse is much less precise than the one standard in theoretical writings. In the United States, 'patriotism' is often used for attitude(s) that would be described in the theoretical literature 'nationalistic'. The problem is that love for a country is not just love for a piece of land; normally it involves attachment to the community of its inhabitants, and this introduces 'nation' into the conception of patriotism.

It is possible to distinguish low-profile patriotism from the high-profile patriotism, very much close to nationalism, or, as Nathanson puts it, moderate, and non-moderate, extreme patriotism.[16] High-profile patriotism can be aggressive to others; the low-profile one is more turned inwardly. High-profile patriotism enjoins its holder to believe in some kind of superiority of one's *patria*, from the innocuous and convention-regulated one in sport, through insistence on the alleged unique virtues of one's land, all the way to contempt, scorn and disdain of others. The low-profile patriotism is compatible with high regard for others and can be combined with a moderate cosmopolitan stance.[17]

15 G. Orwell, 'Notes on Nationalism', firs. pub. Polemic, London, 1945, reprinted in G. Orwell, *Essays*, Penguin, London, 2000, p. 469.

16 S. Nathanson, *Patriotism, Morality, and Peace*, Rowman & Littlefield Publishers, Lanham, 1993, p. 30.

17 *Id.*

5.2.2.1 The Low-Profile Patriotism

I have noted that the low-profile patriotism is benign: it claims that we have only minimal Samaritan responsibilities to foreigners and much more robust obligations to assist compatriots. It is morally acceptable to feel a special attachment to one's own political community and institutions. To take special pride in its just accomplishments is perfectly acceptable.

The low-profile patriotism is hardly attractive to a right-wing populist. It is much more interesting for the left. To illustrate, the intellectuals who fought in International Brigades in the Spanish Civil war, were internationalists, but they also supported the patriotism of their Spanish co-fighters. One talks of a 'left patriotism', or, to follow Orwell's term, 'revolutionary patriotism'.

In his revolutionary patriotic feelings, Orwell is joined by other leftist intellectuals, like the Australian poet and fighter Jack Lindsay, who wrote *Requiem Mass for the Englishmen Fallen in the International Brigade* (1938). Whether the characterization of 'leftist populist' fits these intellectuals is an open question, but if one needs examples, they could perhaps serve this purpose.

5.2.2.2 The High-Profile Patriotism

I will now address a more typical combination: the right-wing populism fits well with the high-profile patriotism. Roger Scruton, the best known British defender of such patriotism, brings it close to nationalism and writes that patriotism/nationalism stress political loyalty. The focus on national comes from the nature of the modern state. Law and legality require jurisdiction, but the safety, continuity and stability, necessary for the rule of law, are unobtainable until territory is secured. The national loyalty is the same as patriotism: loyalty to one's country, the natural love of country, countrymen and the culture that unites them'.[18]

Indeed, patriots are attached to the people and the territory that are theirs by right; and patriotism involves an attempt to transcribe that right into impartial government and the rule of law. Territorial loyalty is at the root of all, it might be claimed.

If one abstracts from Scruton's sympathy for the rule of law, the general tenor of his patriotism would fit a possible populist attitude. For instance, according to the Centre for Brexit Studies, the relevant questions for the study are (among others) the following two:

- What is 'new' about the current populism in austerity Britain? Can we call a combination of anti-welfarism with business protectionism populist?
- How are patriotism and populism shaping Britain's new relationship with the EU?

---

18 R. Scruton, *England and the Need for Nations*, 2nd ed., Civitas: Institute for the Study of Civil Society, London, 2006, p. 4.

The questions suggest that Brexit is linked to a populist patriotism, obviously with the high-profile variant.

The problem here is that the distinction between the high-profile patriotism and the classical nationalism is minimal. The prominent authors like Scruton group the two together in a single attitude since the populist politics is not sufficiently subtle to keep the distinction alive. I would suggest that in the populist context (if not elsewhere), the high-profile patriotism collapses into classical nationalism.

It is worth mentioning non-ethnic regionalism, like the one characterizing Lega Nord in Italy (until this year, when it changed the name and the policy). Such regionalism demands statehood for a particular region, not based on nationalistic-ethnic criteria. For instance, in Italy, Padania was supposed to have a right to become a state since it is economically and politically advanced in comparison to the rest of Italy. The populist moves in this context resemble national populism, and the case of Lega Nord, which has recently given up regionalism in favour of more traditional Italian nationalism. The case well illustrates the affinity between nationalism and the non-ethnic regionalism, with the difference concerning the non-ethnic character of the characteristics that are supposed to make the region eligible for the statist status.

5.2.3 *Classical Strong Ethnic Nationalism (Nativism)*

The relation between the two, populism and the classical strong ethnic nationalism (nativism) is very tight. This has led some theoreticians to present the nationalist populism as *the populism*. The best-known author claiming that patriotism is just a variant of nationalism is Taguieff. One finds his term 'national-populism' ('*national-populisme*') already in his 1984 article on the 'Rhetoric of National-Populism', drawing on the style of the French National Front (at that time led by Jean-Marie Le Pen).[19]

The term has survived to our days,[20] and within this chapter, it will be used occasionally. It seems that it captures exactly the synthesis of populism and the strong ethnic nationalism or nativism. From populism, it takes the general schema of anti-elitism: the leader is addressing the people directly and is allegedly following the people's interest. From nationalism, it takes the characterization of the people: it is the ethnic community, in most cases the state-owing ethnic community, or the ethno-nation. In his work, Mudde documents the claim that purely right-wing populists claim to represent the true people who form the true nation and whose purity is being muddied by new entrants. He uses the term

19 *See* P. A. Taguieff, 'La rhétorique du national-populisme [Les règles élémentaires de la propagande xenophobe]', *Mots. Les langages du politique*, No. 9, 1984, pp. 113-139.

20 A. Pantazopoulos, 'Populism or National-Populism? A Critical Approach to Cas Mudde's Perspective on SYRIZA's Populism', *Telos*, 25 March 2016.

'nativism' to stress these features: "[N]ativism is defined here as an ideology, which holds that states should be inhabited exclusively by members of the native group 'the nation' and that non-native elements (persons and ideas) are fundamentally threatening to the homogenous nation-state."[21]

In the United States, one can talk about populist and reactionary movements, like the Tea Party, that have emerged through the recent experience of immigration, terrorist attacks and growing economic polarization. In his analysis, Randall Curren claims that these movements revolved around fear and aggression, in-group loyalty and racial and religious exclusion, suppression of dissent and deference to authority that tolerated violations of human rights and civil liberties. He rightly notes the contrast of the populist patriotism, the national patriotism, (to use the adopted term in this chapter), with traditional constitutional patriotism, as he calls it.[22] I would call it the moderate statist nationalism.

Of course, for particular cases, one can discuss whether they fit the bill. The French National Front clearly does, but others are less typical and less easy to classify. For example, Pantazopulous claims that SYRIZA is national-populistic.[23] I doubt it. In the second part of the chapter, I will argue that the Croatian ruling party, the HDZ, comes close to being national-populist in this strong sense, but that it is not exactly purely right wing, rather a *centre*-right one, lacking some important populist elements.

One may note the interaction between the conceptual and causal connection. For example, a country that has a strong nationalistic tradition, like France, will be typically the context in which historical nationalism acts upon would-be populist politicians: they see the traditional nationalistic elements (the adoration of Jane of Arc and of her link with the French monarchy embodied in her 'travel to Reims', etc.) as the fine material to integrate with their populist projects. Once this is done, the more constitutive, conceptual link is formed: the populism will take the form of national populism, what else.

In a country in which the nationalist tradition is being shunned for its historical effects, *e.g.* Germany, the project will give birth to populisms that are not so much nationalistic, but rather turn to cultural, religious identities, *e.g.*, Christianity/Islam contrast.

Taguieff argues in favour of his more radical equation of populism with the national populism-nationalism, by ignoring this diversity and claiming that the traditional critics of nationalism have simply replaced the term with the term 'populism'.[24] He rightly notes that some decades ago the term 'populism' was almost synonymous with 'demagogical' and that this has changed. The change, he argues, appealing to examples like Marine Le Pen and Jőrg Haider, went from 'demagogical' to 'nationalist'. Nowadays, one can see that

---

21 *See* Mudde, 2007, p. 19 and Mudde, 2004, pp. 542-563.

22 R. Curren, 'Patriotism, Populism, and Reactionary Politics since 9/11', *in* M. Sardoč (Ed.), *Handbook of Patriotism*, Springer, Dordrecht (due August 2019).

23 *See* Pantazopoulos, 2016.

24 *See* Taguieff, 2015, the discussion in Chapter 4.

the examples are biased; lots of populist aggression is turned not primarily to the ethnic Other, but to the cultural Other. Taguieff perceives this new enemy, offers the obvious example of Islam, but does not build the new material into his definition of populism. Riva Kastoryano calls it 'transnational nationalism'.[25]

Finally, I will briefly turn to the opposite extreme, the authors that minimize or deny the relevance of nationalism for populism. Benjamin Arditi is an example.[26] He claims that "[...]Things have changed quite radically in recent years without dispelling the polemic around the meaning of the term populism. Populism today seems to bear very little in common with its classical reference [...]". He then passes to the question about the referent and claims that, as targets of populist enthusiasm,

> [...]Nationalism and economic protectionism are virtually gone, and popular mobilization tends to be minimized; in its wake, we are left with what some describe as a marriage of convenience between neoliberal economics and neopopulist politics [...].[27]

His only references for these claims concern his native Latin America; no examples of the European or the US populism are given, nor analysed. Nationalism is virtually gone, he claims. In Italy, at the time the book is written, there was Berlusconi, in France the National Front, in Great Britain the UKIP (that started in the 1990s), and in the post-Communist Central Europe, there was no dearth of nationalist parties. No wonder that he is left with the term 'inexact' object borrowed from Deleuze and Guattari[28] But his characterization of populism as the inexact object, just gives a fancy name to the underlying confusion.

Arditi quotes Paul Blokker as an ally, referring to his work on Eastern Europe. However, Blokker merely claims that populism cannot be reduced to 'chauvinistic ethnic homogeneity', which seems to be true. He also notes that the populist critique of existing institutions is at least in part "about the mobilization of the people around the idea of national emancipation and collective autonomy".[29] Why would anyone take these (correct) claims as supporting the idea that nationalism is 'virtually gone' from the populist context, is very hard to say.

To conclude, the classical strong ethnic nationalism (nativism) is very relevant for historical genesis and conceptual understanding of populism; its combination with pop-

25 R. Kastoryano, 'Vers un nationalisme transnational. Redéfinir la nation, le nationalisme et le territoire', *Revue française de science politique*, Vol. 56, No. 4, 2006, pp. 533-553.

26 *See* B. Arditi, *Politics on the Edges of Liberalism Difference, Populism, Revolution, Agitation*, Edinburgh University Press, Edinburgh, 2007; *see also* P. Blokker, 'Populist Nationalism, Anti-Europeanism, Postnationalism, and the East-West Distinction', *German Law Journal*, Vol. 6, No. 2, 2005, pp. 371-389.

27 Arditi, 2007, p. 56.

28 *Id.*, p. 57.

29 Blokker is quoted by B. Arditi in Arditi, 2007, p. 384, fn. 18.

ulism, the national populism, is one of the central kinds of populism, prominent on several continents.

5.2.4 *Moderate Statist Nationalism*

I now turn to the option close to classical nationalism, but with the difference of being centre-right in contrast to 'pure' right. In the case of such moderate statist nationalism, the nationalist programme is tempered by the rule of law (involving the minimal set of accepted human rights, in particular, the minority rights), and also by the requirements of the parliamentary systems.

In the search for examples, I shall refer to Iavor Rangelov's useful book on the recent history of the changes in the Balkan region.[30] He notes, rightly, that

> [L]aw plays a distinctive and rather ambivalent role in the ethnic citizenship construct, [...]: it serves as an instrument of formalization and codification of membership tied to particular projects of the nation-state and, at the same time, it also provides a potential arena for contestation and transformation of citizenship along the lines of alternative logics and normativities.[31]

Now, a classical nationalist agent does not have to take into account these alternatives. He or she proceeds with defending the narrow interest of ethnicity. 'Slovenia to the Slovenians' is the favourite slogan of the Slovenian nationalist populist, sometimes accompanied with the sequel 'Foreigners out!' A run-of-the-mill Slovenian politician cannot allow himself using such a slogan, because of the strong system of the human rights protection, built by the Slovenian state, initiated not only by the Slovenian mainstream politicians, but also by local NGOs, and strongly supported by the EU.

In such a rule-governed arrangement, the ruling nationalist elite could not silence the voice of non-nationalist opposition in the parliament, and in the local representative bodies. In Slovenia, this was the case with the right-wing Janša's government (the Slovenian Prime Minister twice, the second time in the period of 2012-2013), whose nationalist ambitions were at every step frustrated by the very powerful and active opposition. In the context of this chapter, this is important because the rule-governed arrangement might minimize or block the possibilities of a populist solution. The national-populist option needs a free space, and it cannot find it in the situation in which the ruling team is clearly patriotic, and thus above the accusation of being composed of traitors, and where its actions

30 I. Rangelov, *Nationalism and the Rule of Law: Lessons from the Balkans and Beyond,* Cambridge University Press, Cambridge, 2013.

31 *Id.*, p. 20.

are strictly limited by the rule of law, in particular, by appeal to human rights, in a manner that does not leave open space for populist 'spontaneity' of the leader. The United States seems to be going through the symmetric process, where Trump's populism is constantly banging against the wall of the Constitution and the legal system.

Rangelov dedicates a whole chapter to the example important for the Balkans, and potentially important for other regions, which refers to the interference of the international system of the rule of law in the context of the local war crimes:

> The key challenge for transitional justice in Croatia since the turn of the century has been the need to confront two legacies of abuse: one involving atrocities against Serb civilians and ethnic cleansing during the Homeland War; the other concerning the conduct of war crimes trials in its aftermath. Croatian law, like the political class and public, has struggled to confront these legacies in a meaningful way and come to terms with the past. Nevertheless, Croatia's experience with judicial processes in the past decade is useful in illuminating the potential of deliberative transitional justice to interrogate the 'dark side' of nationalism, as well as revealing some of its limitations.[32]

To widen the range of examples, Netanyahu's Israel might be a typical case of the country with moderate statist nationalism as the leading ideology. It would turn into the immoderate, classic nationalist version, were it not for the constant, loud criticism and ongoing fight of the local Palestinian opposition, criticism of the local Israeli opposition, wider Arab condemnation and international surveillance and criticism. To mention the recent dramatic example of Ahed Tamimi, a populist nationalist state could allow itself to arrest and keep in prison a minority teenage girl. Now, that she has become a Palestinian national symbol of the resistance, the arrest and prison seem unreasonable reactions, and the rule of law blocks the possible populist from the negative and violent reaction. Thus, the need to respect the law, even with some amount of cheating, cutting edges, etc., prevents Netanyahu's rule from becoming a clear case of national populism.

The moderate statist nationalism has not been particularly discussed in the literature on nationalism, probably because its main features are just a weakening of the classical nationalism, and therefore, trivial for the theoretician. However, in recent times, it has attracted the attention, not so much for its theoretical importance, but for its great practical-political relevance. This also accounts for the discussion here: the fact that moderate statist nationalism, the centre-right attitude, respects the rule of law and, in particular, human rights (to an important extent, if not completely) as a potential barrier to an all-our national

32 *Id.*, p. 162. I will return to it briefly in the section on Croatia.

populism, should be stressed. The barrier is not perfectly stable and safe, but it is still better than being politically helpless.

Some of the most obvious components of the barrier are the following. First, the respect for minorities blocks the unitary populist phantasy of unique, homogenous ethnicity as the basis of the nation-state. This relativizes the distance from 'the Other'. To use the Croatian example, once Croatia recognized local Muslims as 'ours', it is inconsistent to treat Muslims in general as a different, exotic and threatening group. Alternatively, to turn to the classical case of populism, the French one. It becomes problematic to enjoy the triumph of the French football team in the World Cup, if one cannot count the big majority of players French, because of their race, and far from being typical Frenchmen. However, if one respects one's minorities, one will count them French, but this relativizes the notion of a French-person way beyond the limits acceptable for the national populists.

Second, the respect for the rules blocks pompous radical 'solutions' to current social-political problems, like Trump's idea of separating immigrant parents from their children, or Orban's manoeuvres in the direction of prohibiting the work of the NGOs in Hungary. Similarly, in the context of Russia, that is not clearly populist, had the rule of law and the respect for human rights been more powerful, the arrest and prison-sentences for members of Pussy Riot would not have taken place.

Third, the rules of parliamentary procedure open space for constant criticisms of the party in power: none of its moves are sacred, none is the incarnation of the will-of-the-people as the whole. The number of excuses and justifications of the ruling party, usually performed by its leaders and functionaries in the course of the everyday functioning of the parliament (and its lower-level counterparts), is just unthinkable for the populist in power. Populism is antidemocratic in denying the need for confrontational democratic practice, and inconsistent in its anti-elitism, which ends up proposing a different elite (possibly a one-person elite) in the replace of the old one.

Fourth, in the case of a problematic history, like the Balkan conflicts in the 1980s and 1990s (or perhaps, in a near future, the one of Ukraine and Donbas region), the respect for rules requires self-criticism, admitting having committed war crimes, and requires giving up of 'heroically conquered' territories (from Krajina to Crimea); deeds that the authoritative, not to say authoritarian, populist ruler is hardly capable of performing.

This does not make the centre-right moderate nationalism ideal, nor close to the ideal. For my own rather cosmopolitan taste, it is just lesser evil than the immoderate, purely right-wing one, but it can be instrumental against the rise of the populist threat. I shall try to document this in the second section, using the example of my native Croatia.

5.2.5 Liberal Nationalism

I turn now to the self-proclaimed nationalist option that is farthest from right-wing populist interests, liberal nationalism, promoted by authors like Yael Tamir and Will Kymlicka.[33] The liberal and the nationalist component do not go well together, but liberal nationalists stress the practical importance of ethnocultural membership, various rights to redress injustice, democratic rights of political association, and the role that ethnocultural ties and associations can play in promoting just social arrangements. The liberal culturalists, including Kymlicka, have proposed minimal and pluralistic versions of nationalism built around such arguments. In these minimal versions, the project of building classical nation-states is moderated or abandoned and replaced by a more sensitive form of national identity, which can thrive in a multicultural society. Terminology varies. For instance, for Kymlicka, patriotism is "the feeling of allegiance to a state", and national identity is the sense of membership in the national group.[34] He claims that, probably, any legitimate form of liberal nationalism must be supplemented and constrained by multiculturalism. Patriotism characteristic of overall national identities must be supplemented by public recognition of ethnocultural diversity within a 'shared national identity and narrative'. The idea of 'multicultural nationalism' goes well with liberal nationalism, "and may be needed to ensure that the privileging of national identity does not come at the expense of minorities".[35] Thus, a thinned and multicultural liberal nationalism remains a viable and important political source of solidarity in the contemporary world.

These considerations are quite irrelevant for the right-wing populism. However, the leftist populism might find a liberal perspective attractive, since it involves weakening of the traditional nationalist stance. The first weakening concerns the force of the national claims. For the beginners, the liberal framework takes some values or obligations to be absolute: human rights are a case in point. A dramatic weakening awaits the paradigm nationalist cairn to state. For a liberal nationalist, the right to national self-determination can be satisfied through a variety of political arrangements – including the formation of autonomous communities or the establishment of a federal or confederal state. Similarly, with ethnonational versus civic loyalties, the liberal nationalist typically sees the difficulty and searches for a compromise.

Robert S. Jansen points out that populist rhetoric posits the natural social unity and inherent virtuousness of 'the people', that includes workers, the urban poor, the landed and landless peasantry, and indigenous populations, as well as professionals, the middle

---

33 *See* W. Kymlicka, *Multicultural Citizenship: A Liberal Theory of Minority Rights*, Clarendon Press, Oxford, 1995; K. Banting & W. Kymlicka (Eds.), *The Strains of Commitment: The Political Sources of Solidarity in Diverse Societies*, Oxford University Press, Oxford, 2017; Y. Tamir, *Liberal Nationalism*, Princeton University Press, Princeton, 1993.

34 *See* K. Banting & W. Kymlicka (Eds.), 2017, p. 13.

35 *Id.*, p. 34.

class or even particular segments of the elite.[36] However, then, he notes that "[I]n so doing, they adopt nationalist ways of speaking and framing situations, sometimes alongside tropes of *indigenismo* or *mestizaje,* which sounds exactly like a tactical Kymlicka and other liberal nationalists would recommend for including various 'ethnicities' into a covering statist organization. To take the closer-to-home example of SYRIZA, Tzipras has been recently taken a positive stance towards Macedonia and Macedonians, unbearable for the standard Greek nationalists.

5.2.6 *Communitarianism and 'Transnational Nationalism'*

I now pass to the main populist alternative (or quasi-alternative) to national populism. It has been already mentioned that in some countries some populist groups-parties appeal to properties wider in their reach than ethnonational belonging, typically to religious affiliations. Others combine this appeal with the ethnonational one. These phenomena constitute the main evidence for the wider reach of populism – as against Taguieff's exclusive focus on national populism, and its identification with populism.

I will start with the few illustrations. The German AfD party (Alternative for Germany), quite successful at the parliamentary elections, has produced a series of posters, some focusing exclusively on cultural differences, other, combining wider cultural belonging with the national one. Take one with Muslim burka. It first quotes President Gauck, depicting him covered with a burka; his fault was saying "Burka? I can well live with it." Then, on the same poster, there is a photo of burka with a stop sign and text: "Burka? No, thanks!" Other similar refer to Ramadan fasting. The posters nicely illustrate the exclusive appeal to wider (not narrowly national) cultural belonging. The Austrian political philosopher Harald Stelzer has talked in this context about communitarian attitudes and even communitarianism simpliciter.[37]

Taken in the wide sense, communitarianism is characterized by the thesis that belonging to a community, preferably the one sharing language, tradition, etc., is the pre-condition of one's rich identity. This idea leads to the rejection of strong individualism and almost essentialist view of cultural properties as defining the identity of their individual bearers. In the communitarian tradition, the typical reasoning about matters of belonging starts from the claim that conditions of one's identity are indispensable for one's being a fully human subject, then adds the claim that the crucial role of identification is language-cum-culture, moves to the idea that the availability of a linguistic-cultural community is

36 R. S. Jansen, *Populist Mobilization: Peru in Historical and Comparative Perspective,* 2009 doctoral dissertation, https://search.proquest.com/openview/01908529b18bf630dfd81739a2e36438/1?pq origsite=gscholar&cbl=18750&diss=y, p. 56.

37 H. Stelzer, 'Communitarianism and Right Wing Populism', conference presentation at the philosophy conference on Ethical Issues: Theoretical & Applied, Bled, Slovenia, 4-8 June 2018 (on file with author).

indispensable for one's being a full human subject and concludes that we have a right to demand from others that they respect our communal belonging. This reasoning belongs to Charles Taylor. MacIntyre's version is more nationalistic and demanding, while Walzer and Sandel sound more moderate, but the general shape is common to the communitarian tradition. Many leading communitarian thinkers reject the label, but for the purpose of this discussion, I shall treat the authors below as communitarians.

Harald Stelzer in his work mentioned above on communitarianism and populism lists among their common elements, the importance of 'embedded individual identity in the community', criticism of liberal understanding of democracy, fear of cultural dissolution and assuming the homogeneity of collectives. On a more sophisticated level, I suggest putting an accent on the shared notion of the good, explicit in communitarian theory and implicit in some populist rhetoric, although Stelzer does not draw the implicit/explicit distinction. For him, the deep common element is a criticism of the liberal notion of the self; I am not sure that existing populisms are subtle enough to voice a stance of this topic.

Accordingly, since 'communitarianism', used with no qualifications, usually refers to theories, even philosophical ones, 'practical communitarianism' to distinguish political activism, like the one incarnated in the posters, from theoretical elaborations, should be underlined.

Now, as one would expect, the AfD posters also appeal to ethnonational belonging. Some, for instance, depict young women in bikinis, and comment "Burkas? We prefer bikinis", but then add the slogan: "German, have confidence in yourself." The domain varies: from the national one to the wider communitarian one, to the combination of both. Therefore, I will refer to the stance 'wider practical communitarianism' and concentrate on its non-liberal variety; in philosophy, it would perhaps come close to MacIntyre but in a much less civilized form.[38] Of course, more liberal communitarianism of Sandel or Walzer style variety is not documented in the wider practical context of populist ideology.[39] The idea of circles of cultural belonging, of equal moral weight, stressed by liberal communitarians, is unusable for a right-wing populist. If you tell them that Mexicans are Latinos, so non-Anglo-Americans, but they share the Christian faith with many Anglo-Americans, and Catholic confession with American Irish, Poles or Croats, this would not help. In a given context, a particular belonging of the Other is chosen as the target, and contrasted with the 'opposite' affiliation, characterizing the We-group, period. The strong, right-wing populist option of this communitarian strategy is finely characterized as 'transnational

38 A. MacIntyre, 'Is Patriotism a Virtue?', in I. Primoratz (Ed.), *Patriotism*, Humanity Books, Amherst, 2002.

39 M. Walzer, 'Nation and Universe', https://tannerlectures.utah.edu/_documents/a-to-z/w/walzer90.pdf; M. Walzer, *What It Means to Be an American*, Marsilio Publishers, New York 1992; M. Sandel, *Democracy's Discontent: America in Search of a Public Philosophy*, Harvard University Press, Cambridge/MA1998; *see also* V. A. Spencer, 'Communitarianism' and Patriotism', *in* Sardoč (Ed.), *Handbook of Patriotism*, Springer, Dordrecht (due August 2019).

nationalism': it is transnational in its object of identification, but it is like nationalism in the kind of attitude that constitutes it.

The basic fact, relevant for the topic of this discussion, is the plasticity-malleability of appeals to the practical communitarian belonging. 'Nationalisms' are seen (rightly) as rather fixed in their extensions: Croatian nationalist cheers for Croats and their community, etc. Interestingly, authors writing about the topic, Stelzer among them, have rarely noticed this central piece of news brought by populism, the flexibility and malleability of the particularist option. To reiterate, it can be determined any among a number of factors: by ethnic or, more rarely, statist nationality, or any kind of cultural-linguistic communitarian belonging, contrasted to another one from the typical contrast class at the same level: Catholics versus Orthodox, Christians versus Muslims, we-Germans (typically Christians but also atheists) versus Muslims, etc.

These options will then offer *ad hoc* choices to the populist politicians. Again, the contrast between causal and conceptual connection turns out to be useful. Conceptual connections (or connections of social kinds) are the following: the target *populus* is affiliated to other *populi* by some features, and is contrasted to others by the opposite, or quasi-opposite features. Croats are close to Slovenians by the same Catholic confession and by very similar language, (some dialects are almost common to both). They can be contrasted to Slovenians by being non-Slovenian, the former Yugoslav nation.[40]

Which transnational contrast will be chosen by the populist rhetorician? The decision depends on the causal forces in the relevant context. If the situation calls for the distancing of one's people from its Yugoslav past, which was the favourite context of Janša, one will talk of Čefurji. If the situation demands that one align oneself with the 'West' rather than with one's Central European identity, one will rationally want to stress the 'Western', more 'European' character of the Slovenian nationality and will group Croats into the category of 'the primitive Balkan' neighbours or quasi-neighbours, etc.

The same is present in other countries, in analogous situations. This practical non-liberal populist communitarianism is anti-pluralistic, but here it has to cheat, given the wide varieties of actual belonging, among which the populist has to choose one in a given context, pretending that others do not exist. Suppose one wants to mobilize the listeners against immigrants. If the causal story is one of the Arab and Afghani newcomers, the common denominator will be their Muslim identity. If the causal story revolves around Mexicans, who are Christians, the religion, since it is common, will play no role. The constellation of causal forces will suggest that the main contrast should be the one between Latinos and the Anglo-Americans. The contrast will be put in terms of stable binary

40 There is a special pejorative term for these nationalities, including Serbs and Bosnians, 'Čefurji', very much alive in the extreme right-wing discourse. The term is used to underline that the members of these nationalities are the Balkan people, which Croats themselves prefer to deny.

opposition. Again, it is useful to heed the conceptual-causal distinction, since each of them accounts for the different aspect of practical non-liberal populist communitarianism: the conceptual one for the variety of options that are in principle available to the populists, the causal for the pressure in the direction of a particular choice of one of them.

This concludes the sketch of attitudes suitable for the right-wing populists. Strong, high profile patriotism certainly belongs here, then varieties of nationalism, with the classical, right-wing view being a central candidate and finally the wider practical communitarianism, popular all over the world, in very different context. The low-profile patriotism, liberal nationalism and pluralistic communitarianism of Sandel's and Walzer's variety falls out, naturally aligned with more centre-leftist or possibly leftist political choices.

What is left among stances singularly unsuitable for the right-wing populism, is the cosmopolitan stance.

5.2.7 *Cosmopolitanism*

Cosmopolitan stance involves the view that one's primary moral obligations are directed to all human beings (regardless of geographical or cultural distance); political arrangements should faithfully reflect this universal moral obligation (in the form of supra-statist arrangements that take precedence over nation-states).[41] Again, this stance has nothing to recommend itself to a right-wing populist. There might be elements attractive for a centrist or left-wing populist. James Ingram notes that

> [T]here have been and continue to be more and less cosmopolitan, universalistic, and inclusive populisms, just as there have been and continue to be more and less popular, common, and inclusive cosmopolitanisms. [42]

However, he is relying on Laclau and Rancière, who are primarily interested in the leftist or quasi-leftist populism. He mentions scholars that "have reconstructed a variety of 'rooted', 'subaltern', 'peripheral', 'discrepant' and 'transgressive' cosmopolitanisms devel-

41 For this characterization of 'cosmopolitanism', *see* the reference in Stanford Encyclopedia of Philosophy, https://plato.stanford.edu/entries/cosmopolitanism/; *see also* C. R. Beitz, *Political Theory and International Relations*, Princeton University Press, Princeton, 1979; T. W. Pogge, *Realizing Rawls*, Cornell University Press, Ithaca, 1989; D. Moellendorf, *Cosmopolitan Justice*, Westview Press, Boulder, 2002; S. Caney, *Justice Beyond Borders, A Global Political Theory*, Oxford University Press, Oxford, 2005; K.-C. Tan, *Justice Without Borders: Cosmopolitanism, Nationalism, and Patriotism*, Cambridge University Press, Cambridge, 2004; G. Brock, *Global Justice: A Cosmopolitan Account, Global Justice: A Cosmopolitan Account*, Oxford University Press, Oxford, 2009; D. Held, *Cosmopolitanism: Ideals and Realities*, Polity Press, Cambridge, 2010; M. Risse, *On Global Justice*, Princeton University Press, Princeton, 2012; L. Ypi, *Global Justice and Avant-Garde Political Agency*, Oxford University Press, Oxford, 2012. J. D. Ingram, 'Populism and Cosmopolitanism', *in* C. R. Kaltwasser *et al.* (Eds.), p. 656.

42 *Id.*

oped by marginalized or displaced people, who build and maintain social, cultural, and political networks across national frontiers".[43] Among recent phenomena, he refers to 'Occupy' movement and discusses its populist characteristics and possibly cosmopolitan features as well.

One should also have in mind that Chávez called his somewhat leftist project an 'international integrative nationalism'.[44]

This brings me to the end of the attempt to systematize potential links between populist movements and various sub-species or wider relatives of nationalism (including its opposite, cosmopolitanism).[45]

To recap:

Table 5.1 The Right-Wing Populism and Nationalism

Kinds		Conceptual Link	Causal Link
Patriotism	High-profile	Strong	Strong
	Low-profile	Very weak; possibly, a stronger one with left-wing populism	No link; possible one with left-wing populism
Nationalism	Regionalism (quasi-nationalist)	Very strong	Possible specific features of the region
	Classical ethnic (nativism)	Very strong: National populism	Ties with historical nationalist parties
	Moderate statist	Very strong	Problems with established parliamentary nationalism
	Liberal	Very weak; possibly, a stronger one with left-wing populism.	No historical ties. Possibly, a stronger one with left-wing populism
Wider Communitarianism	Not liberal (MacIntyre style) Transnational nationalism	Very strong with right-wing ideologies	Strong connection with historical right-wing parties
	Liberal (Sandel, Walzer style)	Possible for centrist populism	Possible for centrist populism
Cosmopolitanism	Strong	-----	----
	Moderate (weak)	Weak, compatibility with leftist populism	Latin American solidarism

43 *Id.*, p. 653.

44 For Latin American context in general, *see* A. Mota, 'Cosmopolitanism in Latin America: Political Practices, Critiques', *in* G. Delanty (Ed.), *Routledge Handbook of Cosmopolitanism Studies*, Routledge, Abingdon, 2012, pp. 491-503.

45 The above is summarized in table 5.1.

The main contrast here is between the classical, ethnic nationalism (nativism) and the much wider, transnational kinds of communitarian belonging, often treated by populist politicians in a promiscuous *ad hoc* fashion.

I will conclude the first part of the chapter by stressing how the rise of populism is changing the political playfield one should be working with. Consider the opposite, anti-populist side. The non-nationalistic, tolerant views are confronting new problems in the populist age marked by migration crisis, etc. One is faced with this new playground and the populist challenge. How should we react to it? The crucial example is immigration and immigrants, the favourite topic of population urging. Authors talk of 'souverainism' to describe this populist return to nationalism-cum-xenophobia. For instance, Theodor Tudoroiu in his recent book points out that, in order to understand Brexit, we should look at the new factors that were absent a few decades ago. He lists together populism and its roots in the dissatisfaction of the working class with their economic situation and the threat of immigration.[46] I hope that the analyses of populism offered here can help to understand this new playfield, particularly in the countries discussed in this volume.

5.3 The Curious Case of Croatia

5.3.1 *Approaches and Disagreements*

This section focuses on the relation between nationalism and populism in Croatia: the issue is whether the present politics amounts to national populism and if yes, how strong is it?[47] To anticipate a bit, the question is more difficult than it seems, and the answer is unexpectedly uncertain.

To start with what is certain, Croatia has had a history of fierce and successful nationalism from at least the 1980s, with ethnic cleansing,[48] many victims on both sides engaged in the war, and finally, a lot of nationalist content being built into the ideological foundations of the new state. The enemy was one and only one, the Serbs, although there has been some military pressure upon and some war crimes committed against Bosnian Muslims. The antipathy, not to say hatred towards Serbs, has become one of the marks of high-profile Croatian patriotism. In Croatia, the right-wing populism is thus predominantly, and indeed exclusively, patriotic-nationalistic. The other cultural factors, above all confes-

46 T. Tudoroiu, *Brexit, President Trump, and the Changing Geopolitics of Eastern Europe*, Palgrave Macmillan, London, 2018, p. 104.

47 I am thankful to professors Berto Šalaj and Marijana Grbeša, as well as to the outstanding journalist, Boris Pavelić, with whom I have discussed the issue in Rijeka.

48 In the early 1990s, the Serbian army pushed Croats out of their homes in what was then called Krajina, and then, in 1995, Croats expelled Serbs from their homes in the same region and elsewhere.

sion and language, play a role only within the nationalist framework. For instance, a general anti-Muslim stance is inconsistent with Croatian nationalist claim, according to which Bosnian Muslims are the 'elite (literally 'the flower') of the Croatian nation', their faith being just an accidental result of the Ottoman conquest. The Catholic/Orthodox contrast plays a role only in the context of nationalistic hatred towards Serbs. Macedonians, who are also orthodox, are perceived as friends, or at least as 'neutral'. So, the malleability of communitarian categories of supra-national cultural belonging plays no role, rather it is the ethnic nationality, 'Croateness' that counts.

Back from the brief history. One should note that things have been slowly calming down, to a large extent thanks to the EU pressure. The relevant question here is what has come out of this sad story, in particular, concerning the national populism. Quite surprisingly, there is no consensus on the answer, even among clearly non-nationalistic, or anti-nationalistic authors. One can recognize two extreme answers. The first, very much present among journalists, is the claim that Croatia is "ruled by authoritarian populists", of the nationalistic bent. Thus, Jure Trampuš claims that "all the neighbouring states" of Slovenia, and this includes Croatia, are "ruled by authoritarian populists", while Slovenia is "the island of freedom" in the middle of this populist constellation.[49]

The second answer is provided by Grbeša and Šalaj, who conducted a detailed analysis of the discourse of politicians in the last decade and found a surprisingly little amount of national populism on the scene. Grbeša even claims that "there is no right-wing populism in Croatia".[50]

My view is in the middle: I am less optimistic than Grbeša and Šalaj, but on the other hand, I am incapable of recognizing any authoritarian populist politician among the leaders of the present Croatian government. To remind, the term 'authoritarian populist' has been coined by Stuart Hall to refer to phenomena like 'Thatcherism' in the UK and, later, 'Reganism' in the United States; none of the possible Croatian candidates is in any way like these two original stars. The President, Kolinda Grabar Kitarović, have some populist moments, and some fellow feeling for neighbouring populist leaders, like Orbán, but she lacks authority. She is very far from behaving in an authoritarian manner and lacks any kind of strong nationalistic engagement. The Prime Minister, Andrej Plenković, has been for a decade the representative of Croatia in the institutions of the EU. He has been often criticized for not having an authority (and for obedience to Angela Merkel), rather

49 Jure Trampuš, 'Nevarna igra', *Mladina*, 2 August 2018.

50 She uses 'the right-wing' to refer to minority-hating nationalism, and 'nationalist' to refer to the one that is not based on hating minorities; whether this is realistic, requires a different discussion which is beyond the scope of this chapter; for Grbeša's points *see* M. Grbeša, 'Živi zid su populisti, Most je čudnovat, no u Hrvatskoj ipak nema desnog populizma', ['Živi zid' is populist, the Bridge is Eccentric, but there is no Right-Wing Populism in Croatia], www.tportal.hr/vijesti/clanak/marijana-grbesa-zivi-zid-su-populisti-most-je-cudnovat-no-u-hrvatskoj-ipak-nema-desnog-populizma-foto-20180429.

than for being authoritarian, and is often accused of being an EU bureaucrat lacking real patriotism. Two of them certainly do not fit the image of authoritarian populists.[51]

Finally, my impression is that the force of nationalism in everyday life has drastically diminished in Croatia. The spectacular example is the behaviour of Croat football players at the World Cup in Russia in 2018 and of the Croatian and Serbian water-polo players at the European Championship in July 2018, which went without nationalistic excesses.[52]

5.3.2 *Some Populist Actors*

Back to populism in Croatia. A party that would be a suitable candidate for the right-wing national populist party is Most (The Bridge). Its members have been coming up with clearly nationalistic comments. At the time when this chapter was drafted, there was a heated debate in the newspapers regarding the accusation of Nikola Grmoja, a prominent member of Most, according to which the chief representatives of the Serbian minority in Croatian parliament, Miodrag Pupovac gave scandalous 'tacit consent' to some ultra-chauvinistic remarks made by the Serbian President. The alleged consent consisted simply in being present at a commemoration of the Serbian victims of the operation Storm (Oluja) by the Croatian army, in which Serbian civilians were massacred. The remark by Grmoja is a nationalist-populist, but also the right-wing in the Grbeša-Šalaj sense since it shows extreme antipathy towards the Serbian national minority represented by Pupovac. However, Grbeša and Šalaj claim that the official discourse of Most in two election campaigns, in 2015 and 2016, did not contain such elements:

> "[...] our analysis has detected almost no presence of the 'dangerous others' in the discourse of the Most's leading politicians. The presence of the 'dangerous others' has been detected in only two out of 57 cases (dangerous media and judiciary). Obviously, there was no systematic stigmatization of particular social or economic actors who, alongside political elites, threaten the well-being of the people. The absence of the 'dangerous others' in their discourse also rejects the assumption about Most's predominantly conservative values [...]"[53]

51 The journalists prone to this accusation usually argue for it by pointing to nationalistic excesses by public celebrities, like the pop-singer Thompson, and rightly accuse the Prime Minister of not reacting against them; but this kind of passivity and lack of authority hardly deserves to be characterized as authoritarian.

52 There was no nationalistic excess by Croatian players and spectators in the whole football cup; the only event that did include a nationalistic singer star was staged at home when a part of the team was reaching their home region. The match with Serbian water-polo players was extremely friendly, Croats congratulating Serbs on their victory, some embracing a Serbian colleague, some tapping a Serbian at his back.

53 *See* M. Grbeša & B. Šalaj, 'Populism in Croatia: The Curious Case of the Bridge (Most)', *Anali Hrvatskog politikološkog društva*, Vol. 14, No. 11, 2018, p. 19.

A year later, the situation remained the same:

> An examination of the references to 'dangerous others' in 2016 has conclusively confirmed that 'dangerous others' were only rarely present in Most's discourse. Such remarks were found in only 4.9% of the cases. [54]

The party Most got a higher score on anti-elitism (roughly half of the cases), and a low score on anti-professionalism. It did not show any particularly nationalistic attitudes. The authors conclude that Most is a moderate centrist populist party and an anti-establishment reform party. If this is a correct reading of Most's discourse, then the statements like Grmoja's are atypical exaggerations, provoked by an excellent opportunity to attract attention, and not typical mainstream statements characterizing the discourse.

In sum, Grbeša and Šalaj have stressed that their analysis did not reveal the presence of the strong, intolerant right-wing populism.[55]

5.3.3 *The Riddle: Why Croatia Does Not Have a Strong Right-Wing Populist Party*

The main candidate for being national populist, the ruling party HDZ (Croatian Democratic Union), was founded in 1989 by then Croatian dissidents, led by the former President Franjo Tuđman, and officially registered on 25 January 1990.

Grbeša and Šalaj have analysed the discourse of the following HDZ candidates in election: Milan Kujundžić (an unsuccessful candidate), Tomislav Karamarko (a moderately successful), and two very successful ones, Jadranka Kosor (the former president of Croatia, 2009-2012) and Kolinda Grabar Kitarović, who is the current President of the Republic of Croatia (elected in 2015). Their findings are surprising: none of them was using aggressive, anti-minorities right-wing discourse. Kosor and Karamarko did not speak in a populist manner since they were talking in the name of the ruling elite (no anti-elitist discourse), and, more surprisingly, they were not referring much to the people or nation in a positive way!

Equally surprising is that the present-day President, Kolinda Grabar, did not use the reference to 'people' in an emphatic, positive way, more than twice out of eleven mentions of the word; most references were neutral. She also did not distance herself from the ruling elite, being the HDZ candidate for the President. Besides, there was no presence of a negative attitude to the minorities. The only clearly national populist presidential candidate

54 *Id.*, p. 21.

55 They call it 'the right-wing', but they define it by hatred towards minorities.

Kujundžić, had some anti-elite comments and positive reference to 'people-nation'. As it has been already noted, after losing in the elections, he completely changed his rhetoric.

Now, I agree with Grbeša and Šalaj that the HDZ is certainly not an aggressive national populist party, although some well-known members are tough nationalists. I find the HDZ is not a typical national populist party, either. It is not sufficiently populist to count as populist simpliciter, and its nationalism has become a very moderate one, quite far from what Taguieff presented as a typical attitude of the national populist parties.

If all this holds, one is faced with a riddle. Given the intense and aggressively nationalistic past of the country, and of the HDZ in particular, how is it possible that the ruling establishment is not national populist nor authoritarian populist?[56]

First, there is the problem with the vertical (people vs. elite) dimension of populism: the HDZ is an established party-in-power in Croatia, a clear case of the political elite, so a loud anti-elitism on their part would be perceived as a fraud.[57]

Second, the horizontal dimension (us vs. others) is also represented too weakly in Croatia: there is nationalism, but it is not much present in the discourse of the state officials (the President and the Prime Minister) and is neither systematic nor sufficiently aggressive in the discourse of the establishment as a whole to mark it as national populistic. The typical present-day criticism of the government is that it is not reacting sufficiently against nationalistic excesses made in public (by sport and music celebrities or war veterans), rather than containing accusations of the actual governmental action for its nationalistic direction.

All this makes the riddle more dramatic. Let us agree that the vertical dimension is clearly too weak: the HDZ is an establishment party, there are no clearly alternative elites, so the normal populist anti-elitist route is very difficult for a candidate from the HDZ or close to the HDZ to take. On the supply side, there is thus a blockade. To see it in explicit form, one should remember that in Croatia, the right-wing populism is predominantly, and indeed exclusively, patriotic-nationalistic. Accordingly, any right-wing populist party would have to present a patriotic-nationalist programme. To do this successfully, it has to accuse the political elite of not being patriotic-nationalist enough. However, what if the ruling party is already quite nationalistic? The would-be populists would have to try cohabitation with the ruling party, and this is exactly what the moderately populist party Most did. Moreover, it did not work.

---

56 In what follows, I will abandon Grbeša-Šalaj distinction between nationalist and the right-wing populism, and return to the terminology where the two are treated as a single phenomenon.

57 Grbeša and Šalaj also note that the vertical dimension is extremely problematic; however, they do not develop an explanation of the phenomenon they studied for a decade or more. *See* M. Grbeša & B. Šalaj, *Dobar, loš ili zao? Populizam u Hrvatskoj* [*The Good, the Bad or the Ugly? Populism in Croatia*], TIM Press, Zagreb, 2018, p. 233.

I have already noted that the HDZ is sufficiently nationalistic to block potential populist accusations of betrayal, and not nationalistic enough to be a clearly purely nationalistic party. This suggests that the answer to the riddle lies in this moderate and statist nationalism of the leading party, the HDZ.

The crucial answer to the riddle can be reduced to the HDZ's historical transformation from a purely right-wing into the centre-right party, coming close to the Christian-Democratic tradition. Concerning ideology, in the beginning, the HDZ leaders described the party as a right-wing, while the former president Tuđman himself stated that he was inspired by Thatcherism. Later, the party described itself as centre-right and Christian-Democrats. However, the only official ideology was nationalism, which provoked conflicts in the 1990s. The strong nationalistic tendencies were toned down after the end of the war. The HDZ, concerned with more domestic aspects of politics, became a mainly social conservative party.

Now, consider the more recent situation from two perspectives, the supply, and the demand. First, for a potential right-wing populist voter (the demand side), the most appropriate context would be the one in which one can accuse the political elite of lack of patriotic attachment and nationalism. 'The people wants its identity to be protected, and the damn elite has betrayed it!' The context of the HDZ rule is dramatically unsuitable for such accusations: the party had created the national state, it has proved its patriotism in hundreds of tests, and it has been favouring the interests of the ethnic Croats in comparison with the interests of the potentially most hated minority, the Serbs, etc. It is nationalistic enough to block possible populist criticisms and accusation.[58] In short, the HDZ has pre-empted the issue of patriotic-nationalist sentiment in its favour.

Second, from the perspective of the political elite (the supply side), one should note that it needs popular support, but it has also opted for the membership of Croatia in the EU, aware that the membership is seen as an important advantage by many of its voters, given the fact that Serbia is not (yet) a member. The rational option for the elite is not the populist experimentation but the search for a middle way: to fulfil as much as possible the nationalistic expectations, without giving up on the pro-European attitude. True is, in the course of all these actions, there were some more-or-less populist episodes: Tuđman did carry his nationalism to extremes, and, two decades later, Karamarko tried the same tactics. However, these episodes did not turn the HDZ into a national populist party.

At the Prime Minister's level, the successor of Tuđman was Ivo Sanader. His government (2003-2009) pursued the policies needed to fulfil the basic criteria for joining the European

58 The HDZ has proved its patriotism in its cultural politics, for instance, by supporting cultural organization carrying on quite strongly nationalist policies (*e.g.*, the purging of Croatian language from presumed 'Serbian' words, to be replaced by invented, archaic sounding synonyms), the short-term but quite brutal cleansing of intellectual caste, throwing allegedly non-patriotic intellectuals out of jobs, *etc.* Besides, the HDZ has been pampering Croatian war-veterans, who have developed a long-term, and very stable fidelity to it.

Union, including the return of the refugees to their homes, rebuilding houses damaged in the war, improving minority rights by including minority representatives in the government, cooperating with the ICTY, and continuing to consolidate the Croatian economy. The Croatian government of that time ended up as the centre-right one. This conservative, centre-right line is the ideal middle way, and it opens no space for the victory of a recognizably populist anti-elite behaviour. For example, the Croatian president, Kolinda Grabar Kitarović, also member of the HDZ, has expressed her support for the Visegrad group, but it was done more in terms of economic cooperation, and not in terms of the support for the specific right-wing political choices of Visegrad countries, like Poland and Hungary. Orbán and Kaczyński(s) are not to be followed.[59]

At this point, one should mention the legal framework supporting the rule of law in Croatia.[60] The framework balances the nationalist interests with the human rights, in particular, the minority rights. The preamble of the Constitution, for instance, starts with an emphatic summary of 'thousand years of history' that guarantees Croats their historical right to a state,[61] but then states that Croatia is the state of Croats and the minorities, and explicitly lists 22 minorities who, together with the ethnic Croats, have constituted the state. Article 3 of the Constitution affirms 'national and gender equality' among 'the highest values of the constitutional order'.

Similar balancing has been at work in the context of international justice, in particular, concerning war crimes committed by the Croatian army in the course of the war. In her book on this topic, Jelena Subotić rightly notes that "[…] Croatia's commitment to transitional justice has for many years been best described as one step forward, two steps back".[62] She explains that

> The Croatian government has mostly cooperated selectively, reluctantly, and insufficiently with The Hague tribunal. The pressures coming from the ICTY but also from other international organizations and individual states have created deep divisions within the Croatian state, with the 'Hague issue' dominating domestic political debates and pitting strong domestic interest constituencies against one another.

59 For a comparison with the history of Serbian populism, *see* the contribution of Dušan Spasojević in this volume.

60 I am thankful to my colleague and friend Miomir Matulović for a helpful discussion on these points.

61 The preamble of the Croatian Constitution explicitly mentions "[…] the formation of the Croatian principalities in the seventh century; […] the independent medieval state of Croatia established in the ninth century; […] the Kingdom of the Croats established in the tenth century; […]".

62 J. Subotić, *The Hijacked Justice: Dealing with the Past in the Balkans*, Cornell University Press, Ithaca, 2009, p. 83.

> This lackluster cooperation ended in 2005 when Croatia transferred the last ICTY indictee to The Hague, effectively fulfilling its obligations to the tribunal.[63]

The balance between the political and the legal has turned the dominant nationalism into a statist centre-right one, not very suitable for strong populist rhetoric. To reiterate, this does not make the centre-right moderate nationalism ideal, nor close to the ideal. For my own, rather cosmopolitan taste, it is just lesser evil than the immoderate, purely right-wing one, but it can be very useful against the rise of the populist threat.

Finally, I will briefly address a problem that some readers, in particular, the American, will easily recognize. The Republican Party in the United States is not very different in its patriotic ideology from the HDZ. Besides, the American "nativism" is very much like Croatian, tough nationalism. The question is why did a populist coup, led by Trump, succeeded in the United States, and not in Croatia?

Imagine a parallel fictional story: a successful Trump-like Croatian businessman, Dinko Knavs, member of the HDZ, starts a populist campaign. He claims that the HDZ, should be transformed and turned against the corrupt elite and tries to mobilize war veterans against the Serbs who have returned to Croatia, and are now living normally ('much better than they deserve', he would tweet). He also claims that the establishment was making decisions undermining the economic interest of the country, and promises to build a wall at the border with Serbia and make Croatia great again. The issue is, would this work? I guess it might work one day if Dinko Knavs has enough luck. The main opposition party in Croatia is extremely weak, and relations within the HDZ might change in the direction favourable for Knavs. He might finally trump the opponents. However, some factors go against his victory and make it quite improbable. The main obstacle is the pressure by the EU. Croatia is a member of a supra-state organization, (unlike the United States). The border with Serbia is the border of the EU, and the EU would like it to be as flexible as possible: building a wall would hardly be allowed to Croatia. Any kind of Trump-line economic foreign policy is quite unimaginable within the EU.[64] In sum, there is no certain answer. However, having in mind that the difference is big enough, Dinko Knavs has much less chance than Trump to drag Croatia into the national populist mire.

5.4 CONCLUSION: A NEW PLAYGROUND

This chapter started with a reflection on the conceptual confusion resulting from the many empirical and conceptual ties between populism and nationalism. Throughout the chapter,

---

63 *Id.*

64 On the other hand, Hungarian and Polish national populist governments did allow themselves some moves that go very much against both the spirit and the letter of the EU.

it has become clear that populism and nationalism have been strongly articulated indeed. The chapter has provided insight into the various articulations of populism and nationalism by distinguishing between populist politics and nationalist politics as revolving, respectively, around the claim to represent the people as underdog, constructed through a down/up antagonism between the people-as-underdog and the elite, and the claim to represent the nation, constructed through the in/out distinction between the nation and its outgroups. It is through this clear conceptual distinction that the intricate and complex conceptual and empirical relations between populism and nationalism can be grasped.

In this chapter, I have tried to offer a taxonomy of nationalist attitudes, or those sufficiently close to nationalism, that characterize various populist ideologies. The central one is the right-wing classical nationalism powering national populism. Closest to it is high-profile patriotism and moderate statist nationalism. In the same 'garden' one finds other wider communitarian belongings, determined by religion and language-culture. Rather far from national populism is liberal nationalism, much more suitable for the leftist populist, and also cosmopolitanism-internationalism, that has been associated with important historical left-wing populisms.

I have also stressed the contrast between two kinds of interactions of each attitude and populism: the conceptual proximity and the actual causal link. The conceptual proximity is important in order to describe *in abstracto* the options a would-be populist. I hope the two proposals, taxonomy and the distinction, might help organize further inquiries into populism.

Questions that such inquiry might address in the future include: what do populist nationalisms, in stronger or weaker variety, change in the outlook of nationalism? Did nationalism change its face in its populist incarnation? I conjecture that it did for the following reasons.

First, the classical nationalism implies the need (and the wish) of an ethnic group to have a state. Empires like the Austro-Hungarian, for Slovenians, Hungarians and Croats or the Ottoman, for Serbs, Bulgarians and some other Balkan people, are prime examples. The national(istic) awakenings have reminded some members of the ethnic group of the old glories of the group, the greatness of the Bulgarian, the Croatian and the Serbian kingdoms, the heroic fights against the imperial conquerors, etc. The present-day national populism operates with nationalism mostly in the context of the existing and the functional national states. The ethnonational independence was achieved (or almost achieved) within a federal order. Therefore, the populists have to invent new enemies, often in rather comic inconsistent procedures. ("[W]e want to be members of the EU, but they are at the same time our enemies whom we should distrust at every step.") A very suitable kind of the 'new enemy' is, of course, the migrants. The inconsistency of the effort is nicely highlighted by the slightly inconsistent term 'transnational nationalism'.

Second, because populism is essentially anti-elitist, it brings nationalistic attitudes into a new context, unavailable for the traditional nationalist. I have demonstrated how this complicates the situation for a would-be populist in Croatia. The same demand might make it easier for the populist in some other country with a leftist government, that can be accused of not being sufficiently patriotic. Italy might be a good example. Alternatively, like in Hungary, it might push the mainstream political professional into pretending he is a rebel, ready to govern against his own bureaucrats. The traditional Gellnerian cohabitation of the statist and the ethnonational motivation gets replaced by much more complicated relations.

Third, the new nationalism is ready to morph, in a way unimaginable by its classical predecessor. The invention of new enemies, strong enough to mobilize one's 'people', requires the invention of new solidarities: if the new enemy is a Muslim, the traditional rivalry with the neighbouring Christian states will be pushed into the background, and the brand new Christian identity will replace the ethnic one, or simply cohabitate with it.

Finally, the traditional enemy has changed the face completely. In Europe and North America, the acting hated 'Other' definitely does not appear in the traditional military form, except for negligible exceptions. The new face of the hated 'Other' is the face of an immigrant, either the economic or the political. The dangers traditionally associated with military presence are gone; the national populists have to invent and construct a presumed danger that comes into the country together with the foreign families, including those with the children.

In short, if these conjectures hold, the politicians and theoreticians are faced with a change. The traditional issue of the contrast between patriotism/nationalism and cosmopolitanism has changed its profile: the current drastic contrast is between the populist aversion to the foreigners-migrants and a more generous, a just attitude of the acceptance and the Samaritan sort of help. The aversion inherits some features of the traditional, high-profile patriotism and nationalism, while the acceptance shares the main features with traditional cosmopolitanism. I assume that the future scholarship on patriotism will mainly focus on this new and challenging playfield, with an aim to address the new contrast and locate patriotism(s) in relation to it.

Finally, the populist understanding of 'our people' ('we-community') encompasses not only nationalist options but also goes way beyond it. The important element is a promiscuous character of the populist choices. The traditional contrast has been the one between cosmopolitanism on the universalist side and nationalism on the particularist side. The novelty brought by populism to it is flexibility and malleability of the particularist option: it can be determined by the nationality or by any other kind of communitarian cultural-linguistic belonging. It can also be contrasted with another one from the typical contrast-class at the same level: Catholics versus Orthodox, Christians versus Muslims, etc.

The fact that the playground has been changed is a general message of this chapter, and, I believe of the book, as a whole.

Part II
Comparative Populism: Case Studies

6 Beyond 'Illiberal Democracy': The Case of Hungary

*András Bozóki**

6.1 Introduction

Since the end of the 'transition paradigm',[1] which displayed an optimistic belief in political progress, analysts had to accept that the development from dictatorship to democracy could be halted or reversed. General expectations notwithstanding, the democratic upheaval of 1989-1991 did not end in turning all dictatorships into liberal democracies. Not only the countries of 'democracy by default'[2] became authoritarian, but even formerly consolidated, liberal democracies could backslide to hybrid regimes, "combining democratic and authoritarian elements".[3] While the number of liberal democracies increased significantly, it is even more important to note a growing grey zone lying between democracies and dictatorships, where hybrid regimes thrive.

In the following, I will mostly focus on regime types and not on political speeches and supposed intentions of politicians. As we know, important as they are, political speeches often hide, rather than express, real political intentions. "Do not pay attention to what I say, but what I do" said Viktor Orbán memorably to the US ambassador in Budapest while he was still in opposition.[4] Further, hybrid regimes, in holding on to the name of democracy, are even more likely to use public speeches to obfuscate rather than to reveal the inner workings of the regime.

Thus, here I will focus on the academic issue, the grey zone which contains several mixed regimes and the place of illiberal democracy in this terrain. These regimes have been termed variously: as semi-democracies, semi-dictatorships, 'guided', 'sovereign' or 'managed' democracies, delegative democracies, illiberal democracies, liberal autocracies,

---

* Professor, Central European University, Department of Political Science, Budapest.

1 T. Carothers, 'The End of Transition Paradigm', *Journal of Democracy*, Vol. 18, No. 1, 2002, pp. 12-27.

2 L. A. Way, *Pluralism by Default: Weak Autocrats and the Rise of Competitive Politics*, The Johns Hopkins University Press, Baltimore, 2015.

3 L. Diamond, 'Elections Without Democracy: Thinking About Hybrid Regimes', *Journal of Democracy*, Vol. 13, No. 2, 2002, pp. 21-35.

4 Orbán's remark, back to 2006, became widely known from Wikileaks in 2011, www.origo.hu/itthon/20110906-orban-viktor-reagalt-a-wikileaks-iratokban-szereplo-kijelenteseire.html.

electoral authoritarianisms, competitive authoritarianisms and the like.[5] As early as 1986, O'Donnell and Schmitter already recognized the existence of some transitory regimes, such as *democradúra* and *dictablanda,* based on the Latin American experience.[6] It soon became clear that the defining democracy and dictatorship was not simply an 'either-or' question, but a problem of 'more or less'. Countries in the grey zone contain some elements of democracy and authoritarianism at the same time, albeit in different proportion. But even if it is a 'more or less' issue, one has to be able to identify the Rubicon, a particular historical juncture or moment, which needs to be crossed at times of regime change. Even if it is true that dictatorships do not develop to democracies overnight, nor fall back to dictatorships with the same speed, still we have to able to find the borders between liberal democracies, hybrid regimes and dictatorships. Even on the 'more or less' axis, there are some turning points that separate the three different regimes from each other.

Hybrid regimes have the common feature that they all have competition, although the political elite in power deliberately rearranges state regulations and the political arena as to grant itself undue advantages. For all practical purposes, they are all beneficiaries of an 'uneven playing field'. According to Levitsky and Way,

> [...] competitive authoritarian regimes are civilian regimes in which formal democratic institutions exist and are widely viewed as the primary means of gaining power, but in which incumbents' abuse of the state places them at a significant advantage vis-à-vis their opponents. Such regimes are competitive in that opposition parties use democratic institutions to contest seriously for power, but they are not democratic because the playing field is heavily skewed in favor of incumbents. Competition is thus real but unfair.[7]

6.2 Why 'Illiberal Democracy' Is Not Democracy

In recent years, somewhat surprisingly, the concept of 'illiberal democracy', once introduced by Fareed Zakaria,[8] has enjoyed a spectacular renaissance. While Zakaria defined this concept negatively, considering it as valid description for countries lacking strong consti-

5 Some examples from this literature: G. O'Donnell, 'Delegative Democracy', *Journal of Democracy*, Vol. 5, No. 1, 1994, pp. 55-69; A. Brown, 'From Democratization to Guided Democracy', *Journal of Democracy*, Vol. 12, No. 4, 2001, pp. 35-41; A. Schedler (Ed.), *Electoral Authoritarianism: The Rise of Unfree Competition*, Lynne Rienner Publishers, Boulder, 2006; S. Lewitsky & L. Way, *Competitive Authorianism: Hybrid Regimes After the Cold War*, Cambridge University Press, Cambridge, 2010.

6 G. O'Donnell & P. C. Schmitter (1986), *Transitions from Authoritarian Rule: Tentative Conclusions About Uncertain Democracies*, The Johns Hopkins University Press, Baltimore, 1986.

7 Lewitsky & Way, 2010, p. 5.

8 F. Zakaria, 'The Rise of Illiberal Democracy', *Foreign Affairs*, Vol. 76, No. 6, 1997, pp. 22-46.

tutional-liberal tradition, recently some authoritarian leaders have proclaimed proudly that illiberal democracy was a positive notion. It was presented as an 'anti-core' voice of the periphery against the supposedly elitist, bureaucratic-technocratic, liberal democracy which favoured the upper classes of Western countries. Illiberal democracy was presented as majoritarian, bottom-up, re-politicized democratic alternative to democratic elitism in which working people regain power from the politically correct (but socially less sensitive) elites. However, in reality, it did not lead to higher popular participation, or popular sovereignty; rather it resulted in social apathy and the nearly unlimited power of the sovereign leader.

Theoretically, some promoters of illiberal democracy return to Max Weber's notion of 'leader democracy' (*Führerdemokratie)*, while forgetting that Weber understood the salience of leaders within the realm of liberal democracy.[9] Others offer a right-wing, nationalist interpretation of Antonio Gramsci's theory of hegemony,[10] as they believe that political discourse should be dominated by relentless propaganda. Some others refer to Carl Schmitt's theory of 'the political', which states that the major constitutive element of politics is the conflict between friend and foe.[11] They also like to reinterpret Ernesto Laclau's and Chantal Mouffe's understanding of radical politics[12] to highlight the importance of return to real politics of 'real people'. This approach to politics favours virtue, community and the articulation of conflicts vis-à-vis the dominant neutralizing, legal and moral discourse of the liberal elites. For them, a large dose of populism is vital to reinvigorate politics, and the rise of populist democracies[13] should be considered as healthy reaction to Western democracies which reveal citizens as alienated consumers (and not spirited participants) of democratic politics.

However, despite all these efforts at justification, hybrid regimes, populist politics and illiberal democracies constrain the political activity of citizens and move in an authoritarian direction. The reason why authoritarian leaders like the concept of 'illiberal democracy' so much is that it offers an opportunity for them to present themselves as (some sort of) democrats. Even new dictators want to present themselves as democrats. Maybe 'sovereign', maybe 'non-Western', maybe 'illiberal', but democrats nonetheless. Despite their own role in destroying the rule of law, they make all efforts to convince everyone that they are elected by the people. Former autocrats were not so keen to insist on electoral legitimacy. The notion of illiberal democracy helps the new autocratic leaders to hide their authoritarian intentions as long as possible.

9 M. Weber, *Economy and Society*, G. Roth & C. Wittich (Eds.), University of California Press, Berkeley, 1978.
10 A. Gramsci, *Selections from the Prison Notebooks*, Lawrence & Wishart, London, 1971.
11 C. Schmitt, *The Concept of the Political* [1932], The University of Chicago Press, Chicago, 1996.
12 E. Laclau & C. Mouffe, *Hegemony and Socialist Strategy*, Verso, London, 1985.
13 For an explanation of this attitude *see* T. S. Pappas, 'Populist Democracies: Post-Authoritarian Greece and Postcommunist Hungary', *Government and Opposition*, Vol. 49, No. 1, 2014, pp. 1-23.

By attaching a variety of qualifications to the concept of democracy, to indicate its corruption, academic approaches make a desperate effort to 'rescue' the concept and to stay true to some of its parts. However, this results in a situation where 'too many cooks spoil the broth'. In the final analysis, they come to describe regimes as democracies that, in fact, have nothing in common with the original meaning of the concept. As turned out, populism or illiberalism did not make the regime more democratic, rather less.

What shall we do with illiberal democracies then? Do they exist at all, in the first place? If yes, do they belong to the group of democracies or hybrid regimes? To what extent do liberal values – the rule of law, checks and balances, constitutionalism, civil liberties, separation of powers, human rights and the protection of minorities – belong to democratic values? Does democracy belong to all citizens of the political community or is it just a property of the majority? These questions are equally important for political theorists and students of comparative politics, as much as they are for citizens. Is democracy a universal value or just a particular good? Is it a Western value only or are there non-Western democracies at all?[14] Old problems seem to come back now.

What we have learned around 1989 is that democracy equals Western, liberal democracy. It is the only regime that is based on political pluralism, participation, competition and civil liberties. Therefore, several scholars rightfully questioned the validity of illiberal democracy as a sub-type within the family of democracies. In his essay, Jeffrey C. Isaac already mentioned some powerful criticisms of that concept by Jan-Werner Müller,[15] János Kornai[16] and others. The Hungarian political philosopher, János Kis[17] presents a similar argument. He claims that the key aspect of democracy is that even the minority accepts the legitimacy of decisions. This, however, happens only when the system is unbiased and when people whose opinion ended up in the minority remain legitimate actors in the democratic process because majority decisions are not used to disenfranchise the minority. In modern democracy, it is not possible to marginalize, neglect or dispose of the minority; that is, there is no democracy beyond liberal democracy. Consequently, according to Kis, there is no such thing as illiberal democracy because an illiberal regime could not qualify as democratic.

If we operate within normative democratic theory, I agree with this. Those who systematically attack the rule of law can hardly be seen as defenders of democracy. The concept of democracy gradually changed and by today it has come to embrace the liberal and constitutional components. It is difficult to label any political regime as a democracy outside

14 R. Youngs, *The Puzzle of Non-Western Democracy*, Carnegie Endowment for International Peace, Washington DC, 2015.

15 J. W. Müller, 'The Problem with Illiberal Democracy', *Project Syndicate*, 21 January 2016.

16 J. Kornai, 'Hungary's U-Turn: Retreating from Democracy', *Journal of Democracy*, Vol. 26, No. 3, 2015, pp. 34-48.

17 J. Kis, 'Illiberális demokrácia nem létezik', *Hvg.hu*, 24 November 2014.

the world of liberal democracies, even if we know that democracy is *never* perfect, and that there are defective democracies that do not fulfil all criteria properly.

My approach is summarized in the following typology:

Democracy	Hybrid Regime	Dictatorship
Liberal democracies: Consensual or majoritarian	Various regimes, including illiberal democracy and competitive authoritarianism	Full authoritarian or totalitarian regimes

Others see this differently. Csillag and Szelényi,[18] for instance, present an electoral democracy argument. They judge the example Orbán regime of Hungary as democratic because it came to power by democratic means and there is still a possibility of a change of government. They work with a relatively low threshold and argue that one can speak of democracy when the legitimization of power is based on the will of the majority. They accept Huntington's minimalist reasoning that free and fair elections are the *sine qua non* of democracies and, from the perspective of legitimization, the actual mode of governance is relatively less relevant.[19] The authors do not problematize whether the 2014 elections in Hungary lived up to the criterion of free and fair elections.

There were indeed some regimes in post-communist Europe in the 1990s that we can retrospectively label as electoral or illiberal democracies, like Slovakia under Meciar, Yugoslavia under Milosevic, Romania under Iliescu or Croatia under Tudjman. In the optimistic mood of transitology, it was supposed that these regimes would develop towards liberal democracy. Since three out of those four countries are now members of the European Union, illiberal democracy could be interpreted as 'child disease' of new democracies.

Csillag and Szelényi primarily emphasize the fact that the leadership is elected by free elections. If this criterion is met, they deem the regime democratic, either liberal or illiberal. If the principle of free elections is not met, they automatically see it as authoritarian, which may also be liberal or illiberal. They consider liberal autocracies as being halfway between democracy and dictatorship while only illiberal autocracies are regarded as dictatorships by them. Their typology is the following:

	Democracy	Autocracy
Liberal	Liberal democracy	Hybrid Regime
Illiberal	Illiberal democracy	Dictatorship

18 T. Csillag & I. Szelényi, 'Drifting from Liberal Democracy: Neo-Conservative Ideology of Managed Illiberal Democratic Capitalism in Post-Communist Europe', *Intersections*, Vol. 1, No. 1, 2015, pp. 18-48.

19 S. P. Huntington, *The Third Wave: Democratization in the late Twentieth Century*, Oklahoma University Press, Norman, 1991.

I certainly agree with Csillag and Szelényi that empirical reality displays broader varieties of regimes than normative democratic theory, and illiberal democracies can occur in the real world. But I disagree with them in considering illiberal democracy as type of democracy. In my view, illiberal democracy belongs to the hybrid regimes. If one accepts illiberal democracy as a form of democracy, then he or she not only denies the normative consensus on democracies but inflates the notion of democracy. At the end, we will not able to recognize democracies and distinguish them from other regimes. Isaac is right by stating that we need to accept empirical reality but we need to avoid conceptual stretching as well.[20]

What people commonly call 'illiberal democracy' is, in fact, an empirically existing hybrid regime, in other words, non-democracy. Calling it democracy might be academically misleading and politically disarming. To demonstrate the second: the concept is used in the political discourse of the European Union in a rather diplomatic way to lessen the significance of Hungarian and Polish deviations from mainstream European democracies. That appears to justify the soft attitude of the EU toward these countries, despite their disrespect to commonly accepted standard, liberal democratic values. As long as the EU considers Hungary and Poland as (some sort of) democracies, it will justify its own inability to sanction these countries.

6.3 Hungarian 'Exceptionalism'

Is it possible to have an increasingly flourishing autocratic regime in the European Union? After all, the Union was built on liberal democratic values, as a community with 'ever closer' cooperation. Member states of the European Union are supposed to be liberal democracies, but Hungary, in harbouring authoritarian features under a disintegrating guise of democracy, is rightly called a hybrid regime. As such, it is the first non-democratic member state in the history of the European Union.

In Hungary, the deconsolidation of democracy, widely perceived as elitist, started in late 2006. The opposition Fidesz-party, led by Viktor Orbán, behaved not so much as rivals but definitive enemies of the coalition government, as an already polarized political discourse became increasingly driven by hatred. The economic crisis of 2008 led to the political storm of the 2010 elections, when Fidesz received a qualified majority in the Parliament. Since that time, the quality of democracy steadily deteriorated. At the beginning, supporters of the regime talked about 'majoritarian democracy' as if liberal democracy would survive unharmed. Retrospectively, one can claim that the regime was some sort of damaged, broken or illiberal democracy between 2011 and 2015. Democratic institutions were gradually less respected by the government but important democratic principles,

20 J. Isaac, 'Is There Illiberal Democracy? A Problem with No Semantic Solution', *Public Seminar*, 12 July 2017.

listed by Jeffrey C. Isaac,[21] were still in place. These included open political contestation, freedom of speech, freedom of association, legal equality, egalitarian conception of citizenship, gender-neutral civic status, albeit all of them were somewhat distorted. Finally, however, the regime left 'illiberal democracy' behind and has been relying on increasingly authoritarian measures. The time factor is relevant: the book *Hungarian Patient*, which contains the term 'illiberal democracy' in its subtitle, edited by Peter Krasztev and Jon Van Til,[22] reflects on the political processes occurred before 2015. Any serious discussion about broken, damaged, defective or illiberal democracies should consider the ever-changing nature of these regimes.

In 2016, when Hungarian citizens were prevented from submitting a referendum question by brute 'civilian' force and with the government's tacit consent, *i.e.*, they were barred from exercising their constitutional right, it was time to ask the question again: Does it still make *any* sense to talk about democracy in Hungary? With its outsourced violence and its plan to amend the Constitution claiming a 'state of terrorist threat', the Orbán regime took another step on the road to establishing a power monopoly in early 2016. Just as the far right Jobbik party once had a paramilitary wing, there were indications that a similar team of loosely organized thugs in Fidesz colours was about to emerge whose members, while not wearing uniforms, were deployed to intimidate demonstrators and members of the opposition.

For policy reasons the regime proudly claimed that its enforcement agencies did not use direct force (instead, it had come to prefer existential threats) and the job of intimidation has been outsourced to 'civilian' street fighters, the ultras of some football clubs and others.

All this was not taking place in Milošević's rump-Yugoslavia at the end of the previous century. The policy perfectly fits the Orbán-regime's governance strategy characterized by a deliberate effort to blur the differences between official and unofficial, responsible and unaccountable agents. Decisions are made outside the established institutions, behind their back, in an invisible and grey zone, in a world of shady organizations bearing no political responsibility or liability. Under this scheme, acts of violence that may embarrass those in power are performed by skilled skinheads that, in turn, can be easily disclaimed by Fidesz. Similarly, the budget is not necessarily drafted by the minister in charge, but by private firms (acting as money-laundering operations, according to a former staff member) with no legal ties to the government and whose members may also have access to classified information.

There is a point where even broken democracy comes to an end. At a point where the line between private and public interest is swallowed up, the difference between national-

21 *Id.*

22 P. Krasztev & J. V. Til (Eds.), *The Hungarian Patient: Social Opposition to an Illiberal Democracy*, CEU Press, Budapest, New York, 2015.

ization and privatization disappears, where public interest becomes indistinguishable from the interests of politicians/economic players capturing the state, where mutatis mutandis, the system ends up defending these entrepreneurs. Corruption is legalized. Hungary has arrived at this point: "What is called corruption is in effect Fidesz's most important political aim", the regime's chief ideologist András Lánczi stated with undisguised honesty.[23] Today, corruption in Hungary is no longer seen as deviant behaviour but an integral part of the system itself. Breaking the law has become the new normal. What was once described as the abuse of power, today has become a defining feature of the regime. As Bálint Magyar put it: "The mafia state is a privatized form of the parasitic state", where the patron/client relationship no longer refers to the patronage system also seen in democracies; essentially, it is the "eradication of the foundations of individual autonomy and the shoehorning of all existential issues into a system of dependencies".[24] This already comes dangerously close to a definition of authoritarian regimes.

The concept of 'mafia state' is one of the most consistent theoretical arguments to describe the regime, and its Orwellian communication can be used not only as opposition criticism of the regime, but also for an academically sound analysis of Hungary's political system. We have come to a point where the Orbán regime has slipped the bounds of democracy definitions in the broadest sense, *i.e.*, 'defective', 'electoral' and 'minimal'. There are too many defects, elections are not clean and the democratic minimum is evaporating. Has the time come to take another look and reposition the Orbán regime along the political continuum?

I consider the centralization and personalization of power, the propaganda of 'national unification' coupled with the discrimination and marginalization of underclass elements of the society, the forced change of elites by the predatory (or mafia) state and the practice of power politics as the building blocks of the regime. The regime is rooted in the prime minister's conviction that 'revolutionary circumstances' mandate him to execute exceptional policies.[25]

The Orbán regime of 2018 is largely different from its early days of 2010-2011, although one can trace the origins of its authoritarianism to its beginning. It has experienced a gradual process of transformation since 2010. Excessive majoritarian arguments dominated its early stage of development.[26] The first step toward illiberal democracy was the unilateral writing and approval of a new constitution, the Fundamental Law, by the governing party

23 A. Lánczi, 'Viccpártok színvonalán áll az ellenzék' [The Opposition Is Like a Joke], (Interview by Imre Czirják), *Magyar Idők*, 21 December 2015.

24 B. Magyar, *The Postcommunist Mafia State: The Case of Hungary*, CEU Press, Budapest, New York, 2016, p. 13.

25 A. Bozóki, 'Broken Democracy, Predatory State and Nationalist Populism', *in* Krasztev & Til (Eds.), 2015, pp. 3-36.

26 A. Bozóki, 'Die autoritäre Versuchung: Die Krise der ungarischen Demokratie', *Osteuropa*, Vol. 61, No. 12, 2011, pp. 65-88.

only. As a result, abusing its democratically legitimized power, the government has done away with the rule of law step by step. The best example of this is the fourth modification of the Fundamental Law in the spring of 2013: this modification made the Constitutional Court legally possible to disregard its decisions from before 2010.[27] (Similar processes are observable in today's Poland, although the governing bloc does not have the qualified majority to change the constitution. Therefore, the Polish governing far right PiS party, led by Jaroslaw Kaczynski, goes openly against the Constitution in the hope that the castrated Constitutional Court will give them green light.)

In Hungary, up until the 2014 general elections, the possibility of free and fair elections could not be excluded. Those elections, however, failed to meet the minimal requirements of the democratic process, due to the 'uneven playing field' of the competition. Orbán's statement on building an illiberal state, in July 2014, instead of indicating the launch date of a new order, had simply promised further measures aimed at entrenching his authoritarian system. By that time the regime had the unfair elections safely behind it and was just done with changing rules for municipal election in Budapest, just a few months before balloting.

The system has undergone massive change over the years. By 2014 it already left the illiberal democracy signpost behind. Today, after the 2018 elections, we have no proper terms to describe the phenomenon before our eyes,[28] but the notion of competitive authoritarianism might fit the nature of the regime best. The election results have provoked a set of large scale protests on the streets of Budapest, in which protesters repeatedly accused the opposition parties of collaboration with the rising autocracy. The regime's move toward authoritarianism has continued, which is best evidenced by some recent actions:

- Hiring of enforcers to block violently the opposition's attempt at initiating a referendum and the public prosecutor's failure to press charges. Outsourcing violence to football hooligans and paramilitary groups reminds the observer of the early Putin years in Russia.
- The state's vehement anti-immigrant propaganda campaign during the government initiated referendum in 2016 as well as in the electoral campaign of 2018.
- By using its overwhelming political and economic power, the government closed the biggest left-liberal daily newspaper, the *Népszabadság* in 2016.
- The attempt to close down the Budapest-based Hungarian-American private university, the Central European University.

27 I. Vörös, 'Hungary's Constitutional Evolution during the Last 25 Years', *Südosteuropa*, Vol. 63, No. 2, 2015, pp. 173-200.

28 B. Trencsényi, 'What Should I call you? The Crisis of Hungarian Democracy in a Regional Interpretative Framework', *in* B. Magyar & J. Vásárhelyi (Eds.), *Twenty-Five Sides of a Post-Communist Mafia State*, CEU Press, Budapest, New York, 2017, pp. 3-26.

- The leadership of the governing party has led "an electoral campaign, with disproportionate resources and the explicit backing of state institutions, which focused on fearmongering, employed conspiracy theories and fake news, and issued some open threats. The ruling party neither engaged in open public debate on its governing record, nor presented concrete policy plans".[29]
- Another characteristic of the regime has been its aggressive handling of civic organizations. As an official of the governing party declared, independent NGOs "must be swept out of Hungarian public life" because they interlope in politics. This statement was followed by discriminatory legislation against NGOs, which had received foreign funds.

The language used by the regime serves to hide reality. Propagandistic mass communication, a questionnaire sent to all citizens with a set of biased or manipulative questions, is called 'national consultation'. With this, the primary goal of Fidesz was to refresh the list of its supporters. 'Protection' stands for the collection of protection money. In reality, the 'defence' of retirement benefits means the requisitioning of pensions by the state. Utility-cost cuts have led to higher prices and deteriorating services. The protection of the Hungarian people has resulted in the impoverishment of large segments of the population. As corruption became the norm and a part of daily routine, it has become invisible to the public. Apart from public works programs for the poorest of the poor, utility-cost cuts benefiting the well-off, and a flat tax, the system gains legitimacy through investments demonstrating the symbolic power of the ruling elite (*e.g.*, the prime minister's new office, which is a palace on the Castle Hill in Buda), nationalist campaigns and government-generated xenophobia.

As the growing literature of the topic demonstrates the Orbán regime gradually evolved from its larval stage and today it stands fully formed (if we can talk about 'full formation' at all).[30] This is not to suggest that the leader of the regime follows a pre-calculated blueprint. The authoritarian direction was clear, but there were lots of incidental events, spontaneous reactions, contradictory policies and periods of slower or faster speed of change, as the political situation allowed. Since 2014 the main problem with the regime is not only that it is illiberal, but that it is increasingly anti-democratic.

Moreover, due to the constraining power of the European Union, by now the Orbán regime appears to be relatively more liberal than democratic. The EU is more equipped to sanction deviations in human rights than the deconstruction of democracy. In this regime, a few fundamental rights (freedom of speech, freedom of assembly, right to privacy, freedom of movement) remain protected despite the autocratic monopolization of politics.

29 F. Laczó, 'The Illusion of Choice', *Visegrad Insight*, 24 April 2018.
30 *Cf.* P. Wilkin, *Hungary's Crisis of Democracy: The Road to Serfdom*, Lexington Books, Lanham, 2016; A.L. Pap, *Democratic Decline in Hungary: Law and Society in an Illiberal Democracy*, Routledge, London, 2017; Magyar & Vásárhelyi (Eds.), 2017.

In essence, it is an emerging authoritarian set-up which could be moderately tamed by the European Union with regard to basic human rights and civil liberties.[31] In other words, the international embeddedness of the Orbán-regime hinders or makes slower its slide toward authoritarianism. Because of this external constraint, the leaders of the Orbán-regime have been forced to engage in Janus-faced methods, double talk, double standards and pay lip service to democratic values, in short, to pursue a hypocritical behaviour that they would not do under other circumstances. The government tries to justify their anti-democratic policies by appealing to democratic norms, which softens the autocratic nature of the regime. The regime uses a rhetoric that exploits xenophobia, a nationalist interpretation of Christianity,[32] so as to throw off the European Union's liberal democratic rule of law with limited success. Lately, the developments in politics abroad, particularly in Turkey and Russia, encourage the opponents of pluralist democracy further to eliminate the liberal elements of the regime.

In sum, the Orbán regime could be described as a hybrid regime with mafia state structure, unorthodox economic policy that serves social inequality, ethno-nationalism and re-feudalization. The regime could be called competitive authoritarianism,[33] provided it allowed genuine competition — which it does not, however. There is a dominant party-system with limited competition and elections are held without real options. While opposition forces may win in several electoral districts in by-elections, their hope for victory in the general elections is much constrained. The ruling political clique combines political and economic tools to maintain its power, yet it lacks the intellectual and moral support of the largest part of society. The regime relies on its political loyalists, while it divides and neutralizes its potential opponents, no matter whether they are passive or active.[34]

It appears the downward spiral continues, regardless the country's membership in the European Union. The Hungarian politics of 'worst practices' is quickly copied by the Kaczynski regime in Poland. When citizens' constitutional rights for initiating a referendum are denied even on the apparently trivial issue of whether retail stores should stay open on Sunday, what arsenal would the governing forces deploy should their hold on power be threatened? Perhaps we need to reverse the premise of our analysis: instead of trying to understand why the Hungarian political system – formerly called democracy – is illiberal, let us study what makes this European *autocracy relatively liberal.*

---

31 A. Bozóki & D. Hegedűs, 'An Externally Constrained Hybrid Regime: Hungary in the European Union', *Democratization*, Vol. 25, No. 7, pp. 1173-1189, 13 April 2018, doi:10.1080/13510347.2018.1455664.

32 Z. Ádám & A. Bozóki, "'The God of Hungarians': Religion and Right-Wing Populism in Hungary", *in* N. Marzouki *et al.* (Eds.), *Saving the People: How Populists Hijack Religion*, Hurst & Company, London, 2016, pp. 129-148.

33 Lewitsky & Way, 2010.

34 In this respect, it fits to the model set up by B. B. de Mesquita & A. Smith, *The Dictator's Handbook*, Public Affairs, New York, 2011.

6.4 Conclusions

Finally, we need to understand the spread of authoritarian epidemic and the place of illiberal democracy in the grey zone. For me, illiberal democracy is not so much a popular political project, but a relatively rare empirical configuration among the hybrid regimes. It is a fluid and relatively less authoritarian and less violent regime type among the hybrid regimes which, in the case of formerly democratic countries, appears as part of de-democratization. The contradictory character of illiberal democracy can also be explained by the real tension between internal and external forces within certain international organizations (such as the EU). Illiberal democracy, just as liberal autocracy or competitive authoritarianism, might be described as a temporary co-existence of overlapping political structures that contradict to each other. They might have the following characteristics:

1. The regime is led by an authoritarian leader who comes to power by elections and who is supported by similarly authoritarian-minded leaders internationally.
2. The leader creates a highly personalist, informal, centralized, vertically operating system of rule in which loyalty overrides expertise and where social autonomies (like independent media and independent groups of civil society) are considered dangerous.
3. The political clique, that occupies the state from inside, might behave as an adopted political family including formal party-members and loyal clientele selectively.
4. The regime is in a constant flux, a 'moving target', where consolidation is improbable. In the lack of external constraint, the regime is often transitory on the road to full authoritarianism (as the case of Russia suggests).
5. The leader, who speaks in the name of the native people, condemns international elites (European Union politicians, multi-national business circles etc.) and foreign migrants and considers them enemies.
6. However, an illiberal leader prefers 'clean' and not openly violent methods, just as regular (but unfair) elections, to secure his long-term rule and to be able to present himself as a sort of 'democrat' internationally.
7. The regime promises to re-politicize the public sphere and to mobilize the political community, but it ends up with no politics just central propaganda and confused, chaotic public administration. The so-called 'strong state' is in fact a mafia state where corruption is not external or deviant, but it is an embedded, legislated and networked phenomenon.
8. The regime is rather based itself on fears and traditional mentalities of citizens rather than any coherent ideology.
9. Leaders of illiberal democracy, just as of any hybrid regime, learn from each other: similar autocratic methods and narratives are circulating among themselves (sometimes called as autocracy promotion).

10. Yet, there are a lot of spontaneous actions, accidental and unpredictable events that occur in such regimes. Although authoritarian leaders learn from each other, they do not necessarily implement the same blueprint or follow a pre-calculated political project.
11. Politics is more complicated for authoritarian leaders if their country belongs to a community of democratic states. Subsidiarity principle, formal commitment to basic democratic values, multi-level governance, institutional cooperation etc., which all exist in the European Union, are external factors that condition the behaviour of the national leader. At this point the leader of an illiberal regime enters a cynical and hypocritical game with representatives of the international community by taking the available material benefits from the common basket whilst disrespecting the common democratic norms.
12. In the post-communist context, illiberal democracy often includes rough redistribution of property among the old and new elites. Members of the new power elite use legislation to renationalize private property temporarily in order to reprivatize it for themselves and their clients afterwards.

To conclude in one sentence: illiberal democracy sounds like an oxymoron theoretically, yet it might exist in the real world as a fluid, non-crystallized and often externally constrained set-up in the grey zone as a particular type of hybrid regimes.

7 Populism, Free Speech and the Anti-Entrenchment Principle

Adam Shinar[*]

7.1 Introduction

One salient feature of the new populist tendencies that are seemingly sweeping many democratic regimes is the concentration of power by the executive. To be sure, the rise in executive power has been a persistent feature of the modern administrative state, but the reasons underlying this accretion today are different. In the past, concerns about the rise in administrative power stemmed from a wariness of a growing class of bureaucrats. Administrative power was perceived as challenging democratic principles, because it entailed an ever-growing reliance on experts, who occupied the vacuum opened by legislators. Legislators, on their part, were often happy to delegate important tasks to a growing class of experts, thus removing the setting of important norms from 'the people', who now felt subject to bureaucratic power instead of representative government.

But the recent populist impulse is different. Like its predecessors, it is also suspicious, and even sometimes dismissive, of experts and bureaucracy. But unlike its predecessors, it has little patience for opposition and minority views. Whereas the rise in administrative power in the past led to charges of a democratic deficit, the present populism either minimizes the importance of democracy, or, more accurately, puts forward a conception of democracy that views majority rule as its most important and defining characteristic. It thus conflates the people with the government, while opposition to the government is consequently viewed as unpatriotic, harmful or illegitimate.

This populist tendency will be demonstrated by examining the situation in Israel (though of course it exists elsewhere). In Israel, the right wing has enjoyed unprecedented dominance, governing almost uninterruptedly since 1977. It thus faces little substantial opposition in the legislature, leading it to identify and mark opposition elements elsewhere in order to secure and bolster its rule. Those, perhaps predictably, include the Supreme Court, which sometimes rules against the government, and dissenting voices in the public sphere, mostly the cultural and academic elites.

The chapter will focus on the ways in which the Israeli government is attempting to use its 'power of the purse' to limit speech it perceives as critical of its policies. Crucially,

* Associate Professor, Harry Radzyner Law School, IDC Herzliya.

part of the government's reasoning is that it represents the people, and thus is under no obligation to fund views (mostly through funding of the arts and cultural institutions) that are critical of its values and policies, as those are the policies chosen by 'the people'. The Supreme Court has developed doctrines that limit the government's discretion in the use of its allocative power, yet I will argue that Court has not gone far and deep enough.

The chapter will consequently develop the anti-entrenchment principle, according to which democratic regimes should be suspicious of governments which try to entrench their power beyond their elected term. Much of anti-entrenchment doctrine focuses on election law, but, as I will argue, it should extend to all facets of governance, in this case speech. On my view, the prohibition on government entrenchment should lead to a constitutional principle that requires the government to allocate funds precisely to speech that is critical of the government's values, policies and preferences.

7.2 Israel and the Protection of Speech

It is often thought, at least by many Israelis, that Israel is a liberal democratic state. Indeed, several features indicate it is just that, including the broad legal protection given to speech. As Barak Medina claims, the scope of the protection for speech is a litmus test for a state to considered a liberal democracy.[1] And indeed, Israel's Supreme Court, beginning in the 1950s with the *Kol-Ha'am* case,[2] has developed and entrenched a system of legal rules that, on the one hand, sought to protect speech, but on the other hand, delineated its limits. It thus recognized limits to speech based on state security and public order. After Israel's 'Constitutional Revolution',[3] limits on speech became subordinated to a proper purpose and proportionality analysis.[4]

According to the Court's case law, every type of speech is entitled to *prima facie* protection.[5] Unlike the United States, for example, Israel does not have a category of unprotected speech. This does not mean that every type of speech will end up being protected, but *prima facie* constitutional protection will be given to every speech, including, but not limited to, political speech, artistic speech and commercial speech.[6]

1 B. Medina, 'The Unintended Consequences of Prohibiting Advocacy of Hatred and Regulating Campaign-Finance: The Weakening Status of Freedom of Speech in Israel', *Hebrew University of Jerusalem Legal Research Paper*, No. 17-42, p. 2, https://ssrn.com/abstract=3039940.

2 HCJ 73/53, *Kol Ha'am v. Minister of Interior*, 7 P.D. 871 (Sup. Ct. 1953).

3 *See* A. Shinar, 'Accidental Constitutionalism: The Political Foundations and Implications of Israeli Constitution-Making', *in* D. Galligan & M. Versteeg (Eds.), *The Social and Political Foundations of Constitutions*, Cambridge University Press, Cambridge, 2013, pp. 207-238.

4 *See, e.g.*, HCJ 316/03, *Bakri v. Film Review Council*, 58(1) P.D. 249 (Sup. Ct. 2003).

5 HCJ 399/85, *Kahana v. Israel Broadcast Authority*, 41(3) P.D. 255 (Sup. Ct. 1987).

6 *See Kol Ha'am v. Minister of Interior* (political speech); *Bakri v. Film Review Council* (artistic speech); HCJ 606/93, *Kidum v. Broadcast Authority*, 48(2) P.D. 1 (Sup. Ct. 1994) (commercial speech).

Alongside the constitutional protection of speech, Israel has also enacted several laws that affect the scope of protection given to speech. For example, the Penal Law criminalizes speech which incites violence and racism;[7] the Battle against Terrorism Law criminalizes speech that promotes terrorism.[8] At the constitutional level, Basic Law: The Knesset (Israel's parliament) authorizes the disqualification of candidates and parties who deny Israel's existence as a Jewish and democratic state, incite racism or support an armed struggle of a state or a terrorist organization against Israel.[9] At the administrative level, the Foundations of the Budget Law, alongside other laws,[10] authorizes the denial of public funds due to incitement of violence, terrorism or racism, the rejection of Israel as a Jewish and democratic state, supporting an armed struggle of a state or of a terrorist organization against Israel and for noting the day of Israel's establishment or its Day of Independence as a day of mourning.

Despite the extensive literature and case law on free speech Israel has generated in its seventy years of existence, precious little focuses on the question of subsidizing speech. What happens, or more exactly, what is the law when the state does not directly ban speech, but nevertheless funds expressive activity and that funding leads to privileging some speech over another? Put differently, the question is one of 'speech resources'. In addition to each individual's right to free speech, an expression needs a platform, which may require governmental economic support. The paradigmatic example is the right to demonstrate. The police are often required to secure demonstrations, whether due to violence against protestors or due to the need to regulate traffic in the surrounding streets. These actions require the allocation of economic resources in order to realize the freedom to protest. In these cases, the realization of free speech depends on the monetary allocation of funds from the government. Of course, this is not new. Even though free speech is usually thought of a negative right, it has positive aspects.[11]

The link between free speech and government funding gives rise to some of the most complicated questions when it comes to free expression. Even if we were to say that a person has a right to free speech, it does not follow that there is a right that the speech she wishes to express warrants government funding. Indeed, the distinction between the negative aspect of free speech (the duty not to interfere and censor) and the positive aspect of free speech (the duty to fund and support) has been relied upon in recent years by the Israeli government to justify selective funding of speech, in particular, supporting speech in line with policies, values and ideas the government wishes to advance. At the same time,

7 Sec. 144B and Sec. 144D2 to the Penal Law, 1977.

8 Sec. 24 to the Battle against Terrorism Law, 2016.

9 Sec. 7A of Basic-Law: The Knesset.

10 Sec. 4 of the Law to Prevent Harm to the State of Israel through Boycott, 2011 and Sec. 3B to the Foundations of the Budget Law, 1985.

11 S. Holmes & C. R. Sunstein, *The Cost of Rights: Why Liberty Depends on Taxes,* W. W. Norton & Company, New York, 2000, pp. 35-48.

the government has attempted to deny or decrease funding from entities and expressions which manifest, in the eyes of the government, criticism of the policies and values the government supports.

To name just a few examples, there have been attempts to deny or decrease funding from the Al-Midan theatre in Haifa, which presented a play describing the experiences of Walid Daka, a life-term prisoner in Israel, after having been convicted of commanding a group of terrorists which kidnapped and murdered an Israeli soldier;[12] from the Tel Aviv cinematheque for its decision to hold a Nakba film festival;[13] from the Jerusalem cinematheque for showing films by the human rights NGO 'B'Tselem';[14] and devising funding criteria that incentivize cultural institutions to appear in Jewish settlements in the Occupied Palestinian Territories, while reducing funding for entities that refuse to do so.[15]

These recent events have given rise to a new claim in Israel, formulated most clearly by Minister of Culture Miri Regev, under the name of 'freedom of funding'.[16] According to this claim, the state may not censor expressions (except for the limits mentioned above), but it may support expressions in line with the policy it wishes to further. Selective funding is thus justified because it does not impinge on freedom of speech. Indeed, the government is not preventing anyone from speaking. It is merely choosing which speech to subsidize, and in a world of limited resources, such a choice is inevitable. Moreover, it only makes sense that in a world of limited resources the government will fund speech it supports, since its task is precisely to carry out the will of the voters who put the government in office.

The principle of freedom of funding has intuitive appeal. It sits well with our distinction between negative and positive rights and between the public and the private. In addition, as just mentioned, it has a certain democratic resonance as well. However, the Israel Supreme Court has rejected this principle. Interestingly, the principle has been rejected not because of free speech considerations, but mostly on equality grounds. Government

12 Y. Ashkenazi, 'Culture Ministry Halts Funding to Haifa's Al-Midan Theatre', *Haaretz*, 16 June 2015; N. Shpigel, 'A Victory for Al-Midan Theatre: The District Court Ordered the City of Haifa to Return its Funding', *Haaretz*, 4 November 2015.

13 N. Anderman, 'Israel Culture Minister Wants Tel Aviv Cinematheque Fined for Hosting Nakba Film Festival', *Haaretz*, 16 November 2017.

14 I. Stern, 'Culture Ministry Calls to Reexamine the Budgeting of the Jerusalem Cinematheque for Showing B'Tselem Films', *Haaretz*, 24 August 2017.

15 Y. Ashkenazi, 'Leading Israeli Rights Group Riled Up Over Culture Ministry's Revised Funding Criteria', *Haaretz*, 30 March 2017.

16 L. Grave-Lazi, 'Regev: No Funding for Cultural Institutions that Subvert State, Burn Flag', *Jerusalem Post*, 27 January 2016. ("Freedom of expression is part of the DNA of the State of Israel and I have no intention of harming this, but the state will not fund any cultural institution that subverts it or that burns the flag [...] We all respect the principles of democracy and the State of Israel being a Jewish and democratic state. I will not allow the subversion of the foundations of the state, especially when it is government-funded. What is this outcry? That I ask that a funded institution will abide by the law?").

funds should be allocated according to equal criteria.[17] Giving funds to one and not to another, when there is no relevant difference, constitutes discrimination. The discrimination claim is analytically easier for the Court. It does not raise the complicated questions of free speech which would lead, perhaps, to the determination that free speech entails a positive right to receive government funding.

In this chapter I wish to present a new claim which justifies the rejection of the freedom of finance doctrine. The extant justifications rooted in equality and neutrality provide only a partial response to the challenge presented by the freedom of finance doctrine. Suppose, for example, that the government wished to fund only one area of activity, which is in line with its general policy – strengthening Jewish heritage. Let us further suppose that the government would distribute funds according to neutral and equal criteria. Would there be a constitutional violation in such a case?

In my view, the answer is a tentative yes.[18] To explain why, I develop an 'anti-entrenchment' principle.[19] This principle supplements and complements the extant equality justification and does not seek to replace it. It merely adds a theoretical layer in order to claim that the government cannot remain neutral to different views in the marketplace of ideas. Instead, there may be instances where the government is under an obligation to support values, ideas and principles that seek to subvert the very values, ideas and principles that the government seeks to promote. This obligation might arise when the government uses its allocative power to fortify and entrench its political power beyond its term, thus preventing (or minimizing the chances of) the minority from becoming the political majority or increasing power.

In the next parts I examine the existing legal framework in Israel which regulates speech resources when it comes to state support of expressive activities. I then turn to briefly discuss the shortcomings of current doctrine. Exclusive reliance on equality ignores 'thicker' justifications rooted in free speech and democratic structure. In response to these shortcom-

17 *See* Sec. 3A(d) to the Foundations of the Budget Law, 1985; A. De-Hartoch, 'The State's Support of Public Institutions: The Flourishing of Unique Funds', *Hebrew University Law Review*, Vol. 29, 1998, pp. 82-83; HCJ 59/88, *Tsaban v. Minister of Finance*, 42(4) P.D. 705 (Sup. Ct. 1989) (hereinafter *Tsaban* case); HCJ 1438/98, *The Masorti Movement v. Minister of Religious Affairs*, 53(5) P.D. 337, 360 (Sup. Ct. 1999).

18 One possibility, which I do not develop here, is to claim that because of the importance of culture to society, the government has an obligation to support cultural activities. On this view, the decision not to support culture at all would be unconstitutional, since the state has a duty to promote some type of human flourishing, since only under conditions of cultural diversity will persons be able to develop their personality, re-examine their beliefs and realize what they perceive to be the good life. For support of this argument, *see, generally* M. Mautner, *Human Flourishing, Liberal Theory, and the Arts*, Routledge, Oxford, 2018. A hint of this approach can be found in the Israeli case law. *See* HCJ 175/71, *Abu-Ghosh Music Festival v. Minister of Education and Culture*, 25(2) P.D. 821, 828 (Sup. Ct. 1971).

19 General anti-entrenchment principles have been developed mostly in the context of election law. *See, e.g.*, M. J. Klarman, 'Majoritarian Judicial Review: The Entrenchment Problem', *Georgetown Law Journal*, Vol. 85, 1997, p. 491; J. H. Ely, *Democracy and Distrust: A Theory of Judicial Review*, Harvard University Press, Cambridge/MA, 1980.

ings, the chapter concludes with an introduction of the anti-entrenchment principle, which adds to existing justifications in the literature and case law.

In a nutshell, the anti-entrenchment principle relies on the distinction between government and state, which are often used interchangeably. The government is not the state, and in a certain sense, it does not represent the state. It is one manifestation, albeit an important one, of the state. In a democratic state the government cannot act in order to entrench its power. In order to preserve a democracy, the political majority must maintain conditions that allow competition between majority and minority (however we define them). From this it follows that a political majority cannot entrench its power at every cost and thus prevent the minority from becoming the majority. One way to entrench power is through one-sided support of ideas, opinions and values that are in line with those of the majority, while denying or reducing funding from ideas identified with the political minority. It follows, then, that paradoxically, there will be instances where the government must support messages and entities which oppose the policies it wishes to promote.

7.3 The Regulation of Speech Resources in Israel – Public Funding of Private Expression

In this Part I cannot cover all the public support Israel gives to speech. For example, I will not refer to providing security for demonstrations, allocating radio frequencies or protecting copyright. I will focus only on public funding for private expression, in particular artistic or cultural expression, where the argument of freedom of finance arises most frequently. My claim is that when the constitutionality of an allocation is at question, its legality is determined through equality, while overlooking or giving marginal weight to free speech and considerations of democratic structure.

My point of departure is that a liberal state aspires to separate the right from the good.[20] Rights enable people to pursue their conception of the good life. Consequently, the state cannot grant a privileged status to a certain conception of the good life. It cannot impose its own conception of the good life on its citizens. It thus must remain neutral toward competing conceptions of the good, since it is not possible to develop a free and pluralist environment where the government determines what citizens much see and know. The imposition of a 'good life' undermines the basic idea of agency each of us possess, and it violates, in Dworkin's terms, the state's obligation to treat us with 'equal concern and respect'.[21]

---

20 *See* J. Rawls, *A Theory of Justice*, Harvard University Press, Cambridge/MA, 1971, pp. 30-32, pp. 446-451; M. J. Sandel, 'Political Liberalism', *Harvard Law Review*, Vol. 107, No. 7, 1994, p. 1766.

21 R. Dworkin, *Taking Rights Seriously*, Harvard University Press, Cambridge/MA, 1978, pp. 180-183.

On the other hand, a government is elected precisely so that it can realize the policies its voters wish to promote. This includes, *inter alia*, economic support to purposes, values and policies in line with what the government's preferred position. Otherwise, what is the point of elections if the government cannot advance its policies, which entail, inter alia, selective funding? How should we go about deciding between these arguments?

We can start by thinking of two conceptions of neutrality. Under the first, the state must completely avoid any funding, since funding one activity and not the other already departs from the neutrality principle that requires the non-privileging of one conception of the good over another. We can call this conception the market conception of speech, since the state refuses to play any part in the marketplace of cultural idea and leaves it to the economic market and the power relations inherent to it. The problem is that these economic powers are not necessarily diverse, let alone equal. Without guidance and intervention, the power relations that are the result of the background rules of property and contract will generate only particular messages, those of the economically strong party, the party that can afford to pay for its expressions.[22]

Israel has a different conception of neutrality. On the current view, the state must be neutral toward competing conceptions of the good, but the way to realize this neutrality is not through withholding support, but in giving financial support to provide the conditions which will allow individuals to participate in the public sphere. Millions of dollars are given each year to artists and institutions for plays, movies, exhibitions and a variety of cultural activities. Support for the arts and culture is based on the desire to guarantee a thriving and bustling marketplace of ideas, a precondition for exercising agency. This marketplace of ideas must therefore provide a broad spectrum of ideas, both to shape people's personality and so that people will re-examine their beliefs. From this we can derive the state's obligation of neutrality, since if only certain ideas and opinions receive funding, a true marketplace of ideas will not be able to exist. Instead, we will have hegemony and monolithic thought.

Israel has adopted this conception of neutrality. In the *Abu Ghosh* case, the Ministry of Education and Culture refused to support a music festival, claiming the music that will be played is "church music".[23] Judge Cohn, in a dissenting opinion, held that the type of work of art cannot be a criterion for funding, due to the risk of political intervention in artistic freedom.[24] Political intervention, he held, is "any intervention on behalf of a political body" that attempts to impose on the artist an "act of omission, opinion or belief, that

22 *See, generally* R. L. Hale, 'Coercion and Distribution in a Supposedly Non-Coercive State', *Political Science Quarterly*, Vol. 38, No. 3, 1923, p. 470.

23 *The Abu Ghosh* case, p. 823.

24 It should be noted that the law today, as embraced in the Foundations of the Budget Law, 1985, adopted Judge Cohn's reasoning in his dissent.

he did not choose freely".[25] Moreover, Judge Cohn rejected the market conception of neutrality, recognizing that the arts require government support in order to survive. However, government funding must be allocated without violating free speech.[26] Thus the Ministry could have considered the amount of public interest, the festival's geographic location, whether the festival has alternative means of funding, and any other criterion that would be neutral and content-independent but would allow the Ministry to decide on funding in a world of limited resources.[27] Although Judge Cohn was in dissent, the case was decided on other grounds, and the dissent's rationale came to be accepted in subsequent decisions.

Until the *Abu Ghosh* case, public funding was given according to the exclusive discretion of the relevant agency. After the decision, the Attorney General issued guidelines that enshrine the duty of equality in allocation of government funds.[28]

These were the days prior to the Constitutional Revolution, when the legislature was supreme. Administrative allocations could have been struck down, but laws were immune. This led to a curious situation, where members of the legislature started allocating funds to their pet causes through the budget law (which the court could not strike down), instead of through administrative regulations (which were susceptible to judicial review).[29] The solution was the Foundations of the Budget Law, passed in 1985. The law mandated that allocation of public funds to public institutions in the budget law must be according to equal criteria. In a complementary decision, the Court held that the provisions in the Foundations of the Budget Law were superior to any individual budget law.[30] These moves made equality, and not free speech, paramount. From the outset, then, Israeli case law examined the allocation of public funds through the eyes of equality. A marginal role was given, if at all, to free speech, despite ample opportunities for the Court to do so. Indeed, the most the Court has been willing to say in this context in favour of free speech can be found in Judge Cohn dissenting opinion in the *Abu Ghosh* case. Yet, as I will argue momentarily, this is not enough and leaves the public funding doctrine wanting.

25 *The Abu Ghosh* case, p. 828.
26 *Id.*, pp. 828-829.
27 *Id.*, pp. 829-830.
28 De-Hartoch, 1998, p. 83.
29 *Id.*, pp. 83-84.
30 *See Masorti Movement* case.

7.4 The Anti-Entrenchment Principle

7.4.1 *The Difficulty with the Existing Legal Framework*

The emphasis of the current law is not on free speech but on equality and neutrality. Save for isolated statements, the Israel Supreme Court prefers to steer clear from questions regarding the scope of free speech, primarily whether there is a positive obligation to fund private speech. In comparison, it is much easier to rely on the non-discrimination principle, which does not entail delving into the content of the speech.

The general principles of equality and neutrality, also rooted in administrative law, go a long way in responding to the freedom of finance argument. Yet the problem with these principles is that they do not fully grasp the difficulty in the idea of freedom of finance. To illustrate, suppose that the government decides to only fund plays that promote Jewish heritage. The criteria it adopts are equal and professional, and everyone can apply to receive funds that go toward that end. But let us further suppose that a playwright wants to receive public funding for a play dealing with Palestinian heritage (roughly 20% of Israeli citizens are Palestinian Arabs). The Ministry of Culture will likely not allocate funding, stating that the budget is designated to Jewish heritage. Will the Court intervene? The likely answer is no, since the principle of equality applies to the criteria themselves and not to the decision to promote a particular cultural field over others.[31]

In such a case, the equality-based arguments against freedom of finance are not doing sufficient work, and, as I argued, do not capture an important aspect of the problem with the freedom of finance claim. As I will argue below, the real problem with freedom of finance is that it confuses between state and government, and while doing so, prevents the political minority from becoming a political majority. Freedom of finance is especially problematic when the contingent political majority uses its allocative power to entrench and bolster its hold on power, thus contributing to the weakening of the minority. Thus giving full effect to free speech, not just in its artistic form, but also in its democratic form,

31 This claim was made, for example, by Judge Danziger in HCJ 5239/11 *Avneri v. The Knesset* (Sup. Ct. 2015), translation available at http://versa.cardozo.yu.edu/opinions/avneri-v-knesset. In Sec. 21 he states: "It must be emphasized that the state may support one type of activity but not another. It may promote its policy, *inter alia*, by providing financial support for matters that are the subjects of public debate. But, having decided to support an activity – no matter how hotly debated – the state may not distinguish among entities involved in such activity on the basis of considerations that are not relevant to the purpose of the support and that might violate constitutional rights. Thus, for example, the state may allocate funds in support of Torah study institutes, a matter that may be the subject of public debate [...], but it may not distinguish among institutions operating in that area without relevant justification related to the purpose of the support. It cannot, for example, distinguish between two otherwise identical institutions, even in terms of their religious merits, simply because one of the institutions publicly expresses support for the political views of the ruling party or of a coalition partner, while the other does not."

might require support for ideas and values of the political minority that resists the government. In certain cases there can arise a constitutional duty, which on first blush seems paradoxical, according to which the government must support critical speech of the government's policies. Crucially, this duty is not derived from the neutrality or equality principles, but from the anti-entrenchment principle, to be discussed below.[32]

7.4.2 *State and Government*

In the popular and legal discourse, the words 'government' and 'state' are often used interchangeably. For example, in Israel (but also elsewhere), when a petition is filed against specific bodies in the executive branch, the Ministry of Justice represents 'the state', even though the petition is only against specific bodies in the executive branch. The case law often adopts the same terminology when it states that the 'state' claims so and so, thus equating the state with the government. The reason for this conflation is not the result of ignorance. All know that the government is not synonymous with state; the state is the sum total of the state organs operating in it. Indeed, the government represents the state – for example in international law – but the government is not the state but only a part of it.[33] Usually the conflation does not pose a problem, since it is clear that the two are not identical and that the reason for non-distinction is the result of linguistic convenience.

Things become complicated, however, when the rhetorical unification is leveraged to serve political ends that undermine the distinction. The complication is most acute when freedom of finance is claimed, since at its core is the idea that the government, and only the government, serves as mouthpiece for the 'people'. Indeed, many populist regimes

---

32 Against the equality and neutrality principles, one can make another type of argument, which goes beyond the scope of this chapter. This argument is based on a positive duty to support arts and culture generally. Suppose that the government decides that due to resource constraints it does not have enough funds in the state budget to support plays and theatres and therefore declares that no funds will be given to any theatres this year. To be sure, the government has the authority not to allocate funds in a certain field, and if there is no allocation whatsoever, it is difficult to argue that the equality principle has been breached. In this situation, the conventional arguments against freedom of finance end, since they are not usually based on free speech. In order to obligate the state to support a certain field we there need an argument from free speech that focuses on the social importance of arts and culture, and that this importance generates a positive duty of economic support. Such an argument goes beyond the anti-entrenchment principle, but it should be emphasized that it does not contradict the anti-entrenchment principle and can overlap with it. For example, if the 'free market' reflects significant asymmetries of power, and those leave toward the government's positions, one could argue that the state must support the field, since without such support the free market will entrench the status quo. However, many artistic activities are not directly related to support for the government's messages or opposition to them, so the claim about the importance of the arts as such requires broader justification than the anti-entrenchment principle can provide.

33 *See, e.g.*, Montevideo Convention of Rights and Duties of States, Art. 1. 26 December 26, 1933, 165 L.N.T.S 19, which establishes the criteria for state existence. One condition of the four is that there be a government, hence merely having a government is not tantamount to having a state.

identify themselves with channelling 'the voice of the people'. The difficulty is that since the government equates itself with 'the people', it confuses the government and the state, since the state (and not the government) is the organ through which the people are reflected. Now, because the government unites itself with the people, it can claim that it may promote its policy and at the same time claim that it is actually doing so as a state. However, the distinction between state and government is important precisely because of the limited legitimacy one should accord the government. In Israel, at least (and in many other parliamentary systems), the government is formed from the majority it enjoys in the legislature, and therefore *prima facie* represents those voters who voted for parties that then formed the government. Yet the government also 'represents' those who did not vote for these parties.[34] The state, among others through the government, exercises power on all the subjects in its territory, whether those who voted for it or not. The state is a unit larger than the government; the government is not 'the people'. Therefore, the attempts to unify the people and the government are dangerous, since they undermine the idea of intellectual pluralism; their purpose is to impose monolithic thought and suppress ideas that oppose the government's position. If the government identifies itself as the people ("I do what the people what", "I reflect the people's will"), then there is a leap and confusion between the government as representing party of the public and the state that is comprised of 'the people'. Now, if the government perceives itself as representing what 'the people' want, then what is the point of an opposition or criticism? And how can there be criticism if no one has it? After all, the identity between people and government means that there cannot be criticism from 'the people', since the government is channelling the voice of the people.

Thus, the unification between government and people, wherein the government substitutes the state, is problematic not just at the rhetorical level, when it is directed toward silencing of criticism, but also on an allocative level. In Israel, the government is the organ which allocates funds and decides on priorities. The budget law is enacted in the legislature, but the government is dominant in its planning, design and passage.[35] But because there is no identity between the government and the state, it is important to remember that money it allocates is not of the government or of the political majority from which it is comprised. The money the government spends belongs to the public in its entirety; the government holds the money in trust, and this money must serve the entire public and not just the government's exclusive policies. The view that the government represents the

34 I am simplifying here. Of course, the government, although it enjoys democratic legitimacy in the form of elections, does not necessarily 'represent' the will of those of who voted for parties that then formed the government. For the complex relationship between elections and government, *see* A. Shinar, 'Public Employee Speech and the Privatization of the First Amendment', *Connecticut Law Review*, Vol. 46, No. 1, 2013, p. 44.

35 For this reason, among others, the provisions of the budget law are not considered 'normative' in that they guide behavior. They merely constitute an authorization to spend money. *See, e.g., Masorti Movement* case, p. 356.

people might thus lead the government to believe that allocations that serve its ends are sufficient, since its ends are, as explained above, the 'people's ends.

7.4.3 *The Anti-Entrenchment Principle*

A corollary of the obligation of trust the state owes its citizens is that the government must take care of all the public under its domain. Of course, there is nothing new in this. The requirements of neutrality and equality are based precisely on this logic. Indeed, the government cannot do what it wishes with the public's money, but must distribute it 'equally' (though of course there can be disagreements as to what equality requires). In the context of speech resources, the allocation must be neutral and be based only on relevant criteria. Yet this is not enough. The concern about the unification of the government with the state generates another, deeper, consideration, in favour of supporting critical views. This consideration is derived from the anti-entrenchment principle.

Attempts to silence critical views is wrong, not just because resources must be distributed equally, but also because they harness the power of the contingent political majority – the current government – to prevent the minority from becoming the majority or increasing its power.[36] Put differently, my argument is that when the government allocates funds in favour of private speech, it is possible to assert a constitutional obligation to specifically support speech that expresses messages, principle, ideas and values that oppose those the government wishes to promote. This argument is based on the anti-entrenchment principle. According to the conventional meaning of this principle, the government may promote the policies for which it was put into office, but it must not act to entrench its power, thus preventing its replacement.

The anti-entrenchment principle is familiar in constitutional law.[37] Although the Supreme Court's *Bank Hamizrachi* decision (Israel's analogue to *Marbury v. Madison*) did not decide whether Israeli law adopted this principle,[38] Basic Law: The Knesset did adopt one aspect of the anti-entrenchment principle in the context of elections. Indeed, the anti-entrenchment principle is usually applied to the legislative branch and to the way legislators operate. In this chapter, I wish to extend it to the context of the executive branch and freedom of expression. The conventional assumption is that legislators reflect their voters' will. This is a foundational tenet of the majoritarian system. Yet legislators are often tempted to deviate from that will and act in a counter-majoritarian fashion, for two reasons.

36 They also often prevent the minority (however defined) from becoming stronger in general.

37 *See* E. Posner & A. Vermeule, 'Legislative Entrenchment: A Reappraisal', *Yale Law Journal*, Vol. 111, No. 7, 2002, p. 1665.

38 C.A. 6821/93, *United Bank Hamizrachi Bank v. Migdal Cooperative Village*, 49(4) P.D. 221 (Sup. Ct. 1995), translation available at http://versa.cardozo.yu.edu/opinions/united-mizrahi-bank-v-migdal-cooperative-village.

One, legislators are interested in re-election. This interest might cause them to act in ways that their voters would not approve. This is the ordinary agency problem, which also exists in the political system.[39] The second reason is that a temporary political majority might attempt to entrench its power when it believes that in the future it will lose its majority status.[40]

The institutional solutions for these situations are mostly two: one is giving courts the power to invalidate legislation; the second is legal rules that seek to mitigate the danger inherent in a legislator interested in entrenching his rule. As for the first – on which I will say very little – the concern about the majority's power to entrench its status is commonly cited as a primary justification for judicial review and as an answer to the counter-majoritarian difficulty.[41] John Hart Ely's theory of judicial review is specifically designed to respond to concerns about entrenchment. In particular, Ely emphasized the potential of judicial review to guarantee a proper democratic process and ensure the possibility of political participation.[42] Unlike Dworkin, who justified judicial review as a way to protect substantive democratic values, namely human rights, Ely believed that judicial review should not intervene in substantive decisions but should only ensure that the 'rules of the democratic game' are being observed. Ely was concerned with barriers set up by the majority that prevent the minority from meaningful political participation and from possibly becoming a political majority. For example, rules that *de facto* prevented African-Americans from exercising their right to vote, rules that prevented minorities from representing or being represented (gerrymandering), and discriminatory rules that excluded minorities from public institutions and political life – all these rules undermined representative democracy. Judicial review must therefore, according to Ely, make sure that the rules of the game are being observed by enforcing these rules on the political branches. Correlatively, as long as the rules are maintained, courts should not intervene in the substantive decisions that democracy generates.

Judicial review is one way to prevent the majority from entrenching its power.[43] A second way is by particular arrangements that seek to do the same thing. For example, an axiomatic principle of any parliamentary system is that one parliament cannot bind the subsequent parliament. Every parliament can repeal or amend the laws enacted by the

39 *See, generally* D. A. Farber & P. P. Frickey, *Law and Public Choice: A Critical Introduction*, University of Chicago Press, Chicago, 1991.

40 For a discussion of these problems, *see* Klarman, 1997, p. 498. Concern about losing power might also lead to strengthening other branches, when a majority in one body believes that another body could protect its interests after it loses power. This is a possible explanation for why legislators favour judicial review of legislation. *See* M. C. Stephenson, '"When the Devil Turns…": The Political Foundations of Independent Judicial Review', *Journal of Legal Studies*, Vol. 32, No. 1, 2003, p. 62.

41 For the most famous statement of this difficulty, *see* A. M. Bickel, *The Least Dangerous Branch: The Supreme Court at the Bar of Politics*, Yale University Press, New Haven, 1962, pp. 16-17.

42 Ely, 1980, pp. 73-104.

43 For examples of judicial review exercising this function, *see* Klarman, 1997, pp. 528-539.

previous parliament. Binding the parliament can only be done with a constitutional norm.[44] Another common limitation is parliamentary term limits and the requirement that elections be held at a fixed time. In Israel, for example, Section 8 of Basic Law: The Knesset, provides that "[t]he term of office of the Knesset shall be four years from the day on which it is elected". The concern about the majority entrenching its power is made explicit especially in Section 9A(a) of the Basic Law, which provides that "[t]he Knesset shall not extend its term except by law passed by a majority of eighty members of the Knesset and only if special circumstances exist that prevent holding the elections at their proper time; the period of extension shall not exceed the time necessary due to the aforementioned circumstances [...]". The requirement of a majority of 80 Knesset members (out of a total of 120) is crucial, since it *de facto* obligates part of the political minority to agree to postponing the elections. The special majority requirement stems, of course, from the fear that the political majority will try and use its power to entrench its status by postponing the elections, thus remaining in power beyond its elected term.

In my view, the anti-entrenchment principle is a structural constitutional principle derived from democratic theory and not from a particular constitution. At its foundation lies the basic rationale for democracy. In a democracy, a contingent political majority should not have the power to immunize itself from changes. The mandate the legislature or the government has is limited, not just in law but also in time. In order for a government to receive legitimacy from the people, and so that the principle of self-government will be realized, a democratic regime must determine fixed times for holding election so that the legislature and government can be replaced according to the will of the voters (or, at the very least, the majority of the voters). Indeed, an array of constitutional arrangements determine the frequency of elections, and many countries impose term limits on high-level positions on the view that too much time in power can lead not only to corruption, but also to a consolidation of a particular power arrangement that will seek to preserve and entrench its power.

My argument is that there is little sense in limiting the anti-entrenchment principle, whose purpose is to ensure the smooth transitioning of power necessary for a democracy, only to election related matters. The anti-entrenchment principle is substantive and should *prima facie* apply wherever and whenever the majority seeks to entrench its power beyond its term. Of course, this does not mean that the majority cannot promote the policies for which it was elected. However special attention must be given to attempts by the political majority to silence critical positions, including through the denial or reduction of state funds. This is especially true in the context of the arts and culture, which have traditionally served as sites for challenging the status quo, and whose flourishing will likely not be possible without state support.

---

44 Some, however, dispute this rule. *See* Posner & Vermeule, 2002.

The anti-entrenchment principle should therefore be extended beyond the election context. In the speech context, it stipulates that the government should be prevented from using its allocative power to leverage its positions in a way that will prevent the political minority from speaking and possibly increasing its power and maybe becoming the majority, especially when its speech is critical of government policy. Indeed, precisely because the government's special role in the marketplace of ideas and because of the reliance of cultural institutions on government support, the government must financially support expressions directed at promoting self-governing democratic society, especially when those expressions seek to resist the values and policies of the political majority and government itself.

We can also think of the anti-entrenchment principle through an economic lens. Suppose the government uses its allocative power and leverages the enormous funds at its disposal to support only the policy it wishes to promote. Since arts and culture rely on state supports, it is possible to argue that the purchasing of the public sphere in favour or one system of positions (or positions that do not challenge the government) leads to a monopoly over the marketplace of ideas. Once a monopoly is formed, it is very difficult to take it apart, and it has a natural tendency to enshrine its monopolistic status. The anti-entrenchment principle therefore seeks to mitigate the problem of monopoly. Importantly, it has an advantage over the neutrality principle, since, as I noted above, neutrality need only exist with the activity that receives government funds but does not obligate the government to support critical content. Neutrality's strength (but also its weakness) is that it ignores considerations of content. But precisely because of this, there can be a situation where critical speech will be denied funding without any breach of the neutrality principle. In other words, one can design criteria for government funding without offending the neutrality principle while succeeding the silencing of critical content. The anti-entrenchment principle requires us therefore to consider funding critical speech when the concern about the monopolistic power of the government rises. In these instances, the power of neutrality is limited, and examining the content of the speech is unavoidable.

To sum up, the anti-entrenchment principle provides another explanation why critical speech should receive governmental support. This explanation is rooted in democratic theory itself. It adds to the extant doctrine in the Israel Supreme Court, which focuses exclusively on equality and neutrality. The anti-entrenchment principle links the right to free speech with a political conception of governmental power, which is why its focus is not on a particular expression. It exemplifies the desire to separate those who control funding for speech through allocative power and those who speak, so that those who control funding for speech will not seek to entrench their power.

7.4.4 How to Apply the Anti-Entrenchment Principle?

A different question is how to apply the anti-entrenchment principle, since it will not always be the case that wherever the government promotes its policies we will be able to say that the principle is violated, and that its violation establishes a positive obligation to finance critical speech, even if the government policy survives the government that promoted it. Indeed, I think that in most cases it will be difficult to say when an allocative action is limited to promoting policy and when that same action also violates the anti-entrenchment principle, especially if we will agree that the line separating the two is blurred. In addition, it seems to me that in most cases the principles of equality and neutrality will suffice for treating problematic allocation. Of course, a determination that the anti-entrenchment principle has been violated will require a complicated examination of the circumstances, which will inevitably differ from case to case. In this sense, it is not different from many other public law principles.

In this chapter I cannot provide definitive criteria for implementing the anti-entrenchment principle. However, I wish to delineate several possibilities regarding its future implementation and to distinguish between several conceptions of the principle. One possibility (endorsed in this chapter) is to understand the anti-entrenchment principle as a prohibition on an action that entrenches the government's control of power in contradistinction to an action that promotes its policy. When the government seeks to entrench its control (whether through selective funding or whether through reduced funding or denial of funding), one of two demands can arise. The first demand will be to cease the entrenching allocation. A second, alternative demand will be a positive obligation to allocate funds toward speech that will neutralize the entrenching power of the allocation. So, for example, if the government allocates funds for plays that celebrate Jewish settlements in the Occupied Palestinian Territories, and this will be found to be an entrenching allocation, then the government will be required to either cease the allocation, mitigate the allocation so that it will not rise to the level of entrenchment or allocate funds for plays that criticize the settlement enterprise. Assuming the third option is chosen, then immediately the question is how much should the government allocate for the critical speech? Should we require equality in allocations? A similar allocation? These are complicated questions, since, as I noted above, the government may promote and privilege its policies. This is not a one-size-fits-all scenario, and the answer will vary from case to case.

A second possibility is to focus on the 'free market' and to examine whether it reflects a prohibited situation in the marketplace of ideas. This possibility is different from the first, since it does not ask whether the government's action was prohibited, but whether the government has to support critical messages so that its replacement will be possible, even if the government is not responsible for the marketplace of ideas that reflects, without its intervention, its positions.[45] Indeed, if the government cannot entrench itself, it may be obligated to shape the marketplace of ideas and actively support critical messages that resist those it wishes to transmit. For example, assume that without governmental intervention the political power relations are reproduced in the market. Is the government required to allocate funds to mitigate the majoritarian influence the market possesses? Those who support the second possibility will answer in the affirmative.

The third possibility goes even further. Not only is the government required to provide a platform for critical speech that do receive a sufficient platform through the free market, the government is required to provide a platform that will create an equal marketplace of ideas, and thus overcome the market asymmetries that exist without government intervention.

The difference between the second and third possibility is that the second possibility requires some support, whereas the third possibility requires the government strive for equality, even if the inequality was not its own doing and derives from economic disparities between majority and minority opinions. The difference between the first possibility and the second and third possibilities is that the latter two seek to deal with a situation in which the state decides not to provide any financial support in a particular cultural field or not to make any interventions in that field (as opposed to an activity within a field), whereas the under first possibility the principle is limited to cases where the government chooses to fund a particular message.

Each of the three possibilities generates a different meaning of the anti-entrenchment principle, and each comes with its own difficulties. The first possibility is narrower and limited to situations where the government made a prohibited allocation. An advantage of this possibility is that it is relatively easy to apply. However, the second and third possibilities are more complex, since they require a determination that marketplace of ideas, even without government support, may violate the anti-entrenchment principle. This determination is of course possible, but it requires a factual foundation that will be difficult (if not impossible) to establish and agree upon, and then generating conclusions about the amount of funding required to remedy the harm to the anti-entrenchment principle.

As stated above, the purpose of this chapter was not to develop a comprehensive doctrine regarding the application of the anti-entrenchment principle, but rather to establish its existence and importance as a limiting principle on the government's allocative power, and thus add to extant array of doctrines available today. Its importance is in those cases where allocations survive the neutrality and equality principles.

45 Of course, it is difficult and perhaps impossible to imagine a situation where the government has no effect on the marketplace of ideas, since every governmental regulation distributes the market power relations, which in turn affect the marketplace of ideas.

7.5 CONCLUSION

In recent years, we are witnessing in Israel (but also elsewhere) increasing attempts of government censorship of opinions and activities that are not compatible with those of the elected government. Unlike the past, this censorship is not direct. It does not usually include a prohibition on opinions, plays, movies and so forth. This is a new kind of censorship, one which harnesses the government's economic resources to deny funding to expressive activities that are not in line with the values the government wishes to promote. The underlying rationale for this move is that without government funding many critical expressions will not see the light of day. The efficiency of the sanction is in its existence. Artists and institutions will direct their activities so that those will not stir up controversy which might lead to a decrease or denial of funding.

This policy, which in Israel has been referred to as 'freedom of finance', has been (partially) rejected by the Court and the scholarly literature on the grounds of neutrality and equality. But as this chapter sought to demonstrate, there is another rationale that justifies its rejection. A government that wishes to preserve its power by preventing the political minority from increasing its power or becoming the majority, acts to entrench its rule, thus blocking the channels of democratic political change. All democratic regimes possess various limits on the powers of the government and the legislature to entrench their rule. Yet these limits usually focus on election law. This chapter sought to extend the anti-entrenchment principle to the realm of speech and the government's allocative power. I argued that not only is the government not allowed to deny financial support to critical speech, but that there will be circumstances it will be under a constitutional duty to support the very messages that resist the policies it wishes to promote.

8 Transforming Populism – From Protest Vote to Ruling Ideology: The Case of Serbia

*Dušan Spasojević**

8.1 Introduction

Populism is not a new phenomenon. However, current academic and political popularity of populism is primarily based on its European revival. Interestingly, current European wave of populism is not a new thing, either. Prominent political figures have been connected with populism since the late 1980s, but the real proliferation of populism occurred during the first decade of twenty-first century. This period has been marked by different actors, mostly from the far-right end of the political spectrum, who were able to attract public attention and popular support. Contemporary European populism includes additional actors – populist parties from the left end of political spectrum whose political standpoints have been strengthened by 2008 economic crisis. On the other side, right-wing actors continued to grow due to importance of 'populist friendly' issues such as 2015-2018 immigration "crisis" and general EU crisis.

Furthermore, during the current phase, European populism(s) proved ability to conform and to adapt to different political circumstances. Some of the major recent examples that could support this argument are the emergence and success of left-wing populism (mostly in the south Europe), emergence of populist ruling parties (mostly in the Central and Eastern Europe) and the success of new right-wing populist parties across the Western Europe (Alternative for Deutschland being the most striking and recent example). Some of these parties have proved the ability to rise to and to remain in power and even to reduce the decline in popular support after being removed from the power. In other words, one could argue that many populists' parties have become institutionalized part of party systems and that they are here to stay.

In this chapter, I will depart from fruitful academic field that was mostly devoted to Western European populism, with the intention to adapt theoretical frameworks to be more applicable for transitional and post-communist societies. This step will be the basis for the analysis of post-communist phenomenon – ruling populist parties. Namely, not

* Associate Professor, University of Belgrade, Faculty of Political Science.

only that Eastern European populists have shown that they are able to remain in power for more than one mandate and/or even to return to the power after several years in opposition, but some of them hold the power as the predominant party, almost without any contestation and relevant opposition.

The cases of Hungary, Poland and Serbia are frequently used as examples of this trend and their analysis raises questions about relation between populism and democratic performances of transitional post-communist countries. It seems that significant part of Hungarian Fidesz, Polish PiS (*Prawo i Sprawiedliwość, Law and Justice*) or Serbian SNS (*Srpska napredna stranka, Serbian Progressive Party*) strength and endurance can be linked to intense campaigns against the opposition, independent media, civil society and other scrutinizing mechanisms of liberal democracies (or emerging liberal democracies, in many cases). Therefore, there is a need to question if this illiberal way of ruling is immanent to populists' understanding of democracy, and whether it is the only possible outcome of transformation of populism from the opposition to the position stage?

In this chapter, I will address these issues though the analysis of Serbian case, which is quite underrepresented in the literature on populism. Serbian case is also interesting because of the nature of ruling SNS whose leadership once stood as far right nationalists within Serbian Radical Party (SRS, *Srpska radikalna stranka*); however, after 'catch-all-ization' and transformation into SNS, the party leadership shifted towards EU-friendly positions which partially differentiates them from the Hungarian and Polish cases.

Therefore, I will address the definition problem first and then lay out the framework for understanding of populism. This stage will be followed by analysis of populist elements in the SNS programme, manifestoes and performances. My focus will be on self-perception and self-positioning of the SNS as *people's party* in opposition to the corrupted elite and on their vague and flexible (but ideologically important) interpretation of 'the other'. In both cases, I will stress the difference between three stages of the party development: (1) ideological profile of SNS predecessor party – SRS; (2) SNS ideological positions prior to 2012 elections, when they entered government for the first time; and (3) after 2014, when the SNS has become the key government party. This change was gradual and allows us to understand the development of current SNS ideological position and mechanisms that party used during this transformation. Furthermore, I will also analyse other phenomena usually attributed to populist parties (although they are not their exclusive characteristics) including specific usage of media, personalization of politics and simplification of politics.

My second research task is to analyse the relationship between the SNS as the leading ruling party and the opposition in Serbia with specific emphasis on populist elements. I will argue that SNS populism is most frequently reflected in their standpoints on democratic procedures and practices and on the role of opposition parties and state independent (regulatory and oversight) institutions.

8.2 Ideational Understanding of Populism

In the simplified version, two major approaches to populism are ideational and discursive. The first one understands populism as an ideology,[1] while the latter one argues that populism should be interpreted as a pattern or a style of political communication.[2] Although it is hard to ignore that some populists have unique and recognizable style of political communication,[3] my starting position is that ideology primarily affects the way of communication[4] rather than *vice versa.* Of course, ideologies are constructed through the political communication (among other mechanisms), but this communication is shaped by fundamental social characteristics and divisions – social cleavages,[5] which means that different sides of political spectrum usually communicate in a different manner.

Departing point in this analysis is Mudde's[6] theorization of populism as a 'thin-centred' ideology that needs a host ideology. Populism, therefore, spins *the original* (or the host) ideology by introducing its prime principle – that society is divided between "two homogenous groups – pure people and corrupt elite and that politics should reflect general will of the people".[7] Some scholars differentiate between thin or 'empty populism' (that includes only referring to the people) in opposition to 'thick populism' that can be either 'exclusive populism' (referring to the people and emphasis on out-groups that do not belong to the people), 'anti-elitist populism' (referring to the people supported with an anti-elitism stance) or 'complete populism' (including all three mentioned elements).[8]

The recent populist wave raises the question about popularity of populism or the roots of its success. However, this should not be taken as a surprise – as Katz and Mair 'predicted' in their analysis, de-ideologization of the mainstream parties and stability of party systems in Europe led to cartelization of politics (or establishment of formal and informal obstacles for the newly emerging parties), which means that new actors on political scene have to be more radical, more provocative and more anti-systematic in order to attract voters' attention.[9] Recent developments at the beginning of the twenty-first century provided more incentives for populism – economic crisis revealed the ties between political and

1 C. Mudde, 'The Populist Zeitgeist', *Government and Opposition,* Vol. 39, No. 2, 2004, pp. 541-563.
2 J. Jagers & S. Walgrave, 'Populism as Political Communication Style: An Empirical Study of Political Parties' Discourse in Belgium', *European Journal of Political Research,* No. 46, 2007, pp. 319-345.
3 Although, it is also quite hard to ignore the differences between *e.g.,* Podemos and Donald Trump.
4 T. van Dijk, *Ideology,* Sage Publications, London, Thousand Oaks, New Delhi, 1997.
5 J. Kleut & D. Spasojević, 'Europeanization Discourse of Serbian Political Elites: *Peščanik and Nova Srpska politička misao*', *in* T. Zimmermann & A. Jakir (Eds.), *Europe and the Balkans: Decades of Europeanization?*, Königshausen & Neumann GmbH, Würzburg, 2015, pp. 57-67.
6 Mudde, 2004, pp. 541-563.
7 *Id.*, p. 543.
8 Jagers & Walgrave, 2007, pp. 322-323.
9 R. Katz & P. Mair, 'Changing Models of Party Organisation and Party Democracy: The Emergence of the Cartel Party', *Party politics,* Vol. 1, No. 5, 1995, pp. 5-28.

economic elites and strengthened perceptions of alienation between politicians and the voters. As Taggart points out, populists (as new politicians) decided to "challenge the functioning of representative democracy in contemporary Europe while at the same time championing the virtues of representation".[10]

Additional seductive element of populists comes from their standpoints on democracy – populist parties present themselves as the defenders of democratic order and its true values. In contrast to populists of the 1980s and 1990s, who were perceived as homophobic and/or racist and separated by *cordon sanitaire* from the other parties (*e.g.*, Vlaam block in Belgium), new actors use the democratic vocabulary and values more often. By doing so and in their attempt to bring democracy 'back to the people', populist actors feed from different kind of dissatisfaction with democratic performances and occupy anti-party (and sometimes anti-systematic) positions.

These issues bring us back to our main question – can populism be a ruling ideology? Does it have a unified outcome regarding the style of governing or it depends on the ideological profile of populism? Are illiberal tendencies observed in Eastern Europe[11] the outcome of populism or of systematic crisis of new democracies – in other words is populism in Serbia, Hungary and Poland a symptom or a cause?

Again, those issues are quite new in populist literature. For example, Taggart argued that "populist politicians, movements or parties emerge and grow quickly and gain attention but find it difficult to sustain that momentum and therefore will usually fade fast",[12] while Mueller points out that "populist parties are primarily *protest parties*" and that they are usually successful in opposition, but failure in the government.[13] In similar manner Albertazzi writes that populist parties' participation in the government leads to their de-radicalization.[14] However, recent trends and recent literature clearly shows that populist parties have the ability to remain in power, to do so without reducing the level of populism (or radicalization) and to become long-lasting elements of the party systems.[15]

Therefore, in the following parts of the chapter I will use the Serbian example as the case study of ruling populist party. I will first analyse the ideological shift of SNS between opposition and position stage. This will be followed by insight into the style of governing in Serbia in order to deduce if populism has any effect on it. The Serbian case will provide

10 P. Taggart, 'Populism and Representative Politics in Contemporary Europe', *Journal of Political Ideologies*, Vol. 9, No. 3, 2004, p. 269.

11 For example, *see* Freedom House, 'Nations in Transit 2017: The False Promise of Populism', https://freedomhouse.org/report/nations-transit/nations-transit-2017.

12 Taggart, 2004, p. 270.

13 J. W. Mueller, *What is Populism?*, University of Pennsylvania Press, Philadelphia, 2016.

14 D. Albertazzi, 'Reconciling 'Voice' and 'Exit': Swiss and Italian Populists in Power', *Politics*, Vol. 29, No. 1, 2009, pp. 1-10.

15 *See, e.g.*, D. Albertazzi & D. McDonnell, *Populist in Power*, Routledge, London and New York, 2015.

us with many uncertainties and shades regarding the causes and the effects, but it will also improve the clarity of research questions that should be addressed.

8.3 The Case of Serbian Progressive Party: Once Radical and Now Progressive – Is It the Same Populism?

8.3.1 *Serbian Progressive Party (SNS) – The Opposition Phase*

SNS was founded in 2008 after another electoral defeat of nationalistic SRS. SRS was an old-styled right-wing party, founded in 1992 by charismatic leader Vojislav Šešelj. Some scholars define SRS as a populist party that "profits from the fact that political populism, more broadly defined, plays an important role within political mainstream".[16] The party occupied nationalistic position and used the issues that were related to the break-up of Yugoslavia. SRS moved from opposition to the position status several times during Milošević rule in Serbia (1990-2000) and acted as his 'favourite opposition'.[17] SRS finally joined Milošević regime in 1998 after the NATO intervention in Kosovo and remained in the government until the fall of Milošević in 2000. Government officials from SRS were perceived as the most militant ones, especially regarding the media freedoms and civil society. SRS accused political opponents and independent media of being the traitors and 'the fifth column' of NATO or international community. But journalist and opposition were only one of the targets; the concept of *out-group* or *the others* in the case of SRS included ethnic minorities in Serbia, Albanians from Kosovo and almost all ex-Yugoslav nations.

After the democratic changes in 2000, SRS remained a right-wing stronghold and continued with preservation of Milošević's political legacy searching for the support in two camps – transitional losers (economic voters) and radical nationalists and conservatives.[18] Due to radical anti-reformist and strong anti-EU positions, other parties were not willing to make coalitions with SRS even when they had almost one third of popular support and equivalent (or larger) share in the Parliament (*e.g.*, after 2004 and 2008 parliamentary elections) which positioned SRS as the party without coalition potential, but with strong blackmail potential.[19]

16 C. Mudde, 'In the Name of Peasantry, the Proletariat, and the People: Populisms in Eastern Europe', *East European Politics and Societies*, Vol. 15, No. 1, 2000, p. 45.

17 M. Spoerri, *Engineering Revolution: The Paradox of Democracy Promotion in Serbia*, University of Pennsylvania Press, Philadelphia, 2015.

18 D. Spasojević, 'Serbian Political Parties and the Kosovo Question', *in* L. Mehmeti & B. Radeljić (Eds.), *Kosovo and Serbia: Contested Options and Shared Consequences*, Pittsburgh University Press, Pittsburgh, 2016, pp. 106-126.

19 Đ. Sartori, *Stranke i stranački sustavi*, Politička kultura, Zagreb, 2002.

This inability to enter power sharing mechanisms initiated gradual de-radicalization process of SRS (facilitated by President Šešelj's surrender to ICTY in 2003 and appointment of Tomislav Nikolić for acting president), but this limited transformation was not enough to change SRS position substantially. After the defeat in decisive 2008 presidential and parliamentary elections,[20] two remaining SRS leaders – acting President Nikolić and secretary general Aleksandar Vučić decided to form a new party – SNS declared as centre-right, pro-EU and *popular* party. Party was designed as *catch-all* party aiming at promotion of economic issues in order to decrease damaging nationalistic ideological baggage. SNS was almost unanimously welcomed by the public and even by majority of other parties;[21] foundation of SNS was also perceived as the end of initial transitional phase and point of no return regarding the consolidation of democracy in Serbia.[22]

What was the ideological profile of the SNS at this stage – was it a populist party, like its predecessor? The short answer would be – it was not *only* a populist party, but it was a party with strong populist characteristics. The possible starting point in the analysis of SNS populism is tackling *the core* populist characteristic – the idea that society can be divided into two groups: the corrupt elite and the honest, true people. The initial concern regarding this characteristic in the case of SNS is that they cannot be treated as representatives of 'true people' because their leaders belonged to political (and from time to time governing) elite for almost 25 years, in contrast to other populist leaders who are truly new political actors (although, it might be debated how to define who is truly new and what would be the criteria of newness). However, this issue was gradually and carefully formulated by SNS communication strategy which emphasized that SNS as a party is something *new*, with clear break regarding *the old* SRS policies. This process was facilitated by gradual changes of Serbian Radical Party that had already begun. Good examples of these changes were SRS participation in the drafting process of new Serbian Constitution in 2006 and their contribution to successful referendum, which confirmed the Constitution. However, final and crucial rejection of the radical ideological baggage happened only after the foundation of the new party.

Newness of SNS was also supported by the 12 years spent in opposition between 2000 and 2012, while different ruling coalitions, including (almost) all other parties, governed Serbia. The cartelization character of Serbian politics prevented new parties to emerge during that period and for many voters in Serbia, SNS made a full circle and in 2012 it was their turn to try again.

---

20 On the election of 2008, Serbian pro-European forces (led by Democratic Party – DS) won narrow but crucial majority and restarted EU integration process of Serbia.

21 M. Jovanović, 'Predsednički izbori u Srbiji 6. i 20. maja 2012. godine', *in* Đ. Vuković (Ed.), *Oko izbora 18*, Centar za slobodne izbore i demokratiju, Nacionalni demokratski institut za međunarodne odnose, Beograd, 2012, pp. 11-26.

22 D. Spasojević, 'Odblokirana tranzicija – političke podele u Srbiji nakon 2000. godine', *Godišnjak Fakulteta političkih nauka*, Vol. V, No. 5, 2011, pp. 119-138.

More importantly for the 'true people-corrupted elite' dichotomy, SNS managed to position itself as the ordinary people's party due to electoral agenda based on economic and anti-corruption issues.[23] Namely, corruption has been perceived as one of the main problems in the transitional Serbia, both by transitional losers, who believed that privatization gained more wealth to tycoons and criminals, and by transitional winners, who believed that corruption comes as the mid-term consequence of the destruction of legal institutions during the Milošević's decade. Therefore, once the Kosovo versus Europe dilemma has been resolved in favour of the latter after the 2008 elections, corruption has become the ultimate catch-all issue of the Serbian politics. Due to its long oppositional status, SNS was in a better position to reach medium voters based on anti-corruption agenda compared to incumbent Democratic Party (DS, *Demokratska stranka*). Also, the idea of anti-corruption as the core campaign issue better suits conservative voters who always demand more 'law and order' policies. It would also be accurate to say that SNS acted as 'the movement of discontented'[24] during 2012 campaign.

The second core characteristic of populism deals with *the other* that presents a treat to ordinary people or to homogeneity of the people. However, *the other* group can refer to different social groups in different societies. In many EU countries, older populist, radical and right-wing parties, often have chosen immigrants as target group, while some post-communist populist parties mimic that regardless of the low-level immigration rate. However, in contemporary Eastern-European cases larger populist parties (or parties with strong populist flavour), such as Fidesz or PiS have chosen both internal and foreign enemies as *the other*, which enables them to develop more comprehensive ideological standpoints. Those enemies usually include liberal or leftist groups, international banks and capital, but also Brussels as the centre that represents EU administration and, in their opinion, lack of understanding for cultural and historical differences.

SNS ideological baggage was full of potential *others*, but in order to present themselves as moderate pro-EU party and to become acceptable for international community and possible coalition partners, the new party had to abandon many of the old animosities. The political situation was in favour of those changes due to the decreased importance of identity issues and gradual growth of the economic ones.[25] Therefore, SNS followed strategies of mainstream populist parties, which are based more on hints than on clearly articulated animosities. We could name this strategy *moderate otherness* and argue that it includes: (a) formal EU-friendly attitude but with certain reservations that are ambiguously

23 Z. Stojiljković, 'Izborna obećanja i postizborna realnost: javne politike u izbornoj ponudi u Srbiji', *in* Z. Stojiljković & G. Pilipović (Eds.), *Javne politike u izbornoj ponudi*, Konrad Adenauer Fondacija, Beograd, 2012, pp. 9-24.

24 M. Jovanović, 'Parlamentarni izbori u Srbiji 2012. godine – rezultati i političke posledice', *in* M. Jovanović & D. Vučičević (Eds.), *Izbori u Srbiji 2012. godine: (Ne)očekivana promena*, Institut za političke studije, Beograd, 2013, pp. 9-30.

25 Spasojević, 2011, pp. 119-138.

directed at some EU policies and mechanisms of EU integration (*e.g.*, unfair treatment of Serbia) and regular expressions of deep cultural connections with Russia; (b) limited resentment towards other post-Yugoslav states which includes old SRS discourse on Serbian victims and breakup of Yugoslavia, with a twist that SNS supports reconciliation and regional cooperation based on economy and mutual interest (which again reinstalls the economy at the top of agenda and decreases identity elements); (c) pragmatic relationship with ethnic minorities in Serbia; and (d) constant low-scale negative comments regarding liberal groups or human right activists.

In sum, SNS has a moderate standpoint regarding all *other* groups targeted by SRS, which enabled them to transform radical and nationalistic standpoints to moderate centrists and acceptable political standpoints (from the perspective of Serbian median voter and the international community). It is important to note it was easier for SNS to formulate this approach compared to the previous government led by Democratic Party and their similar catch-all attempts (symbolized by 'both Europe and Kosovo' slogan). A good example of the catch-all positions of the former government was the international affairs strategy that was formally based on '4 pillars of cooperation' – EU, USA, Russia and China. This was an attempt of DS to occupy position in the middle of political spectrum and consequentially to reduce identity-based issues and polarization that was perceived as a root of support for SRS/SNS.

While the 'old enemies' – international community, national minorities and former Yugoslav republics – received a moderate treatment, the position of the primary 'Other' was assigned to political opponents,[26] and they were treated in a much harsher manner. DS and their coalition partners were accused of high-level corruption during the transitional and privatization period, and during 2012 presidential campaign Nikolić promised that he will "kill the dragon and arrest all criminals".[27] The intensity even increased between the two electoral circles when SNS accused DS for electoral fraud of 500,000 votes; since these accusations were more aimed at public instead of Electoral Commission[28] (who supposed to formally investigate this kind of claims), I can conclude that this was a successful publicity stunt and a good indicator of the level of distrust (at least among the opposition voters) in political processes at the time.

However, the ideological profile of SNS should not be reduced to a negative campaign. For example, the important parts of the campaign were claims that private sector needs to be liberated from state interference and fiscal burdens. This element of liberalism was

26 D. Spasojević, 'Može li populizam biti vladajuća ideologija?', *in* M. Simendić (Ed.), *Demokratski otpori normalizaciji autoritarizma*, Udruženje za političke nauke Srbije, Fakultet političkih nauka, Beograd, 2017, pp. 75-91.

27 S. Atlagić & A. Ugrinić, 'Teme u izbornoj kampanji u Srbiji 2012. godine', *in* Jovanović & Vučičević (Eds.), 2013, pp. 181-182.

28 Jovanović, 2012, pp. 11-26.

important as an attempt to bring new voters like small entrepreneurs into SNS camp,[29] but it was also used to strengthen the primary arguments. Namely, SNS argued that corrupted and captured state (by DS government) is providing subsidies only to foreign investors, that DS is using state resources for employment of their voters and that there are many state agencies and bodies that are not performing their function but only serving as a part of a spoils system.

To conclude, SNS's ability to create a coherent electoral and ideological platform with the main frame stressing that DS is being guilty of corruption and clientelism,[30] was the first pillar of their success. The second pillar was promoting economic issues at the top of their agenda. The third pillar was completed once SNS convinced international community and Serbian medium voters that they will not represent a threat to the established pro-European consensus.

8.3.2 *Incumbent Populism – How Does It Work?*

SNS won 24% votes in the parliamentary elections in 2012 and became the governing party together with the Socialist Party of Serbia (SPS) and the United Regions of Serbia (URS, former G17). SNS President Nikolić was elected for Serbian president, so he resigned and party elected Vučić as a new leader. The main question is whether becoming the part of government shifted SNS's ideological profile and is it somehow related to populist values?

This new phase allows me to broaden the analysis into the way of governing, as well. And only when we observe SNS in (political) action, it becomes obvious that populist characteristics represent the core values and driving force of SNS and the foundation of their popularity.

Initial rise of SNS popularity can be traced back to the period immediately after the elections. The crucial event in this period was the arrest of Mišković, owner of the largest Serbian company Delta, the most important tycoon and unofficially the most influential person in Serbia. Although Prime Minister Dačić was minister of interior at the time, Vučić and SNS claimed all credits as this was their electoral promise and platform. Arrest of the most powerful person and the symbol of post-transitional inequality promoted Vučić as the protector of the poor, ordinary people. This was only strengthened in anti-corruption campaign against previous government members (with the exception of SNS coalition partners at that time – Socialists and URS) that led to the arrest of almost 100 members of DS, including former ministers, mayors and other officials (it should be noted that almost no one has been convicted so far). Some of the arrests coincided with electoral

29 Stojiljković, 2012, pp. 9-24.
30 Spasojević, 2017, pp. 75-91.

periods, especially on local level. Arrests have been followed by strong media campaign,[31] including not only party-controlled communication and human *bot* activity, but also party-friendly tabloids and TV stations (*e.g.*, Pink television) that had special programme dedicated to the police activities. Severe attack against the opposition continued unrelated to corruption activities, so it become customary that DS officials were named by SNS officials as 'lunatic and psychopath'[32] or 'seeds of evil'[33] while the party itself was often labelled as 'criminal organization'.[34]

Media attention in these cases hat set high standards of media presence and confirmed thesis on populist focus on media outreach. In Serbian case, this outreach included information leakage from prosecution office and police investigation teams to selected government-friendly tabloids (*e.g.*, *Informer* and *Kurir*), followed by frequent statements by prime minister or minister of the interior on these cases even before the official indictment has been confirmed.

Following this initial success in anti-corruption campaign, SNS demanded more power and this led to a snap parliamentary election in 2014. This election had the expected outcome: SNS won 48% votes and Vučić was elected as the prime minister (SPS remained the main coalition partner). On the other side, the unexpected outcomes of the elections were complete collapse of anti-European parties (SRS and Dveri failed to win the 5% threshold) and division between the Democrats. Besides the formal takeover of power by Vučić, this election brought about additional narrowing of the ideological space covered by parliamentary parties in Serbia,[35] with two additional consequences: (1) compared to other party manifestos, populist thin ideologies did not stand out as underdeveloped; and (2) centripetal tendencies provided more space at the ends of political space for arrival of new parties.

Elections in 2014 also represented a milestone in the SNS governing mode. Namely, in contrast to the first 2 years marked by rather moderate positions, significant support from international community (also because of delivering promises/results regarding Kosovo agreements) and even Serbian civil society, period after 2014 represented the gradual increase of conflicts.

As stated before, populists have specific grudge on checks-and-balances mechanisms of liberal democracy. This can be rooted in the understanding that there is one popular will that should not be obstructed by other powers or power-sharing mechanisms. Of

31 Z. Stojiljković, 'Izbori 2014. godine: šta se zapravo Srbiji dogodilo', *in* Z. Stojiljković & G. Pilipović (Eds.), *Izborne ponude i rezultati – evropski izbori i izbori u Srbiji 2014. godine*, Konrad Adenauer Stiftung, Beograd, 2014, pp. 7-20.

32 www.blic.rs/vesti/politika/medusobne-optuzbe-pajtica-i-mirovica-nakon-hapsenja-vrebalova/vpmhtj1.

33 www.glas-javnosti.rs/aktuelne-vesti/2014-02-21/da-se-iskoreni-seme-zla-oliceno-u-miskovicu-i-dilasu.

34 www.blic.rs/vesti/politika/medusobne-optuzbe-pajtica-i-mirovica-nakon-hapsenja-vrebalova/vpmhtj1.

35 Z. Stojiljković & D. Spasojević, 'Serbian Party System', *in* Z. Stojiljković, D. Spasojević & J. Lončar (Eds.), *How to Make Intra-Party Democracy Possible?*, Fakultet političkih nauka & CeMI, Beograd, Podgorica, 2015, pp. 49-68.

course, within transitional framework those oversight institutions are not functional and strong,[36] and even a weak pressure can lead to their malfunction and lack of results. Also, it is not a unique populist phenomenon that they reject scrutinizing mechanisms; to a greater or lesser extent, it was the trend of all Serbian governments in the post-Milošević's period.[37] However, during SNS's first government (2014-2016), we had witnessed several very harsh conflicts with independent and regulatory bodies. The most striking example was conflict with Serbian Ombudsperson who tried to engage in several prominent cases and to challenge governmental standpoints. Similar attacks were launched on representatives of civil society and independent media with specific attention given to a small number of investigative journalism teams. Populist affection for social media provided SNS with another tool – aggressive and organized campaign against opponents and all criticism on Twitter and Facebook.

Gradual increase of the level of conflict was also observable in relation to the out-groups ('*the other*'). Due to many unresolved issues that are linked to the break-up of Yugoslavia and because of their importance for internal politics in post-Yugoslav countries, relations between them are still very fragile and can be easily changed based on political preferences and interest. So, SNS continued with moderate *otherness*, but in this phase moderation can be observed as the sum position out of all SNS communication activities. However, a more nuanced insight shows specific *division of labour* within SNS party camp. To be more precise – if one follows only President Vučić communications, it is easy to conclude that SNS changed their ideological standpoints compared to SRS period. However, if this analysis includes other government and party officials, party position becomes more radical and nationalistic.

Similar dual (or multi-level) tactic can be observed regarding some other salient identity-based issues, like LGBT Parade that has long tradition of attempts and failures after the democratic changes. On one side, former Vučić's government supported the organization team and helped LGBT activist to organize the first Parade in Belgrade and Major of Belgrade (from SNS) joined the parade; on the other side, then Prime Minister (and current President) Vučić clearly stated that he does not support the cause and that "he would not consider to join the parade even if he was in Belgrade at the time".[38] This means that Vučić always tries to take the pivotal, centrist position within the party, but also to cover as wide ideological space as possible. For example, in international relations this means that the

36 P. Kopecký & M. Spirova, 'Parliamentary Opposition in Post-Communist Democracies: Power of the Powerless', *The Journal of Legislative Studies*, Vol. 14, No. 1-2, 2008, pp. 133-159.

37 D. Spasojević, 'Control Function of the National Assembly of the Republic of Serbia', *in* S. Orlović (Ed.), *Comparative Analysis of Democratic Performances of the Parliaments of Serbia, Bosnia and Herzegovina and Montenegro*, Faculty of Political Sciences, Belgrade, Sarajevo Open Centre Sarajevo and Faculty of Political Science, Podgorica, 2012, pp. 141-153.

38 http://rs.n1info.com/a283145/Vesti/Vesti/Vucic-Necu-da-setam-na-paradi-ponosa.html.

main focus of SNS is on Brussels, with occasional flirts with other international centres of power like Russia, China or non-alignment countries.

In order to avoid accusations that they rule in a similar manner as their predecessors and that they are decreasing democratic standards further, SNS tries to pre-emptively portray itself as a victim of political forces that have the agenda to prevent changes in Serbia. As one of the ministers argues "attacks on Vučić are attacks on the state".[39] Additional layer in this strategy is to create associations between state officials and the state itself and to frame all criticism against officials as anti-patriotic activity. This strategy resembles discourse from the last decade of twentieth century and Milošević's perception of the opposition as 'the fifth column' or 'NATO infantry'. Therefore, the core idea of the strategy is to divide society between true, decent patriots that support the government and corrupted opposing elite and their supporters (who are supporters only for financial reasons), – or something between classic populist dogma and old SRP standpoints.

The division of the society goes beyond the limits of the political field – it encompasses media and civil society, as well. Furthermore, in contrast to what is defined by SNS representatives as 'the American media' (regional N1 TV station) or 'professional civil society', there is a number of new media outlets and freshly founded civil society organizations that are government-friendly, performing formal functions but without actual challenging of power-centres government policies or without representation of independent grassroots interests. These new pro-governmental actors are also in advantage regarding state funding of civil society, which creates a corruptive and clientelistic network.[40]

This division within society, and perception of it, is not easy to sustain, especially when SNS popularity is also partly rooted in centric, moderate and formally pro-EU attitudes. This is the crucial difference between the Serbian and the Polish or Hungarian case; namely, as these countries are already EU member states, they do not depend on the Brussels administration as much as SNS, and they have more space for political manoeuvres before facing criticism or more concrete actions from Brussels. In the Serbian case, SNS still needs to play carefully between vote-seeking strategies based on confrontation with opposition and office-seeking strategies that presume pro-EU and moderate positions.

That is why this party opted for constant production of high-intensity politics aimed at Serbian public. On the institutional level, this presumes high level of uncertainty achieved through continuous production of political crisis – *e.g.*, government were reshuffled in 2013, and in 2014 – there were extraordinary parliamentary elections. In addition, after only 2 years of mandate and despite having 80% majority in the Parliament, a new round of election was held in April 2016. Periods between national elections were characterized

39 www.b92.net/info/vesti/index.php?yyyy=2015&mm=11&dd=29&nav_id=1068727.

40 D. Spasojević, 'Serbia', *in* P. Vandor, *et al.* (Eds.), *Civil Society in Central and Eastern Europe: Challenges and Opportunities*, Erste Foundation, Vienna, 2017, pp. 266-281.

by constant threat of government reshuffles, presidential or provincial election, or number of municipality elections that attracted unusual attention of national media.

In the general scheme, after taking the leading role in the government, SNS increased intensity of conflict with many opponents, but still tried to maintain some balance when communicating with EU and neighbouring countries. Due to significant decline of democratic standards in Serbia, the term 'stabilocracy' has been frequently used to depict current circumstances.[41] This means that Brussels will turn a blind eye regarding illiberal tendencies in Serbia, as long as Serbian government remains cooperative regarding Kosovo issue. In the national context, it means that SNS will have support as long as they keep general pro-EU directions and does not endanger the basic democratic rules. However, it seems that the fulfilment of the second task is not successful, which aligns Serbia together with Hungary and Poland regarding the illiberal tendencies and 'the false promises of populism'.[42]

8.4 Concluding Remarks

The aim of this chapter was to present ideological transformation of SNS from radical, populist and nationalistic party without any governing potential towards the ruling, predominant, pro-EU, centre-right populist party. Ideological shift of SNS can also be understood as a departure from the old-style populism of SRS, that was ideologically more defined and 'thicker', towards the contemporary, more acceptable and adaptable 'thinner' version.

SNS populism has initially been carefully shaped between general pro-EU standpoints, harsh conflicts with the members of the former DS government – represented as corrupt elite and moderate conflicts with the inherited out-groups. However, governing position placed many challenges in front of SNS and moderate positions are hard to keep in the long run under unfavourable circumstances.

As this analysis showed, longer period in government results in increased level of conflicts and broader scope of actors included in the conflict. In other words, corrupted elites, defined by SNS, are getting bigger and include not only political opponents, but also representatives of oversight and regulatory state institutions, civil society and media.

With this pattern of governing that insists on majority rule without respect for constitutional design or protection of different minorities, SNS comes really close to what has been observed in Hungarian and Polish cases. I could, therefore, conclude that politics of conflict production and illiberal understanding of democracy are at the core of right-wing

41 *See e.g.*, www.cirsd.org/en/horizons/horizons-winter-2018-issue-no-10/the-rise-and-fall-of-balkan-stabilitocracies.

42 Freedom House, 2017.

populism in Eastern Europe and that they represent the driving force behind populist ruling parties and their success.

Part III
Courts Under the Populist Challenge

9 Poland: From Paradigm to Pariah? Facts and Interpretations of Polish Constitutional Crisis

Marcin Matczak[*]

9.1 Introduction

This chapter is divided into two parts. The first one, entitled 'Facts', presents briefly the crucial events of what I call 'the Polish constitutional crisis' or 'crisis' for short, and what has been widely described as a backsliding on the part of Poland into authoritarianism. The second part, entitled 'Interpretations', attempts to explain the nature and possible causes of the crisis. In that part I present three explanations of the crisis. The first explanation is historical and looks for the possible causes of the crisis in the unique nature of the Polish transition from Communism to democracy, in particular in the smoothness of this transition understood as the absence of vindictiveness against the previous regime. The second explanation, a legal one, ascribes the crisis to the immaturity of Polish legal culture, in particular its excessive formalism. The third explanation is a sociological one. It interprets the crisis as one of liberal values in contemporary Polish society, a society whose aspiring middle class needs to redefine itself after 30 years of making money, and whose youth do not appreciate a negative liberty (freedom from) as much as their parents did.

In this chapter, I will limit myself to discussing the commandeering of three institutions which underpin the rule of law in Poland: the Constitutional Tribunal, the National Council of Judiciary and the Supreme Court. One should, however, bear in mind that there were several other elements of that assault. These included the government's taking control of the national public media and undermining competencies of the authority protecting media pluralism. They also included several assaults on civil rights, including the enactment of invigilation laws and limitations of the right to assembly and to protest.

* Professor, University of Warsaw, Faculty of Law and Administration. The chapter is based on the lecture delivered by the author in Wolfson College, University of Oxford, on 8 March 2018, during the seminar "Poland: From Paradigm to Pariah?", organized by The Foundation for Law, Justice and Society.

9.2 FACTS

The Polish constitutional crisis started in November 2015, just after Law and Justice (Prawo i Sprawiedliwość, further 'PiS') won the country's parliamentary elections. The first stage consisted in cancelling the earlier appointment of five Constitutional Tribunal judges and packing the Constitutional Tribunal with new judges, as well as in a series of attempts to commandeer the Constitutional Tribunal by enacting six bills aimed at paralyzing its operations. This first stage ended in December 2016, when the new head of the Constitutional Tribunal was appointed by the President of the Republic. The second stage of the crisis started at the beginning of 2017 and consisted in the political takeover of the National Council of Judiciary, a constitutional body responsible for protecting the independence of judges, and for their appointment and promotion, as well as in commandeering the Supreme Court.

9.2.1 *The First Stage*

The first crucial event of the crisis took place in November 2015 when the newly elected Parliament, in which PiS gained a majority, nullified the appointment of the five Constitutional Tribunal judges by the previous Parliament. Immediately after this, the new Parliament appointed five new judges. The problem was that the previous Parliament had overstepped its constitutional power as it only had the right to appoint three, and not five judges to the Constitutional Tribunal. However, the new Parliament's response was both premature and disproportionate, and constituted a clear example of court-packing. The response was premature because a constitutional review of the previous appointments was already underway, and it was disproportionate because three out of five of the previous appointments were in full compliance with the Polish Constitution.[1]

Some of the events that took place at the beginning of December 2015 would not seem out of place in a political thriller. In a late night, just before the Constitutional Tribunal was to assess their constitutionality, the lower house of the Parliament (the Sejm) nullified the appointments of the judges elected by the previous MPs and appointed five new judges. The newly appointed judges rushed to the presidential palace to be sworn in by the president later that night, and then rushed from the palace to the Constitutional Tribunal building to take on their duties. The newly appointed judges were accompanied by the agents of the Government Protection Bureau into the Constitutional Tribunal building and given office space, despite the doubts concerning the legality of their appointments.[2]

1 *See* European Commission, Reasoned Proposal in Accordance with Art. 7(1) of the Treaty on European Union Regarding the Rule of Law in Poland, 2017/0360 (APP) of 20 December 2017, p. 3, Sec. 2.1(9).

2 *See* M. Kisilowski, 'Poland's "Overnight Court" Breaks All the Rule', *Politico Europe*, 12 August 2015.

The following day, the Constitutional Tribunal issued its awaited decision confirming that three out of the five previous appointments were fully constitutional.[3] It was against such a decision that the Parliament had taken such extraordinary 11th-hour measures. Despite the decision, the president refused to swear in the previously appointed judges on the grounds that all 15 places in the Constitutional Tribunal were now already occupied, thanks to the late night appointments. This resulted in a legal limbo: three legally appointed judges could not take their places in the Constitutional Tribunal, and meanwhile the President of the Constitutional Tribunal, Andrzej Rzeplinski, did not assign cases to the three pseudo-judges with whom PiS had packed the court.[4] The months that followed were marked by a permanent conflict between the Parliament and the PiS government on the one side and the Constitutional Tribunal on the other. The government refused to publish the critical Constitutional Tribunal judgment, despite a clearly stated constitutional obligation to do so.[5] As Rzeplinski, then the President of the Constitutional Tribunal, explained,

> the government's refusal to recognize the legitimacy of a number of the court's rulings threatened to create a double legal system, with some courts upholding our rulings, and others not. Judges really don't know what is the law, and without that, in a continental system, courts cannot operate.[6]

The Parliament adopted several legislative enactments to paralyze the operation of the Constitutional Tribunal including those which:

- increased the Tribunal's required majority to strike down legislation;
- forced a delay in deciding a constitutional case (by imposing a minimum of 6 months from its filing before a case is decided);
- gave the minority of judges and the Ministry of Justice a right to impede the operation of the Constitutional Tribunal;
- introduced amendments with immediate effect (without a *vacatio legis*) to force the Constitutional Tribunal to operate according to a set of rules whose constitutionality the Tribunal was simultaneously assessing.[7]

---

3 The Constitutional Tribunal, Judgment no. K 34/15, 3 December 2015.

4 M. Matczak, 'Self-defense of Public Institutions in the Polish Constitutional Crisis', *VerfBlog*, 3 June 2017, https://verfassungsblog.de/self-defence-of-public-institutions-in-the-polish-constitutional-crisis.

5 Art. 190(2) of the Polish Constitution reads: "Judgments of the Constitutional Tribunal regarding matters specified in Article 188, shall be required to be immediately published in the official publication in which the original normative act was promulgated."

6 C. Davis, 'Poland is "On Road to Autocracy", Says Constitutional Court President', *The Guardian*, 18 December 2016.

7 M. Goettig, 'Polish Parliament Passes Contentious Amendment to Top Court Law', *Reuters*, 22 December 2015.

The government's legislative attack on the Constitutional Tribunal was accompanied by public harassment of its judges, attempts to move the Constitutional Tribunal's seat from Warsaw to a remote town in Eastern Poland, the rejection of the Constitutional Tribunal's annual budget, public accusations of laziness by the Minister of Justice.[8]

The key moment of the crisis took place in March 2016, when the Constitutional Tribunal heard the case concerning the constitutional review of the PiS government's amendment to the Constitutional Tribunal Law.[9] The Constitutional Tribunal operated without the three pseudo-judges in the panel and refused to base their operations on the procedure stipulated by the new law while assessing it. Instead, the Constitutional Tribunal based its proceedings directly on the Polish Constitution. The Constitutional Tribunal's objective was to avoid a 'Catch 22' situation: if it were to base its proceedings on the new rules and then find them unconstitutional, the legal validity of that very judgment would be undermined.[10]

The Constitutional Tribunal's judgment was to strike down the amendments proposed by the government. However, its decision not to apply the new law when simultaneously assessing it, provided the prime minister, who claimed that the judgment was procedurally flawed, with a justification for not publishing it.[11] This claim was made with little regard for the fact that the judgments of the Polish Constitutional Tribunal are final and irreversible by any authority.[12]

Andrzej Rzepliński, the Head of the Polish Constitutional Tribunal, played a crucial role during this first year of the crisis. Not only did he bar the pseudo-judges from sitting on the Constitutional Tribunal panels, he also strongly criticized the PiS government for undermining the rule of law. Rzeplinski's term of office ended in December 2016, and with it ended the first stage of the crisis.[13]

---

8 *See* www.dw.com/en/justice-minister-threatens-polands-constitutional-tribunal-judges-with-legal-action/a-19167885.

9 Case K 47/15; *see also* the opinion of the Venice Commission concerning the issues decided by the Constitutional Tribunal in case K 47/15 (Venice Commission, Opinion on Amendments to the Act of 25 June 2015 on the Constitutional Tribunal of Poland, CDL-AD (2016)001, Venice, adopted on 11-12 March 2016).

10 For a more detailed analysis of the legal reasoning behind that CT's decision *see* P. Radziewicz, 'Refusal of the Polish Constitutional Tribunal to Apply the Act Stipulating the Constitutional Review Procedure', *Review of Comparative Law*, Vol. 27, No. 1, 2017, pp. 23-40.

11 www.theguardian.com/world/2016/mar/09/poland-constitutional-court-law-and-justice-government-reforms.

12 Art. 190 (1) of the Polish Constitution reads: "Judgments of the Constitutional Tribunal shall be of universally binding application and shall be final."

13 M. Steinbeis, 'Christmas Showdown in Poland', *VerfBlog*, 3 December 2016, https://verfassungsblog.de/christmas-showdown-in-poland/.

9.2.2 *The Second Stage*

The next stage of the crisis, comprising the commandeering the National Council of the Judiciary and the Supreme Court, started in January 2017. After Rzeplinski's retirement, the Constitutional Tribunal was fully taken over by PiS with their appointment of a new head, Julia Przylebska, and deputy head, who was one of the pseudo-judges. This raised significant constitutional doubts, not least because Rzepliński's Deputy, Judge Biernat, should have replaced him after his retirement.[14]

Predictably, the first decision of the new head of the Constitutional Tribunal was to allow the three pseudo-judges to sit on its panels.[15] Somewhat less predictably, several weeks later, the new head suspended three judges appointed in 2010 in response to the Minister of Justice questioning the legality of their appointment. In a further move to clear the decks, Ms. Przylebska forced Judge Biernat to take leave from his duties.[16]

The result of these three actions was that the Constitutional Tribunal operated with eleven judges, six of whom were appointed by the PiS government. Such a configuration allowed for setting up new panels or changing the previously set panels (the latter with no legal basis) in a way which ensured a majority of the judges elected by PiS on each one.[17]

Commandeering of the Constitutional Tribunal allowed the PiS government not only to remove an obstacle to promoting their often-unconstitutional policies, but to actively use the Constitutional Tribunal for political ends. Following its executive takeover of the Constitutional Tribunal, the government started using it in a way akin to a thief who regularly requests a court to confirm that he has still not stolen anything: the applications filed with the Constitutional Tribunal in the first six months of 2017 by the Minister of Justice and PiS MPs, were not aimed at assessing constitutionality, but were simply tools in a political battle. Some applications were requests for the Constitutional Tribunal to legitimize constitutionally doubtful measures, some were clear attacks on the government's opponents.

A particularly shocking example of using the Constitutional Tribunal for political purposes – and the next step in undermining the rule of law – took place on 20 June 2017, when the Tribunal heard a case concerning the election of the National Council of the

14 M. Matczak, 'Poland's Constitutional Tribunal under PiS control descends into legal chaos', *VerfBlog*, 1 November 2017, https://verfassungsblog.de/polands-constitutional-tribunal-under-pis-control-descends-into-legal-chaos/.

15 *See* European Commission, 2017, p. 8, Secs. 2.3(38) and 2.3(39).

16 *See id.*, p. 9, Sec. 2.4(42).

17 M. Muszynski, one of the Constitutional Tribunal pseudo-judges, admitted in one of his recent dissents that the manipulations concerning Constitutional Tribunal panels indeed took place; *see* A. Grzelak, 'Choosing between two Evils: the Polish Ombudsman's Dilemma', *VerfBlog*, 6 May 2018, https://verfassungsblog.de/choosing-between-two-evils-the-polish-ombudsmans-dilemma/.

Judiciary of Poland.[18] This constitutionally enshrined body is responsible for preserving the autonomy of Poland's courts and the independence of its judiciary; its main power is to appoint new judges and make decisions regarding the promotion of currently serving ones. The National Council of the Judiciary is composed in a manner intended to ensure cooperation between the legislative, executive and judicial branches, in line with the principle of checks and balances provided for in the Constitution.

The Constitutional Tribunal decided that certain provisions of the Act governing the National Council of the Judiciary were unconstitutional.[19] By doing so, the Tribunal conceded to the motion of the Minister of Justice, who had questioned those provisions in the course of work on reform of the Council. The motion to the Constitutional Tribunal was a smokescreen to confuse the public and allow the government to take control of the courts at a lower political cost. Its trivial challenges against the Act were either doubtful or contrived. Yet, with the help of the Constitutional Tribunal, the Minister created an impression that the unconstitutional procedure of electing the members of the National Council of the Judiciary requires a decisive and broad intervention from the Parliament, even if this intervention is totally disproportionate to the unconstitutionality it ostensibly addresses. And so, with the help of the recently subjugated Constitutional Tribunal, the Minister received a carte blanche to demolish the body constitutionally responsible for the protection of the independent judiciary.

As a consequence of the Tribunal's judgment, the Parliament was able to pass a bill which gave politicians full control over the appointment and promotion of judges. Parliament also passed a bill to amend the Courts Act, which gave the Minister of Justice huge influence over the presidents heading the work of the courts.[20]

As if this were not enough, soon another bill on the judiciary was passed to the Sejm which supplements the above steps in PiS's plans for unitary state power. The party's executive takeover of the National Council of the Judiciary would be of little use if there were no vacancies that board could fill. The aim of the latest bill targeting the Supreme Court was to create vacancies at the very top of the judicial hierarchy.[21] Almost overnight, all Supreme Court judges, except those chosen by the Minister for Justice, were to be sent into retirement.

---

18 M. Matczak, 'How to Demolish an Independent Judiciary with the Help of a Constitutional Court', *VerfBlog*, 23 June 2017, https://verfassungsblog.de/how-to-demolish-an-independent-judiciary-with-the-help-of-a-constitutional-court.

19 Case K 5/17.

20 *See* Helsinki Foundation for Human Rights, 'New Threats to the Rule of Law. The Reform of the Judiciary in Poland', 11 December 2017, www.hfhr.pl/wp-content/uploads/2017/12/New-threats-to-the-rule-of-law-brief-12-2017.pdf.

21 S. Grela, 'The End of Independent Judiciary in Poland. PiS Government Violates the Constitution and Assumes Control Over All Courts', *OKO-Press*, 15 July 2017.

This flagrantly unconstitutional onslaught on the independence of the judiciary showed how far PiS's multistage process of violating the Polish Constitution had progressed. The process, which started with an attack on the Constitutional Tribunal, was obliged by PiS's political programme of changing the state system without officially amending the Constitution. The PiS government did not have a sufficient parliamentary majority for such an amendment, but once the Constitutional Tribunal was fully under its control, the Constitution became something of a dead letter.

The government's attack on the separation of powers was objected to in almost all legal environments: advocate and attorney-at-law councils and even prosecutors' associations. The changes were condemned by the parliamentary opposition, which has called for mass protests. Strong criticism has also come from abroad.[22]

Following huge street protests in the summer of 2017 against the legislative changes, President Duda vetoed the draft legislation that would have allowed PiS to commandeer the NJC and Supreme Court.[23] That glimmer of hope for those increasingly disillusioned with the president's distance from his own political stable was in fact an *ignis fatuus*, a will-o'-the-wisp.

President Duda's veto of the legislation did not signal a refusal to sign it on the grounds of merit: in fact, he did not present any criticism of the draft law, and his silence on this matter showing his acceptance of the principle (promoted by PiS in their draft legislation) that members of the Council should in future be appointed by politicians rather than by judges, as had previously been the practice. Rather, Duda's objection was a means to his own political ends: he chose to propose his own bills for taking political control over the judiciary, thus wresting control over the Supreme Court from the Minister of Justice, under whose power the legislation he vetoed would have placed it.[24]

Ultimately, the president proposed new bills on the National Council of Judiciary and the Supreme Court in September 2017, and after several weeks of private consultations between him and the leader of PiS – who does not even hold any public office – the bills became law.[25] The outcome of these entirely opaque negotiations came in the final set of presidential proposals, namely:

- the removal of 40% of judges from the Supreme Court, including its president, thereby shortening her constitutionally enshrined term of office;

22 R. Lyman, 'The Polish Parliament Reshapes Courts, Drawing Criticism', *The New York Times*, 8 December 2017.

23 M. Matczak, 'Is Poland's President Duda on the Road to Damascus?', *VerfBlog*, 26 July 2017, https://verfassungsblog.de/is-polands-president-duda-on-the-road-to-damascus/.

24 C. Davies, 'Why Suspicion Remains Over Polish President's Veto of Contentious Laws', *The Guardian*, 25 July 2017.

25 R. Lyman, 'Poland's President Offers New Path to End Court Crisis', *The New York Times*, 25 September 2017.

- the establishment of a new Supreme Court Chamber which will be responsible for assessing the validity of elections; and
- the appointment of a new National Council of Judiciary whose judicial members will be, contrary to the Polish Constitution, elected by Parliament.[26]

This last appointment will result in shortening the constitutionally enshrined terms of office of the National Council of Judiciary's incumbent members. The newly appointed, politically controlled National Council of Judiciary members will be responsible for filling the vacancies created in the Supreme Court by the removal of 40% of its judges and the establishment of a new Chamber.

This flagrant upsetting of the balance of power between the judiciary and the legislature, where PiS have a majority, led judicial associations and the political opposition to call for a boycott of appointments to the new National Council of Judiciary.[27]

The call was a success: out of 10,000 Polish judges, only 18 agreed to stand for appointment to the new National Council of Judiciary. An overwhelming majority of them have links to the Minister for Justice and their candidacies are questionable to say the least.[28] After its establishment, the National Council of Judiciary will be completely dependent upon politicians, allowing them to influence the process of appointment of all Polish judges. This influence will extend to those who take up seats in the new chambers of the Supreme Court. The official line of argument given by the government to support the proposal of these 18 politically vetted candidates is that every judge represents judges, irrespective of who appoints them and whether they are independent of the appointing person – an argument that does not hold water.

To conclude, the commandeering of the Constitutional Tribunal and the National Council of the Judiciary displays two characteristics typical for any assault at the rule of law in pre-authoritarian regimes. First, it displays a preference for mediocre appointments, the choice of second-rate actors to play starring roles. Second, the appointments represent a phenomenon known as 'the hollowing out' of institutions[29] responsible for protecting the rule of law. When the core of those institutions, which is independence, is removed,

---

26 M. Matczak, 'President Duda is Destroying the Rule of Law instead of Fixing It', *VerfBlog*, 29 September 2017, https://verfassungsblog.de/president-duda-is-destroying-the-rule-of-law-instead-of-fixing-it/.

27 W. Sadurski, 'Bad Response to a Tragic Choice: The Case of Polish Council of the Judiciary', *VerfBlog*, 16 April 2018, https://verfassungsblog.de/bad-response-to-a-tragic-choice-the-case-of-polish-council-of-the-judiciary/.

28 *See* Fact 8 in M. Matczak, '10 Facts on Poland for the Consideration of the European Court of Justice', *VerfBlog*, 13 May 2018, https://verfassungsblog.de/10-facts-on-poland-for-the-consideration-of-the-european-court-of-justice/.

29 L. Diamond, 'Facing Up to the Democratic recession', *Journal of Democracy*, Vol. 26, No. 1, 2015, p. 149.

they become useful props for the ruling powers to move about the stage in a purely theatrical show of legitimacy.[30]

9.3 Interpretations

I will now present three interpretations to help understand the causes of the backsliding of Poland into authoritarianism: a historical, a legal and a sociological one.

9.3.1 *The Historical Explanation*

In order to understand the current crisis, one needs to go back to the beginning of the Polish transformation, namely to the year 1989. That was the year of hope for everyone who had suffered under Communism.[31] Both the key players in the PiS government and their supporters believed that the collapse of Communism would bring to justice all the servants of that regime. Yet the Polish transformation went in another direction – a direction marked out by the 'thick line', announced by the first post-communist prime minister Tadeusz Mazowiecki.[32] This thick line was to be drawn between the present and the past; the consequence was that no revenge was taken and that a smooth transition ensued.

For those who support PiS, such an approach was tantamount to a treason. At the time, they perceived the round table talks between the pre-Communist and post-Communist regimes as collaboration.[33] That perception never abandoned them, and their desire for vengeance went unfulfilled.[34] The realization of their desire came close to fulfilment in 1992, when Antoni Macierewicz, then Minister of Internal Affairs, attempted to reveal the list of those who had collaborated with the Communist secret service.[35] What followed, however, was not revenge, but the deposition of revenge-seeking parties from power. What was even worse for those people who sought retribution, the new Polish parliament, elected in 1993, enacted the first post-Communist Constitution, in 1997, without the involvement of those parties.

---

30 S. Biernat, 'The Rule of Law in Poland', https://trema.nvvr.org/uploads/documenten/downloads/2018-05-Artikel-Biernat.pdf.

31 For the details of Polish post-communist transformation *see* M. J. Chodakiewicz, J. Radzilowski, & D. Tolczyk (Eds.), *Poland's Transformation: A Work in Progress*, Transaction Publishers, New Jersey, 2006.

32 *See* the script of Mazowiecki's speech in Polish parliament: www.archiwum.wyborcza.pl/Archiwum/1,0,6039698,19890825RPDGW,PRZESZLOSC_ODKRESLAMY_GRUBA_LINIA.html.

33 D. Ost, *The Defeat of Solidarity: Anger and Politics in Postcommunist Europe*, Cornell University Press, Ithaca, 2005, p. 107.

34 C. Davies, 'The Conspiracy Theorists Who Have Taken over Poland', *The Guardian*, 16 February 2016.

35 R. Rapacki & G. Blazyca (Eds.), *Poland Into the New Millennium*, Edward Elgar Publishing, Cheltenham, 2001, p. 298.

It is for these historical reasons that both PiS and their supporters perceive the current Polish Constitution as illegitimate. From their point of view, the Constitution (enacted in 1997) promotes leftist and liberal values, including the protection of acquired rights and the safeguards of procedural justice.[36] They believe the Constitution was enacted in bad faith: they believe its real purpose was to protect the beneficiaries of Communism and to secure the status quo.

PiS's suspicions concerning the legitimacy of the Constitution found confirmation (at least in their eyes) after the party gained power as the dominant partner in a coalition government in 2005.[37] One of their crucial political projects was the so-called 'Lustracja' bill: a piece of legislation aimed at revealing the co-operation of Polish citizens with the Communist secret service.[38] This legislation was struck down by the Constitutional Tribunal in 2006 on the grounds of non-compliance with Article 2 of the Constitution – the principle of the rule of law.[39] The Constitutional Tribunal found the 'Lustracja' bill's definition of cooperation with the secret service to be too vague: a charge perceived by PiS as a pretext for not bringing the collaborators to justice.

Shortly after this decision by the Constitutional Tribunal, the leader of PiS, Jarosław Kaczyński, coined the term 'legal impossibilism' to refer to the situation as he saw it: namely, that the principles of procedural justice make it impossible to bring about real, material justice.[40] In this view, the Constitution is an implement whose purpose is to protect post-communist elites and to block the rescindment of their rights, the revocation of their benefits and the redistribution of their ill-gotten gains.

However surprising it may sound, PiS's legal and constitutional doctrine bears a great resemblance to postmodernist claims concerning meta-narratives[41] – that they are publicly disseminated stories whose purpose is to mislead the people and to subdue them to the

36 Ost, 2005, p. 84.

37 B. Stanley, 'Confrontation by Default and Confrontation by Design: Strategic and Institutional Responses to Poland's Populist Coalition Government', *Democratization*, Vol. 23, No. 2, 2016, pp. 263-282.

38 On the process of Polish lustration *see* D. Roman, *Lustration and Transitional Justice: Personnel Systems in the Czech Republic, Hungary, and Poland,* University of Pennsylvania Press, Philadelphia, 2011, and M. Łos, 'Lustration and Truth Claims: Unfinished Revolutions in Central Europe', *Law & Social Inquiry*, Vol. 20, No. 1, 1995, pp. 117-161.

39 *See* Case K 2/07.

40 "Many years ago, Jarosław Kaczyński criticised the 'legal impossibilism,' being in his opinion at the source of the problems with governing Poland, in other words 'as special way of interpreting the law leading to nothing being permitted.' As a PiS leader and a Prime Minister (2006-2007), Jarosław Kaczyński decided that the Constitutional Tribunal was the main source of such 'legal impossibilism.' This is when PiS developed a project for changing the rules of the Tribunal's functioning in order to radically limit its competences, which would unblock the activity of the executive supported by a parliamentary majority. These changes were implemented with the electoral victory of October 2015." A. Balcer, *et al.*, 'Change in Poland, but What Change? Assumptions of Law and Justice Party Foreign Policy', The Batory Foundation, Warsaw, 2016, p. 6.

41 *See* J.-F. Lyotard, *The Postmodern Condition: A Report on Knowledge*, University of Minnesota Press, Minneapolis, 1984.

oppression of those in power. Thus, in the same way that 'patriotism' was a meta-narrative for the pacifists opposing the Vietnam war because it masked the oppression of a US government willing to force people to give their life for the country, so the rule of law in Poland became a smokescreen for shady interests rather than the disinterested expression of an ideal.

Analysing the crisis from a historical viewpoint leads to the conclusion that the subjective experience of the rule of law in Poland – in particular the belief that the law is an obstacle on the road to justice – created in the leaders of PiS and their supporters a very peculiar understanding of the relationship between procedural justice and substantive justice (fairness).

As we know, procedural justice is attained through compliance with formal legal requirements and by basic procedural guarantees: the right to have a case heard by an independent court, the right to defence, the freedom from self-incrimination and the lawfulness of the evidence submitted. Meanwhile, substantive justice is achieved by giving every person what he deserves: penalizing the bad, rewarding the good, giving the innocent peace of mind.

Among experts, procedural justice is considered a necessary means of achieving substantive justice, but the current Polish government sees it as an obstacle to doing so. Originally expressed ten years ago, those convictions are now back in full force under an invigorated (majority) PiS government, whose eagerness to pursue substantive justice has most recently imperilled the separation of powers. The perceived redundancy of procedural justice is reflected in the government's approach to the Constitutional Tribunal and the judiciary: the independence of the Constitutional Tribunal is secondary to the need for it to be composed of people who understand the government's sense of justice; the independence of judges in the courts is secondary to the achievement of the government's substantive objectives.[42]

These convictions are reinforced by the appointment of a re-privatization commission, which, in line with the intention of its creators, is to replace inefficient courts in restoring justice in this politically charged area. Managed by a non-lawyer and composed of politically-aligned members, the commission has judicial powers. Ultimately a kangaroo court, the commission is a manifestation of the belief that it is not institutions but individuals that ensure fair judgments. What is more, it has been hailed by PiS leader Jarosław Kaczyński as the prototype for a solution that may be used in other areas if it works in the current one, heralding the systematic waiver of the guarantees provided by procedural justice.[43]

42 M. Matczak, 'One Law, Two Justices', *VerfBlog*, 30 August 2017, https://verfassungsblog.de/one-law-two-justices.

43 *Id.*

History teaches us that attempts to achieve substantive justice at the cost of procedural justice have always led to disaster: the Inquisition, witch-hunts, kangaroo courts such as the *Volksgerichtshof* and politically-motivated trials, provide ample evidence that the perception of justice and justice itself are seldom aligned.

It is such historical experience of substantive justice that has led Western culture to have so much faith in procedural justice. Its basic elements are checks and balances: the defence attorney weighs in against the public prosecutor, the Constitutional Tribunal checks the parliament, the executive authorities are counterbalanced by independent judicial ones. This balanced structure ensures a thorough examination of facts and elimination of bias to arrive at truth and justice.

For historical reasons, PiS leaders and supporters have no faith either in procedural justice or in checks and balances. Their frustration concerning what others perceive as a great Polish success, namely the smooth transition from Communism to constitutional democracy, impelled them towards a massive assault at the rule of law when their time to wield power finally came. In the next part of this chapter I will interpret the crisis through the lens of legal culture, and we will see why this assault was so successful. Not wishing to give the game away, let me just say it was connected as much with the weakness of the defence as with the strength of the attack.

9.3.2 *The Legal Explanation*[44]

Those following the Polish constitutional crisis from abroad may see it as a traditional clash between law and politics. Analysed in Schmittian terms, law as a system of rules represents an obstacle to the realization of the current political will, and as such must yield to politics. When law and politics clash, politics represents a set of values external to law; law, in turn, represents its own values, mostly formal, which cannot be reconciled with the external values of politics. Analysed in Radbruchian terms, law secures legal safety, politics promotes effectiveness. When law and politics clash, politics trumps law to change the society in accordance with the political will, even if this involves breaking the law.

From this perspective, the nature of the political attacks aimed at the rule of law in Poland may seem familiar: they are attacks through which political values prevail over legal values, and procedural justice yields to the promotion of material justice. The meaning of material justice is defined by those who won the elections. Such attacks recall the actions against the formal values of law undertaken by the authoritarian regimes of the twentieth

44 This part of the chapter is a shortened version of my article 'The Strength of the Attack or the Weakness of the Defense? Poland's Rule of Law Crisis and Legal Formalism', *Review of Central and East European Law*, 2018, forthcoming.

century, so I call them "old-school attacks". A typical example can be found in Lenin's 1917 attacks against 'formality':

> We'll tell the people that its interests are higher than the interests of democratic institutions. There's no need to go back to the old prejudices, which subordinated the interests of the people to formal democratism.[45]

Shocking as it is, similar statements have recently been formulated in Poland – a country deeply affected by the trauma of totalitarianism. During the debate on nullifying the appointment of five Constitutional Tribunal judges on 26 November 2015, the parliamentarian Kornel Morawiecki, said:

> Law is something important but it is not sacred [...] Above law stands the good of the Nation. If law interferes with this good, we shall not treat law as something inviolable or unchangeable. What I say is this: law shall serve us! Law that does not serve the nation is lawlessness!

A similar position was presented in the Report of the Team of Experts appointed to respond to the Venice Commission's 2016 reports concerning the rule of law in Poland.

In the construction of a democratic state based on the rule of law (such as Poland), the principle of democracy prevails over the abstract legal order, the latter being the quintessence of constitutional democracy.[46]

The above quotations may suggest the current attack on the rule of law in Poland resembles the old-school totalitarian attacks seen under the Weimar Republic or communist Russia. Those attacks consisted in establishing a clear and explicit hierarchy in which law is subservient to politics, and the values of the latter prevail over those of the former. However, the kind of attack on the rule of law we currently encounter in the Central and Eastern Europe is different: even if in unguarded moments politicians explicitly declare that politics should prevail over law, when they execute their policy and justify it, they rather pay lip service to the law than ignore or dismiss it completely.

The reason why illiberal governments in contemporary Europe do not openly proceed with illegal action is easy to identify. The rule-of-law values are well-entrenched in public life and memories of the totalitarian regimes that preceded and followed World War II have not yet faded from the public memory. Politicians who wish to achieve an unconsti-

---

45 Lenin's speech from 1 December 1917 (quoted by J. Burbank, 'Lenin and the Law in Revolutionary Russia', *Slavic Review*, Vol. 54, No. 1, 1995, p. 38).

46 Report of the Team of Experts, 15 July 2016, www.sejm.gov.pl/media8.nsf/files/MGOK-ACFDR3/%24File/Raport%20Zespołu%20Ekspertów%20do%20spraw%20Problematyki%20Trybunału%20Konstytucyjnego.pdf.

tutional goal, such as commandeering the judiciary, have to use a much more sophisticated technique than overtly disregarding the rule of law. To succeed, they have to convince the general public they are acting in accordance with the law, whether it takes the form of a national constitution or of EU regulations. The impression they want to produce is that politics is subservient to the law, thus allowing their actions to appear legal even if their effects are not. To do so, they draw on ostensibly legal tools to achieve illegal (unconstitutional) goals.

Paying lip-service to the rule of law allows Poland's politicians to mask their attacks on the independence of the judiciary. The disguised character of their attack makes it difficult for the general public to recognize that an attack is really taking place. As a consequence, the public is not motivated to defend the judiciary or its independence, thus giving free rein to politicians. What is more, the fact that the attack on judicial independence is carried out in a way that seems to secure its superficial compliance with the letter of the law makes it difficult for the judiciary itself to expose the real nature of the attacks.

Let me present two short examples of the new-kind of attack at the rule of law based on the Polish experience. As we have heard, in the course of 2016, the governing majority drew on Article 197 of the Constitution to enact a total of six statutory amendments or full statutes concerning the Constitutional Tribunal, ultimately allowing them to commandeer by the end of the year. Article 197 reads: "The organization of the Constitutional Tribunal, as well as the mode of proceedings before it, shall be specified by statute." This was presented as the sole basis for the parliament's right to regulate the operations of the Constitutional Tribunal in a way the parliament finds proper. No reference was made to constitutional principles stipulating the functions of the constitutional review performed by the Constitutional Tribunal, and no reference was made to the principle of independence of the judiciary, or the separation of powers. Of course, the mere fact of a regulation, imposed by Parliament on the Constitutional Tribunal, being compliant with Article 197 is not sufficient to make that regulation compliant with the Constitution, especially if it hinders the Constitutional Tribunal from performing its constitutional duties.

The second example occurred after the government had successfully commandeered the Constitutional Tribunal, and when it set out to take over the Supreme Court. The first proposed bill Minister of Justice announced in June 2017, stipulated the instant removal of all incumbent Supreme Court judges and the appointment of new ones by him. The constitutional justification for such a brazen move was derived from Article 180(5) of the Polish Constitution, which reads:

> Where there has been a reorganization of the court system or changes to the boundaries of court districts, a judge may be allocated to another court or retired with maintenance of his full remuneration.

Article 180(5), allowing for the retirement of the judges, was presented to the public as an isolated basis for the removal of all Supreme Court judges, with no reference to other constitutional regulations. For example, Article 31(3), which expresses the proportionality principle and requires all the limitations of rights be proportionate to the goal of the limitation. In particular, no substantiation was provided on how the very limited reorganization of thc Supreme Court justified the removal of all judges.

Both of these examples show that the perpetrators of the new-school attack on the rule of law go to great pains to convince others that their actions are justified within the existing legal framework. The main argument they provide is that their actions are compliant with the letter of the law – even if the consequences of those actions cannot be reconciled with its spirit, as expressed in the Constitution.

A specific type of legal argumentation is at work here: one can call it 'isolated constitutional interpretation', which enables a misuse of powers. Isolated constitutional interpretation targets a particular constitutional provision without regard to other provisions or the Constitution as a whole and its outcome is a decontextualized interpretation. The crucial feature of this type of legal argumentation is a much-vaunted compliance with individual bright-line rules of the Constitution, even if the consequences of the actions based on those rules infringe general constitutional principles, in particular the independence of the judiciary and the separation of powers. In other words, isolated constitutional interpretation allows for using lawful means to achieve unlawful ends.

The illegality of the new-school attacks on the independence of the judiciary can be revealed only by a non-formalistic strategy, namely by showing that those attacks infringe constitutional principles, even if they are compliant with isolated, bright-line rules, and by considering the real-life effects of the application of those bright-line rules. As several studies have shown, however, judges in Central and Eastern Europe have been trained in the tradition of judicial formalism, according to which formal compliance of one's actions with the law is sufficient basis for their legality.[47] In other words, to repel the attacks, judges must go beyond the letter of the law and into the realm of its spirit. Yet, this is a step too far for formalistically trained judges.

My thesis is that the rule-of-law crisis in Poland has not been caused so much by the strength of the political attack on the rule of law, but by the weakness of the defence mechanisms that should have been triggered once that attack started. Primary among those mechanisms is the maturity of legal culture, a key feature of which is the ability to carry out complex legal reasoning when interpreting legal text and assessing the validity of legal actions. Both the phenomenon of isolated legal interpretation and the misuse of powers it enabled can be effectively refuted by judicial reasoning if that reasoning is suffi-

---

47 *See, e.g.*, M. Matczak, M. Bencze & Z. Kuhn, 'Constitutions, EU Law and Judicial Strategies in the Czech Republic, Hungary and Poland', *Journal of Public Policy*, Vol. 30, No. 1, 2010, pp. 81-99.

ciently complex. But if a judicial culture's preferred form of reasoning is formalistic argumentation, such a refutation is difficult, if not impossible. The legal culture in Poland, and more broadly in Central-Eastern Europe, has not developed adequate tools to defend itself against recent attacks on the rule of law.

This is not to say that all attempts to exploit formalistic judicial reasoning as a basis for political attacks on the judiciary were successful. The Constitutional Tribunal, for instance, was able to defend itself against the isolated interpretation of Article 197. It did so by refusing to base the constitutional review of the new law concerning the Constitutional Tribunal's operation, and based it directly on constitutional principles. Alas, the Constitutional Tribunal's readiness to deploy a principle-based argumentation to protect the independence of the judiciary should be perceived as an exception rather than a rule. As a constitutional court whose source text is principle-based, the Constitutional Tribunal has a particular inclination to use principle-based reasoning, but this inclination is not an entrenched element of the Polish legal culture as a whole.

Notwithstanding such exceptional cases, the very fact that patently superficial formalistic argumentation was provided to justify attempts to commandeer the Polish judiciary, indicates that those presenting the argumentation considered it to be legally valid. This implies that a legal culture in which such justifications can be put forth is indeed underdeveloped, and as a consequence, all but defenceless against politicians' new-school attacks on the rule of law.

9.3.3 *The Sociological Explanation*

No constitutional crisis is only about the law. Even if lawyers in Poland and in the European Union have a tendency to perceive the Polish crisis as solely a legal one, it is not. The violations of the Polish Constitution and obligations arising from EU law have deep sociological grounds. This needs to be kept in mind, especially by those responsible for building an argumentation that could alleviate the conflict between the Polish Government and the European Commission.

In this, lawyers engaged in the Polish crisis may feel a little like Atticus Finch, the protagonist of Harper Lee's book *To Kill a Mockingbird*, who found himself defending a black man accused of rape. In both cases, their legal arguments are strong, their words are clear and convincing, and yet they seem to lose their case. The jury they address is unimpressed. Why is it so? Ultimately, the problem Atticus Finch was facing was not a legal one; it was social and psychological, namely racism. Lawyers struggling with the assault on the rule of law in Poland also face a similarly multidimensional problem. A large section of Polish society has no time for the niceties of the constitutional order, they want reform to address social problems.

The government's narrative presents the dismantling of the rule of law as the cure for several social ills, including historical injustice and the dangers of globalization. With governmental propaganda presenting the assault on the rule of law as a cure for multiple ills,[48] those opposing the treatment are at risk of losing their patient. By perceiving the dismantling of the rule of law as a purely legal problem, the defenders of the rule of law seem to be denying the very need for treatment. They might be better advised to go beyond the purely legal dimension and recognize the symptoms of the disease, namely the social dimension, and propose an alternative treatment. The failure to take into consideration the underlying social problems which have motivated this attack on the rule of law is a dangerous oversight on the part of those who wish to put Poland back on the road to recovery. That is why I would like to dedicate the last part of my chapter elaborating a little on those underlying social symptoms.

A recent sociological study carried out in a medium-sized Polish town may be of some help.[49] According to this study, the supporters of the governing party display features of a neo-authoritarianism syndrome. What is neo-authoritarianism? The prefix 'neo' indicates the novelty of this kind of authoritarianism – in fact, it is deeply democratic. The Polish people are ready to provide their elected representatives with an absolute right to change the rules, including the constitutional ones, even without the formal legitimacy to do so. The abstract legal order must yield to the will of the people.

In other words, the supporters of PiS do not recognize the distinction put forward by Bruce Ackermann between long-term constitutional politics and the short-term regular variety.[50] Constitutional politics is carried out in line with the values agreed upon during a so-called 'constitutional moment' – a point in time when a society decides upon the fundamental values that will shape its existence. By contrast, regular politics is carried out by parties in the course of the regular electoral and representational process. Contrary to Ackermann's distinction, both PiS and its supporters believe that winning the regular election gives them a sufficient mandate to change constitutional politics at will. And this is how democracy defeats constitutionalism.

As for regular authoritarianism, its main elements are:

- domination over the weak and the alien, including ethnic and sexual minorities, refugees and whoever else can be perceived as an enemy;
- a preference for a politically effective strong-hand approach to social problems; and

48 *See* the argumentation presented in Chancellery of the Polish Prime Minister, 'White Paper on the Reform of Polish Judiciary', Warsaw, 7 March 2018, www.premier.gov.pl/files/files/white_paper_en_full.pdf.

49 M. Gdula, (in co-operation with K. Debska and K. Trepka), 'Dobra zmiana w Miastku. Neoautorytaryzm w polskiej polityce z perspektywy małego miasta', *Krytyka Polityczna*, 2017, pp. 3-39.

50 I. Berlin, 'Two Concepts of Liberty', *in* I. Berlin (Ed.), *Four Essays on Liberty*, Oxford University Press, London, 1969.

- belonging to a national community that provides its members with aspirations far beyond the typical needs of a middle class.

All those elements can be explained by Erich Fromm's concept of 'the authoritarian personality'.[51] This concept, originally constructed by Fromm to explain the psyche of the Germans under the Weimar Republic, provides an excellent basis for a diagnosis of Poland's reversion to authoritarianism.

In essence, whenever social unrest occurs (the threat of terrorism, an immigration crisis, a difficult labour market) a feeling of uncertainty and danger spreads and the government deftly kindles it (Islamization of Europe, the threat of unemployment and fear of disease).[52] The broader social uncertainty reinforces what Fromm identified as the social masochistic component of the authoritarian personality – the wish to dissipate in something larger than oneself: in the idea of a nation, patriotism, in some grand plan imposed by a charismatic leader. This leader's plan brings order to the lives of those who cannot muster the strength to organize their own. By making their world more clearly defined, by making it clearer who is friend and who is foe, the leader's plan gives such individuals the impression of being able to regain control over their fate.

Aggressive criticism of supporters of the leader only increases the sense of danger that has been instilled within them; in confirming the existence of enemies, such criticism enhances trust in the leader who intends to combat them. In Poland's case, this mechanism explains the positive correlation between intervention by EU authorities into the Polish affairs and popular support for the governing party.

The narrative provided by the neo-authoritarian parties also appeals to the youth. Young people are a generation more interested in 'freedom to' than 'freedom from', to use Isaiah Berlin's famous distinction.[53] Unlike their parents and grandparents, they have never needed to fight for freedom from coercion, nor have they experienced oppression. Free from coercion and oppression, they have been left to organize their lives as they want. The problem is, they do not really know what to do with this excess of freedom and, returning to Fromm, they may feel an urge to escape from it. Escape routes are provided by such normative ideologies as patriotism and nationalism, which provide clear paths for thinking and acting. However anachronistic it may sound, patriotic values appeal to today's youth, even if the patriotism peddled to them by our authoritarian-inclined leaders is one of

51 E. Fromm, *Escape from Freedom*, Holt, Rinehart and Winston, New York, 1941.

52 The results of the opinion polls carried out in Poland showed that between 2015 and 2016, *i.e.*, during two years of the PiS government, the level of distrust towards Arabs and Africans significantly increased. *See* the report of IPSOS (for the International Organization for Migration), 'Badanie na temat postaw wobec cudzoziemców w Polsce', http://poland.iom.int/sites/default/files/IOM_Cudzoziemcy_raport_IX_2016.pdf.

53 B. Ackerman, 'Constitutional Politics/Constitutional Law', *The Yale Law Journal*, Vol. 99, No. 3, 1989, pp. 453-547.

failure, sacrifice, struggle and hate, not the patriotism of victory, tolerance, cooperation and openness.

A recent notorious example of the appeal to patriotic emotions was Poland's so-called Holocaust Law, a new piece of legislation which criminalized the act of accusing the Polish nation of crimes against humanity. From a practical point of view, the law did not make much sense: the phrase 'Polish death camps' was only used sporadically before the law was enacted and was effectively combatted by a combination of NGOs, state bodies and strategic allies. However, the law allowed PiS's aggrieved supporters to unite in an unprecedented defence of their nation against the whole world when its narrow nationalistic agenda raised protests worldwide. This feeling of unity is exactly what the authoritarian personality craves, and what the current Polish government is pleased to deliver, at whatever cost.

Returning to ideologies, but of the non-rule-imposing variety, liberalism joins the rule of law in being in crisis. Unlike nationalism, it is a social notion for individuals who know how to lead their lives. The rule of law and constitutionalism underpin the liberty of living one's life without the threat of coercion. However, a large number of our fellow citizens do not have a clear idea on how to lead their lives and are relieved to be provided with ready-made solutions. Liberalism has nothing to offer them. Creating plans for people's lives would be an anomaly in the liberal DNA, as it would limit people's freedom.

Thus, liberalism by definition fails in creating an attractive narrative for people who are unwilling or unable to create one for themselves. In fact, for some, the target of creating a social space free from coercion threatens them as it obliges them to take responsibility for their own lives. Liberalism thereby loses the battle to the effective narrative-generating, life-organizing machines such as nationalism supported by institutionalized religion, which are ever-ready with clear and comprehensive life plans. Such plans offer simple solutions to complex problems and allow their adherents to dissolve themselves into something greater than their individuality: the nation, a patriotic frenzy or historical pride.

9.4 Conclusion

What lessons can we derive from Poland's predicament? In line with my interpretations of the crisis, I would propose three. First, the historical interpretation teaches us that there is no such thing as a complete and successful post-authoritarian transition. Transitional societies are like cancer survivors – even when they seem healthy, they require constant monitoring. Social frustrations need to be addressed, especially if the style of the transition did not give them room for adequate expression.

Second, the legal explanation teaches us that to transform a legal order from a totalitarian one into one based on the rule of law requires more than the changing of the law in the books. The way the law is applied by the courts and the way the legal reasoning is carried out is of at least equal importance. The promotion of the rule of law in the post-communist countries must transform what we call the law in action by encouraging judges to embrace a more holistic, principle- and consequence-based approach to applying laws. As we have seen, a superficial understanding of the rule of law as compliance with bright-line rules only, and a lack of understanding of the role principles play in the legal system, may both contribute to backsliding into authoritarianism.

Third, the sociological interpretation teaches us that freedom never can be taken for granted. Even if the older Polish generation remembers a world in which, as the Polish Constitution states, "fundamental freedoms and human rights were violated", the younger one does not. To secure the freedoms of those who, for historical reasons, do not fear that they will lose it, we need to rewrite the liberal values into a new language. This is no easy task.

10 Populism and the Turkish Constitutional Court: From a Game Broker to a Strategic Compromiser

*Bertil Emrah Oder**

10.1 Introduction

Populist strategies have for some time been an integral part of Turkish political life employed dominantly by the right-wing political parties.[1] Appealing to a 'national will', populists in Turkey typically embrace the genuine citizens who are forced to abandon their original cultural identity particularly as Muslims by the bureaucratic elite with its belief in secularization and reform.[2]

After the transition of Turkey into the multiparty system and adoption of competitive elections, the Democrat Party (DP) first deployed this populist discourse in the 1950s, successfully mobilizing the masses against the bureaucratic, statist and secularist elites. The legacy of the DP has been taken over by the succeeding conservative right parties and their leaders, including Süleyman Demirel, Turgut Özal and Recep Tayyip Erdoğan. Their indisputable electoral success supported by the populist discourse and policies has shaped

---

* Professor of Constitutional Law at Koç University Law School, Istanbul. This chapter is based on my blog article for Debate on Constitutional Courts and Populism on Verfassungsblog and ICONNECT. *See* B.E. Oder, '*Populism and the Turkish Constitutional Court: the Game Broker, the Populist and the Popular*', *VerfBlog*, 2 May 2017, https://verfassungsblog.de/populism-and-the-turkish-constitutional-court-the-game-broker-the-populist-and-the-popular; B. E. Oder, '*Populism and the Turkish Constitutional Court: the Game Broker, the Populist and the Popular*', *Int'l J. Const. L. Blog*, 2 May 2017, www.iconnectblog.com/2017/05/populism-and-the-turkish-constitutional-court-the-game-broker-the-populist-and-the-popular. I am grateful to Michaela Hailbronner for her comments on an earlier version of the manuscript. I also thank Samuel Issacharoff, Miodrag Jovanović and Violeta Beširević for their truly valuable comments regarding my submission in International Conference on New Politics of Decisionism in October 2017 (University of Belgrade Faculty of Political Science and Faculty of Law, and IVR Serbian Association of Legal and Social Philosophy).

1 For populism as a discursive strategy in Turkey *see* Z. Toprak, 'Popülizm ve Türkiye'deki Boyutları', in *Tarih ve Demokrasi*, Istanbul, Cem Yayınevi, 1992, pp. 41-62; R. Kasaba, 'Populism and Democracy in Turkey, 1946-1961', *in* E. Goldberg *et al.* (Eds.), *Rules and Rights in the Middle East*, University of Washington Press, Seattle, 1993, pp. 43-68; N. Erdoğan & T. Bora, "Biz, Anadolu'nun Bağrı Yanık Çocukları…': Muhafazakar Popülizm', *in* T. Bora & M. Gültekingil (Eds.), *Modern Türkiye'de Siyasi Düşünce, Cilt 5, Muhazafakarlık*, İletişim Yayınları, İstanbul, 2006, pp. 632-644. For Turkey's rightist parties and populism *see also* N. Mert, *Merkez Sağın Kısa Tarihi*, Selis, Istanbul, 2007.

2 For the authentic people argument of populism *see* J. Müller, *What is Populism?*, University of Philadelphia Press, Philadelphia, 2016, p. 4 and p. 21.

contemporary Turkey. Demirel and his Justice Party (AP) complemented the national will discourse with calls for economic development and the 'Great Turkey' slogan in the 1970s. Özal's and his Motherland Party's (ANAP) neoliberal populism emphasized market-oriented economic reforms and the empowerment of the middle class after the coup in 1980.[3] Erdoğan and his Justice and Development Party (AK Party) have portrayed themselves as the protector of the victims of ignorant, secularist, unwise or corrupt policies undertaken by previous governments in the 2000s. Leaving aside the recent illiberal discourse in Turkey, the AK Party has initially combined the democratization, Europeanization, majoritarian and religiously sensitive discourse with the anti-establishment argument of populism.[4] It still insists on the exclusive representation of the 'nation' against elites dynamically redefined according to the context.

After the 1950s, Turkey's right-wing leaders have represented the dominant political preference of the voters constantly. As the 'people's authentic representative', they have regularly claimed to be free from the limits and checks of the bureaucratic elite. This point is the key to identify the complex relationship between populism and democratic politics in Turkey which suffered from overt and subtle forms of the military tutelage especially after 1980. It points out difficulties to draw a line between democratic politics, which should be free from military and any other tutelage, and the populist politics refusing a real sense of checks and balances. In fragile democracies like Turkey, the anti-tutelage argument can easily mask the illiberal populism which usually leads to polarization and resentment politics, colonization of institutions and the suppression of civil society. Here, welfare policies and state funds can easily serve populism to fuel mass clientelism.

Demands for 'being free from external limitations' are the major cause of the conflict between the Constitutional Court and the conservative right governments of Turkey. The conservative governments have defined the elite not only as alienated modernists, secularists, supporters of the state-centred economy, the (Westernized) middle class or wealthy industrialists but also as judges. Being a counter-majoritarian institution, the Constitutional Court has been mostly perceived as another tutelage body confining the national will illegitimately, ever since it was established after the 1960 military coup. The activist case-law of the Court in critical policy preferences, which is sometimes extensively politicized and lack of the sound legal argumentation, has strengthened this image.

Until the 2010 constitutional amendments, the Constitutional Court has frequently clashed with powerful and populist governments in high-profile cases as a game broker.

---

3 For Özal's neoliberal populism *see* Z. Öniş, 'Turgut Özal and His Economic Legacy: Turkish Neo-Liberalism in Critical Perspective', *Middle Eastern Studies*, Vol. 40, No. 4, 2004, pp. 113-134.

4 For conservative populism and conservative modernism of AK Party *see* Y. Taşkın, 'AKP's Move to "Conquer" the Center-Right: Its Prospects and Possible Impacts on the Democratization Process', *Turkish Studies*, Vol. 9, No. 1, 2008, pp. 53-72; Z. Öniş, 'Conservative Globalism at the Cross Roads; The Justice and Development Party and the Thorny Path to Democratic Consolidation in Turkey', *Mediterranean Politics*, Vol. 9, No. 3, 2009, pp. 21-40.

However, after the 2010 constitutional amendments which have reshuffled the Court and the Supreme Council of Judges and Prosecutors, it has increasingly provided judicial support for populist policies. The 2010 amendments have reregulated the number, term limits, selection procedure and eligibility criteria of constitutional judges. While governmental circles presented it as the 'rule of law reform' against tutelage, the opponents voiced the concerns of court-packaging and judicial independence.[5] In the meantime, the Court's reputation as a 'defender of defenseless' in human rights cases has risen. This is triggered in 2012 by the introduction of an individual complaint procedure for constitutional rights also guaranteed under the European Convention for the Protection of Human Rights and Fundamental Freedoms (European Convention on Human Rights).

In the rest of the chapter I will address these changing roles of the Court from a game broker to a strategically compromising figure which, after the coup attempt in July 2016, encounters with illiberal populism and democratic decay. The future of the Court will be discussed in concluding remarks, taking into account the recent amendment introducing a type of presidential system in Turkey.

10.2 THE CONSTITUTIONAL COURT IN HIGH-PROFILE CASES AND POPULISM: THE GAME BROKER

The Constitutional Court's previous role as game broker in high-profile cases has often been perceived as an illegitimate intervention into the political sphere. Three critical areas are of particular interest to observe the relationship between the impact of the Court's decisions and the rise of populist discourse. These include the constitutional amendments, the dissolution of *Refah Partisi* (Welfare Party) and the presidential election process.

After banning the *Refah Partisi*, the Court closed the political sphere to a religiously motivated political party, which was not only anti-secularist party but also the party which incited to hatred and violence using the tools of populism.[6] The Court's approach was approved by the European Court of Human Rights (ECHR).[7] Considering the moderate approach of the newly established AK Party, which has refused the Refah's legacy and favoured democratization in its initial years, the religiously conservative right seemed to

5 For the 2010 amendments *see* L. Gönenç, '2010 Proposed Constitutional Amendments to the 1982 Constitution of Turkey', *TEPAV*, 2010, www.tepav.org.tr/upload/files/1284468699-0.2010_Proposed_Constitutional_Amendments_to_the_1982_Constitution_of_Turkey.pdf; A. Bali, 'Unpacking Turkey's Court-Packing Referendum', *Middle East Research and Information Project*, 5 November 2010, www.merip.org/mero/mero110510; A. Bali, 'Courts and Constitutional Transition: Lessons from the Turkish Case', *International Journal of Constitutional Law*, Vol. 11, No. 3, 2013, pp. 666-701; B. E. Oder, 'Turkish Constitutional Transformation of the EU: Europeanisation towards Constitutionalism?', *in* Ç. Nas & Y. Özer (Eds.), *Turkey and the EU: Process of Europeanisation*, Ashgate, Farnham, 2012, pp. 69-98.

6 E. 1997/1, K. 1998/1, 16 January 1998.

7 *The Welfare Party and others v. Turkey*, ECHR (2003), Applic. No. 41340/98, 41342/98, 41343/98, 41344/98.

have learned from the perils of hatred based populism defeated by the Court and the ECHR. However, the decision of the Court in 2008, which sanctioned the AK Party in a controversial dissolution case to the deprivation of the state aid on weak grounds, has represented a turning point.[8] In dissolution cases, the deprivation of state aid is an alternative and less drastic sanction to be applied to the unconstitutional political parties under Turkey's closure regime of militant democracy. Nonetheless, the Court lost the confidence of the AK Party government by this ruling. It has subsequently been labelled an ally of secularist and bureaucratic forces.

Under the Court's unamendability jurisprudence, its 2008 decision on the removal of the headscarf ban in higher education institutions is also of specific importance to understand the populist backlash in Turkey.[9] The veiling issue has never been discussed by politicians from of a real perspective of rights and freedoms or the status of women in society. It was, of course, an agenda item of democratic politics, but availing intense populist discourses and strategies of polarization. The uncompromising stand of the secularist opposition (People's Republican Party-CHP) has also prevented a deliberative approach to the veiling issue. In such political climate, the Court has followed its own institutional choice purporting the review of constitutional amendments that are well established in its previous case-law. It has reiterated the entrenched constitutional interpretation prescribing headscarf ban as backed by the ECHR.[10] Accordingly, the Court struck down the constitutional amendments aimed at removing the ban in higher education institutions. This decision has been perceived as an attack to the primacy of politics for the constitutional amendments which prefers more inclusive secularism.

The case-law on presidential elections in 2007 has also triggered the anti-tutelage debate. Here, the Court had to deal with an unprecedented and scholarly controversial issue regarding the interpretation of the parliamentary quorum of the election process.[11] AK Party, which proposed the strongest presidential candidate, claimed that the initial quorum for the election had to be determined in line with the general constitutional provision on parliamentary decision-making. This provision prescribed the one-third majority of the deputies at the Parliament (184 deputies) unless otherwise was provided in specific constitutional provisions. However, the constitutional provision on presidential election was defining a specific procedure referring to the two-thirds majority (367 deputies) in a less eloquent wording. In the end, the Court interpreted the quorum as a two-thirds qualified majority on the ground of textual and teleological evidence ('consensus for presidency'). The Court's conclusion in this case (the so-called 367 ruling) was not groundless, but it had deficiencies to consider the preparatory works of relevant quorum

8 E. 2008/1, K. 2008/2, 30 July 2008.
9 E. 2008/16, K. 2008/116, 5 June 2008.
10 *See, e.g., Leyla Şahin v. Turkey*, ECHR (2005), Applic. No. 44774/98.
11 E. 2007/45, K. 2007/54, 1 May 2007.

norms and parliamentary practices which were inconsistent. More significantly, it was a direct challenge to the religiously conservative AK Party government and its presidential candidate Abdullah Gül.

The Court's jurisprudence in such high-profile cases has neither lessened the populist discourse against the tutelage nor tamed the leading political actors who have mobilized the voters massively against the secular elites and gained their confidence. Instead, its efforts to challenge majoritarian preferences have created a backlash against the Court. The Court has been repeatedly categorized as a tutelage institution that chains the authentic representatives of the people.

The Court's poorly structured reasoning in high-profile cases could be deemed as a factor that undermines its credibility. In politically sensitive matters, one should have expected for the Court to adopt a more careful and diligent approach towards legal argumentation to avoid *petitio principii*. However, the over-politicization of these issues due to harsh public debate seems more decisive to explain the backlash against the Court.[12] The uncompromising attitudes of the opposition and the involvement of military actors in the discussions also hardened to make a rational political analysis. This fed the populist stance challenging the elite's tutelage including the judiciary. The tutelage debate surrounding the Court and the judiciary led to the 2010 constitutional amendments.

10.3 THE CONSTITUTIONAL COURT'S JUDICIAL POPULISM AND POPULARITY

The 2010 constitutional amendments meant a new episode in shaping judiciary. The amendments retained the incumbent judges at the Constitutional Court but increased the seats on the bench by adding new judges. The judicial appointment procedure and qualification requirements for the judges were changed where the parliament was involved in the selection procedure. Moreover, an individual complaint procedure was introduced allowing the access to the Court for constitutional rights violations.

The amendments also changed the structure of the Supreme Council of Judges and Prosecutors by allowing all senior judges and prosecutors to elect a part of the Council's members. When the amendments were challenged before the Constitutional Court, the Court adopted an unsuccessful strategy.[13] It annulled a part of the amendment. Without any reasonable argumentation, it declared the 'one judge/prosecutor one vote' principle for the Council's elections unconstitutional. This preference of the Court paved the way

12 For sharp moves of the Court and the narrower public-facing toolkit of the judiciary *see* A. Huq, 'Democratic Erosion and the Courts: Comparative Perspectives', *New York University Law Review*, Vol. 93, No. 27, 2018, pp. 21-31.

13 E. 2010/49, K. 2010/87, 7 July 2010.

to the election of candidate lists prepared by the government. This initiated the discussions in the Council and questions regarding the capture of the judiciary by the executive.[14]

Since 2010, the Court has increasingly supported the legislative choices of the government in critical cases. This new deferential approach is distinctive in that it represents not restrained deference but offers explicit judicial backing for controversial policy choices. This ideological change has required major shifts in the Court's case-law and established doctrines. The interpretation of the secular state principle is one of the areas portraying such a paradigmatic shift. The constitutional review of educational reform based on the so-called Law 4+4+4 can be a good example.[15] The relevant law is a touchstone for populist policies fostering the majority religion, particularly Muslim identity. In this case, the Court upholds the law providing for courses of Islamic instruction in the middle and high schools curricula. Turkey has already a compulsory religious education system in primary, middle and high schools which has been critically reviewed by the ECHR as indoctrination of Sunni Islam denying plurality.[16] The law provides extra elective courses of Islamic instruction fully endorsed by the state. It does not prescribe such courses for any other religion. Drawing on a new concept of 'flexible *laicité*' for Turkey that embodies the 'positive obligation of the state' to facilitate and provide religious services for the majority religion (Islam), the Court upheld the new law. Such an obligation is hardly deducible from the Constitution with its neutral guarantees for freedom of religion and the secular state principle. The Court's judicial populism based on a judge-made theory of the 'flexible *laicité*' has enhanced religiously populist policies of the government.

Another new phenomenon is that the Court's popularity has been rising after 2012. The reasons for this seem to be attributable to the introduction of the individual complaint mechanism implemented since 2012. Complaints can be initiated for violations of the constitutional rights and freedoms guaranteed by the Turkish Constitution as well as the European Convention on Human Rights and its protocols ratified by Turkey. Until now, judgments of the ECHR have been observed in a variety of critical cases. Despite the limited argumentative creativity of the Court and extensive translations from Strasbourg jurisprudence, the individual constitutional appeal has had a positive impact overall. Receiving appeals from different segments of the society has enhanced the Court's accessibility and visibility in citizens' eyes. Its case-law on Twitter and YouTube bans, headscarf bans for attorneys, patriarchal surname regulations, freedom of expression issues and particularly cases involving journalists, or environmental protection have raised the

---

14 For the colonization of institutions as a populist technique *see* Müller, 2016, pp. 44-45.

15 E. 2012/65, K. 2012/128, 20 September 2012.

16 *See, e.g., Hasan and Eylem Zengin v. Turkey*, ECHR (2008), Applic. No. 1448/04; *Mansur Yalçın and others v. Turkey*, ECHR (2015), Applic. No. 21163/11.

expectations and public confidence in the Court. In these cases of public interest, the Court supported *pro libertatis* stance against state interventions.[17]

10.4 THE FRAGILE POPULARITY OF THE COURT: STRATEGICALLY SUPPORTIVE AND DEFIANT STANCES AFTER THE COUP ATTEMPT IN 2016

The Court's popularity is fragile due to the formal boundaries of the complaint mechanism and its self-restrained approach. In general, the Court has tended to dismiss claims regarding electoral fairness or fraud cases as political questions which could have been, in fact, a touchstone to review the constitutional limits of populist strategies.[18] The Court's popularity also seems endangered, because of its tendency to delay dealing with constitutional appeals in recent politically significant cases, such as the detainment of journalists under severe criminal charges of anti-terrorism legislation. The freedom of expression issues have become crucial for testing the Court's integrity in rights-based cases against AK Party's populist policies.

After Turkey experienced a fierce intervention in the form of a coup attempt in July 2016, the incremental democratic backsliding towards illiberal democracy became visible.[19] The constitutional retrogression process that began after 2010 as a result of constitutional amendments on the reshuffling of the judiciary, has been complemented by decline of the freedom of expression, the rights to peaceful assembly and association. The Turkish constitutional judges seem either strategically to support or disobey the regressive shift. To illustrate the Court's approach, I will present several post-coup cases regarding emergency decrees, journalists and libel suits.

17 *See especially Yaman Akdeniz ve Diğerleri Başvurusu,* Applic. No. 2014/3986, 2 April 2014; *Youtube LLC Corporation Service Company ve Diğerleri Başvurusu,* Applic. No. 2014/4705, 29 May 2014; *Tuğba Arslan Başvurusu,* Applic. No. 2014/256, 25 June 2014; *Sevim Akat Eşki Başvurusu,* Applic. No. 2013/2187, 19 December 2013; *Mehmet Kurt Başvurusu,* Applic. No. 2013/2552, 25 February 2016; *Erdem Gül ve Can Dündar Başvurusu,* Applic. No. 2015/18567, 25 February 2015; *Sencer Başat ve Diğerleri Başvurusu,* Applic. No. 2013/7800, 18 June 2014; *Mehmet İlker Başbuğ Başvurusu,* Applic. No. 2014/912, 6 March 2014.

18 *Oğuz Oyan Başvurusu,* Applic. No. 2015/8818, 14 July 2015. In this inadmissibility decision, the Court has refused to consider the complaint alleging that the principle of electoral fairness was violated in parliamentary elections of June 2015 by President Erdoğan's rallies. The applicant claimed such rallies undermined the presidential impartiality clause of the Constitution. *See also Mahmut Tanal Başvurusu,* Applic. No. 2014/11368, 23 July 2014; *Mahmut Tanal (2) Başvurusu,* Applic. No. 2014/11438, 23 July 2014; *Nurullah Efe ve Halkın Kurtuluşu Partisi Başvurusu,* Applic. No. 2017/20127, 7 June 2017.

19 For incremental democratic backsliding as a constitutional retrogression *see* A. Huq & T. Ginsburg, 'How to Lose a Constitutional Democracy', *University of Chicago Public Law Working Paper,* No. 642, 2017, p. 16.

10.4.1 Constitutional Review of Emergency Decrees

The state of emergency declared after the coup attempt in July 2016, a political trauma both at the institutional and social level, has a decisive impact on the Court.[20] The Court's approach to the state of the emergency regime has been twofold.

First, the Court's stance was disappointing and unreliable from the perspective of the rule of law because in 2016 it refused to review emergency decrees by reversing its well-established case-law on the matter.[21]

In a leading decision from 1991, the Court declared the constitutional review of emergency decrees admissible although they were exempted from judicial review by an explicit constitutional rule (Article 148, para. 1 of the Constitution).[22] This leading decision gives the precedence to the compliance with the substantive requirements of the Constitution prescribed for the emergency regime, and not to the formal title of the act. Here, the *telos* of the rule of law and the real nature of legal acts overwhelmed the legal formalism. The Turkish Constitution has extensive norms on extraordinary situations. Even though it provides a non-reviewability clause for emergency decrees, it sets forth territorial, time and circumstantial limits for them for the sake of the rule of law. Accordingly, in 1991 the Court stated that there was a sham emergency decree if it did not comply with the constitutional limits regarding the territory, time and emergency issues to be regulated.[23]

In its reversed decision in 2016, the Court nullifies its previous argumentation based on the purposive interpretation in support of constitutional review.[24] It concludes that the preparatory constitutional documents and the wording of the Constitution confine solely with the parliamentary control of emergency decrees as stipulated in the Rules of Procedure of the Parliament.

This U-turn of the Constitutional Court in a unanimous decision does not represent only a preference for judicial deference but also shows the full support of constitutional judges to the government in administering emergency measures without being threatened by abstract review. This has created a free zone for the government, with a lack of effective checks and balances. The government seizes the opportunity to make excessive regulations by emergency decrees subject to a weak political oversight mechanism not legally enforceable.

---

20 *See also* the decision of the Constitutional Court which orders removal of two constitutional judges from the office after the coup attempt in July 2016, E. 2016/6, K. 2016/12, 4 August 2016.

21 E. 2016/171, K. 2016/164, 2 November 2016; E. 2016/172, K. 2016/165, 2 November 2016.

22 E. 1991/6, K. 1991/20, 3 July 1991; *see also* E.1990/25, K. 1991/1, 10 January 1991; E. 1992/30, K. 1992/36, 26 May 1992; E. 2003/28, K. 2003/42, 22 May 2003.

23 Therefore, the Court upheld the reviewability in a case of circumvention where an emergency decree has regulated the areas under the clause of 'neighbor cities' outside the territory of emergency declaration, *see* E. 1991/6, K. 1991/20, 3 July 1991.

24 E. 2016/171, K. 2016/164, 2 November 2016; E. 2016/172, K. 2016/165, 2 November 2016.

Second, the Court was strategically defiant in the individual constitutional appeal case-law concerning the emergency regime. Strikingly, it interprets the individual constitutional appeal as a potential corrector of injustices that may arise from the aforementioned judicial ruling on non-justiciability of emergency decrees. This makes the individual constitutional appeal proceedings a substitute mechanism of single-issue rectification that can mitigate the detrimental effects of politically significant and judicially controversial judgments declared in abstract review cases.

The Court's stance in *Aydın Yavuz* case is a good example of such strategic defiance. In *Aydın Yavuz*, the Court declares the admissibility of the individual constitutional appeal claiming a violation of the fundamental rights during the state of the emergency regime.[25] The admissibility decision disregards the constitutional ban on the review of emergency decrees as a barrier for individual constitutional appeal. Instead, the Court examines the factual background of the emergency regime, the course of events during the coup attempt and the various emergency decrees in details. It also draws attention to the standards of constitutionality for assessment of the emergency regime, namely the protection of core rights, compliance with the obligations stemming from international law and the principle of proportionality. In a separate assessment on the emergency regime after the coup attempt, the Court testifies its constitutionality. Particularly, the legal remedies provided during the state of the emergency regime are deemed as evidence of proportionality for less strict implementation measures.[26] All in all, the Court comes to a conclusion:

> It is understood that the measures implemented during the state of emergency, considered in parallel with the public authorities' above-mentioned assessments on the facts leading to the declaration of state of emergency, aims at eliminating the threats and dangers arising from terrorism and the FETÖ/PDY ['Fettullahist Terrorist Organization and Parallel State Structure'] that is revealed to be the perpetrator of the coup attempt of 15 July.[27]

10.4.2 Journalism Cases as a Judicial Battle Field

The state of the emergency regime after the coup attempt in 2016 has affected the freedom of expression predominantly. The free media, academic freedom and free speech are the core areas of deterioration, where the disrespect of constitutional guarantees as a form of constitutional transgression becomes a systemic issue by a variety of illiberal measures.

25 *Aydın Yavuz ve Diğerleri Başvurusu*, Applic. No. 2016/22169, 20 June 2017.
26 *Id.*, para. 230.
27 *Id.*, para. 229.

The illegitimate interventions into the freedom of expression have been a long-standing problem of Turkey in times of crisis, first under the military regime of 1980, and then under the state of emergency or anti-terrorism legislation of the 1990s which aims at combating Kurdish separatist terrorism.[28] However, the legislation on free media has been amended in the EU accession process after 2004. The training of judges and prosecutors in line with the case-law of the ECHR also made a positive impact on media jurisprudence despite challenges sustained. This progressive trend seems to have dramatically changed after the coup attempt in July 2016. The retrogressions as regards free media go hand in hand with the substantial regression in the rule of law, the incremental decrease in checks on government by emergency measures, and the constitutional amendment prescribing a strong presidentialism (April 2017).[29]

The rapid increase in criminal investigations against journalists after the coup attempt is the remarkable feature of illiberal populism purported by AK Party government.[30] The decline in freedom of expression covers not only journalism but also academic freedom and social media that has a chilling effect on dissent with removals from the office on insufficient grounds or controversial investigations, accession bans to Wikipedia, the use of criminal and civil norms on insult and compensation.[31]

Under the growing trend of criminalizing the journalism, the opponent journalists have accused the government of media witch hunt.[32] According to the data of the Council of Europe, 109 journalists have been in detention as of October 2018.[33] The state of emergency declared shortly after the coup attempt facilitated the convictions under anti-terrorism and similar legislation on crimes against the constitutional order. Pre-trial detentions

---

28 Committee to Protect Journalists, 'Turkey's Press Freedom Crisis, The Dark Days of Jailing Journalists and Criminalizing Dissent', New York, 2012, https://cpj.org/reports/turkey2012-english.pdf; K. Altıparmak & Y. Akdeniz, 'The Silencing Effect on Dissent and Freedom and Expression in Turkey', *in Journalism at Risk: Threats, Challenges and Perspectives*, Council of Europe, Strasbourg, 2015, pp. 145-172.

29 For data on Turkey's democratic backsliding in a comparative perspective *see* IDEA, *The Global State of Democracy, Exploring Democracy's Resilience*, IDEA, Stockholm, 2017, p. 14, p. 16 and p. 22, www.idea.int/gsod/files/IDEA-GSOD-2017-REPORT-EN.pdf.

30 Regarding the data and analysis on freedom of expression *see also* Office of the United Nations High Commissioner for Human Rights, 'Report on the Impact of the State of Emergency on Human Rights in Turkey, Including an Update on the South-East, January–December 2017', March 2018, pp. 21-28; Commissioner for Human Rights, 'Memorandum on Freedom of Expression and Media Freedom in Turkey', Council of Europe, 15 February 2017, CommDH, 2017, p. 5, https://rm.coe.int/ref/CommDH(2017)5.

31 According to the report of the Monitoring Committee of Council of Europe, 200 academics had their hearings as of 26 April 2018 on the ground of a petition allegedly supporting Kurdish terrorist organization PKK (Academicians for Peace petition). Out of these academics, 13 were sentenced to 1 year and 3 months in prison and all of the sentences were suspended, except one. *See* Parliamentary Assembly of the Council of Europe, 'Honouring of Obligations and Commitments by Turkey, Information Note Following the Visit to Istanbul and Ankara (28-30 March 2018)', Declassified AS/Mon (2018) 07, 17 June 2018, amondoc07_2018.

32 K. Shaheen, 'Turkish journalists accuse Erdoğan of media witch-hunt', *Guardian*, 2 May 2016.

33 The Council of Europe Platform to Promote the Protection of Journalism and Safety of Journalists, www.coe.int/en/web/media-freedom/turkey.

exceeding 1-year, solitary confinement measures and long imprisonment sentences including aggravated life sentences are observed in cases against journalists.[34]

In the meantime, there have also been changes in media ownership so that pro-government dailies represent at present the overwhelming majority. The top-selling mainstream daily owned by the Doğan Group, namely *Hürriyet*, has been recently sold to a media tycoon who publishes two pro-government dailies.[35] During the acquisition process, the news broadcaster CNN Türk and other media companies under the Doğan media group have also been transferred to the pro-government media conglomerate. Under these circumstances, the media pluralism and independent news coverage are severely endangered where the opponent dailies are either low-circulated ones with weak financial structures or online alternative publications. This is equally valid for broadcasting channels.

More recently, a court sentenced 13 members of the *Cumhuriyet* newspaper – the oldest and secular daily as one of the few opponent publications – to imprisonment. The *Cumhuriyet* journalists are charged with supporting the terrorist group Fethullahist Terrorist Organization (FETÖ), which infiltrated the state institutions to form a 'parallel state structure' and organized the coup attempt in July 2016.[36] However, these are the journalists who warned of the cleric Fethullah Gülen and his terrorist group FETÖ for many years but by being also critical against the governmental policies. The international community, including the European Parliament and European Commission, pays careful attention to the *Cumhuriyet* case as a major journalism case.[37] The charges imposed on the *Cumhuriyet* journalists are based on the information about the AK Party government allegedly supplying weapons to Islamist militants in Syria and the claims purporting the change of the publication policy for support to terrorism. The chilling effect of these charges on the media freedom in Turkey is still a matter of concern as stated by the Secretary General of the Council of Europe.[38]

Indeed, the information on weapons was previously subject of the criminal investigation against two journalists of *Cumhuriyet*, Erdem Gül (Ankara representative) and Can Dündar

---

34 For the aggravated life imprisonment sentences *see* 'Turkish court upholds life terms of Nazlı Ilıcak, Ahmet Altan, Mehmet Altan', *Hürriyet Daily News*, 2 October 2018.

35 E. Ersoy, K. Karakaya & T. Ozsoy, 'Turkey Media Baron to Sell After Long Battle with Erdogan', *Bloomberg*, 22 March 2018, www.bloomberg.com/news/articles/2018-03-22/dogan-in-talks-to-sell-turkish-media-assets-to-demiroren-group.

36 C. Gall, 'Turkish Court Convicts 13 from Cumhuriyet Newspaper on Terrorism Charges', The New York Times, 25 April 2018.

37 European Parliament, 'Current Human Rights Situation in Turkey', EP Resolution of 8 February 2018, OJ 2018 C 254/16, (2018/2527(RSP)).

38 The applications of Cumhuriyet journalists were treated as a priority case by the ECHR and the Commissioner for Human Rights became the third party. See 'Cumhuriyet trial: Secretary General deeply worried by the chilling effect the heavy criminal sentences may have on media freedom', Council of Europe, 3 May 2018, https://www.coe.int/en/web/media-freedom/resources-reshuffling/-/asset_publisher/PyxkqhJDYqAj/content/cumhuriyet-trial-secretary-general-deeply-worried-by-the-chilling-effect-the-heavy-criminal-sentences-may-have-on-media-freedom?_101_INSTANCE_PyxkqhJDYqAj_viewMode=view/.

(editor-in-chief) in a separate case. At that time, the government rejected the allegations strongly. It claimed that weapons were an aid to Turkmens, a vulnerable ethnic minority in the region.[39] The Constitutional Court played a vital role in *Erdem Gül and Can Dündar* case, which was upheld before the coup attempt. Due to pre-trial detentions of Erdem Gül and Can Dündar, the claim of violation regarding the freedom of the press was reviewed by the Constitutional Court after the two journalists lodged an individual constitutional appeal before it. The Court ruled in favour of these two Cumhuriyet journalists. It ordered the urgent removal of pre-trial detentions by praising the watchdog role of the free media and the prevention of the chilling effect on press freedom in a democratic society.[40] This was a majority decision of the Court where three of twelve judges dissented. The government heavily criticized the Court's decision as an unconstitutional interpretation, which cannot be respected and abided.[41] In the course of trials, Can Dündar was later sentenced for five years for revealing state secrets but also survived a gun attack on the courtyard.[42] During the appeal proceedings, he moved to Germany and claimed he faced persecution that made him be accused of a fugitive militant by pro-government media.[43]

The *Erdem Gül and Can Dündar* case reflects the Court's journalism friendly approach, but still raises huge criticism by the government. It is also closely related to the aforementioned Cumhuriyet case where the relevant publication on weapons' transportation to Syria has been used again as evidence of support to terrorist organization FETÖ on the ground that the information stemmed from the news source of FETÖ infiltrated into the state bureaucracy and judiciary.[44] It remains to be seen how the Constitutional Court will

39 S. Girit, 'Turkish journalists charged with spying over weapons report', *BBC*, 26 October 2015.

40 *Erdem Gül ve Can Dündar Başvurusu*, Applic. No. 2015/18567, 25 February 2015.

41 'Constitutional Court releases detailed ruling on the release of Dündar, Gül', *Daily Sabah*, 9 March 2016.

42 C. Letsch, 'Turkish journalist Can Dündar jailed after surviving gun attack', *Guardian*, 6 May 2016.

43 'Fugitive Can Dündar a convict, spy, Erdoğan says', *Daily Sabah*, 28 September 2018; M. Altıok, 'Can Dündar in Germany: An innocent journalist or a fugitive militant?', *Daily Sabah*, 3 October 2018.

44 The evidence gathered by the prosecutors against the Cumhuriyet journalists consists of testimonials of a rival group who have been removed the administration of the daily, and publicly available materials such social media posts and newspaper clippings. Cumhuriyet case represents the landmark case against journalism with its large content of allegations and number of journalists accused in a collective action. During the trial process before the inferior court Cumhuriyet journalists were released from detention gradually, but at the end 13 journalists are sentenced to long imprisonments for up to more than 7 years. Currently, the case is in the appeal process. For international reactions see particularly the joint statement of the human rights and media organizations, including PEN International, the European Centre for Press and Media Freedom and the Association of European Journalists, 'Joint Statement denounces verdicts handed down at Cumhuriyet trial', Association of European Journalists, 5 May 2018, www.aej.org/page.asp?p_id=634. In Turkish journalism cases before the ECHR regarding pre-trial detention, the UN Special Rapporteur Professor David Kaye intervened under Art. 36 of the European Convention on Human Rights and Rule 44 of the Rules of the European Court of Human Rights, *see* 'Intervention of United Nations Special Rapporteur on the Promotion and Protection of the Right to Freedom of Opinion and Expression', 20 October 2017, www.ohchr.org/Documents/Issues/Expression/AmicusFiling-ECHR-Turkey-UNSR.pdf.

respond to the Cumhuriyet case if the ongoing appeal proceedings confirms the imprisonment of other Cumhuriyet journalists.

Considering the hostile environment against journalism and increasing number detained journalists, the Constitutional Court's role for the protection of free press is crucial. As evidence of its rising popularity in recent years stands the fact that in its individual application case-law after 2012 the Court has interpreted the freedom of expression in line with the ECHR as a fundamental for a democratic society. In general, in freedom of expression cases decided between 2012 and 2016, the Court extended the limits of free speech even in the controversial cases regarding the hate speech and publications of the imprisoned leader of Kurdish terrorist organization PKK, Abdullah Öcalan.[45] In the aforementioned *Erdem Gül and Can Dündar* case, the Court weighed the non-detention of journalists during the trials higher than the governmental concerns on national security, such as the protection of state secrets and the prevention of espionage. After the coup attempt in 2016, the Court seems to be hesitant to preserve its interpretation in other journalist cases. It does not grant them any priority in its agenda. It has responded belatedly in cases against the journalists despite the pre-trial detentions.[46]

The Court's late response has been in line with its previous pro-journalist case-law. It brought a sparking backlash of the lower courts and governmental actors.[47] The first instance courts claimed that the Constitutional Court exceeded its limits of review by assessing the evidence and therefore acted *ultra vires*. They questioned the binding force of the Court's decisions in the individual constitutional appeal cases. Consequently, the Constitutional Court had to release the second decision in respect of unconstitutionality of the lower courts' disobedience.[48] Due to disrespect of the first instance courts, Mehmet Altan, one of the journalists sentenced to aggravated life sentence for engaging in the coup attempt, was released by a regional appellate court, five months after the Constitutional Court rendered its decision.

After the Constitutional Court's disrespected case-law, the ECHR also delivered its own decision on the matter. In *Mehmet Hasan Altan v. Turkey*, the ECHR engaged in a dialogue with the findings of the Constitutional Court – regarding the lack of evidence other than articles and comments of the journalists – to draw attention to the issues of

---

45 *Sinem Hun Başvurusu*, Applic. No. 2013/5356, 8 May 2014; *Abdullah Öcalan Başvurusu*, Applic. No. 2013/409, 25 June 2014; *see also Bejdar Ro Amed Başvurusu*, Applic. No. 2013/7363, 16 April 2015; *Fatih Taş Başvurusu*, Applic. No. 2013/1461, 12 November 2014; *Mehmet Ali Aydın Başvurusu*, Applic. No. 2013/9343, 4 June 2015; *Mehmet Ayata Başvurusu*, Applic. No. 2013/2920, 7 July 2015.

46 *Şahin Alpay Başvurusu*, Applic. No. 2016/16092, 11 January 2018; *Mehmet Hasan Altan Başvurusu*, Applic. No. 2016/23672, 2016/23672, 11 January 2018.

47 'Courts Don't Release Alpay, Altan Despite Constitutional Court's Decision', *Bianet*, 12 January 2018, https://m.bianet.org/english/media/193240-courts-don-t-release-alpay-altan-despite-constitutional-court-s-decision; B. Çalı, 'Will Legalism be the End of Constitutionalism in Turkey?', *VerfBlog*, 22 January 2018, https://verfassungsblog.de/will-legalism-be-the-end-of-constitutionalism-in-turkey/.

48 *Şahin Alpay (2) Başvurusu*, Applic. No. 2018/3007, 15 March 2018.

silencing the dissent and intimidating the civic society.[49] Strikingly, the ECHR's role in Turkey's recent journalist cases under illiberal populist attack goes beyond the supervision of the European Convention on Human Rights. It maintains the functionality of the Constitutional Court against the disobedience crisis of the courts.[50] This crisis represents an unprecedented transgression form of the rule of law, as a constitutional disrespect in Turkey after the constitutional review was introduced in the 1961 Constitution.

10.4.3 *Criminal Law on Insulting the President of the State*

As a matter of chilling effect, the rise of illiberal populism in Turkey is depicted with the extensive use of the libel suits, particularly the criminal law on insulting the state president (Art. 299 of the Criminal Code). This law has been a seldom-used provision for many years. After President Erdoğan came to the office in 2014, the criminal prosecutions based on the law on insult of the state president have incomparably increased.

The relevant provision on insult prescribes a crime punishable by imprisonment up to four 4 years. There were 6,272 cases filed in the first two years of Erdoğan's presidency, between 2014 and 2016.[51] The total number of the cases filed between 2010 and 2014 was 588. In the period 2010-2016, a total of 1,315 cases resulted in convictions. Out of these 1,162 were rendered during Erdoğan's presidency. This unprecedented and systematic use of the criminal legislation against citizens including high school students, celebrities, opponent politicians and journalists is a new phenomenon in Turkish politics, perceived as a trend of weaponizing the law against dissents. The cases include a variety of insult allegations including not only real sense defamations, but also strong criticism of the state president or political satire. It is to be noted that these criminal convictions on insult have mostly resulted in the suspension of punishments, not in imprisonment. Such an extensive, but a mitigated application of insult provisions cannot be classified as a form of traditional oppression, but as a new pattern of illiberal populism. Here, the chilling effect is secured by the least intrusive judicial measure, namely the suspension of the punishment. However, the constant victim status of the state president as the subject of defamation is also secured in the eyes of his proponents.

Against the quantification of presidential insult cases, the strategic litigators have initiated concrete review of the insult legislation before the Constitutional Court. This could

49 *Mehmet Hasan Altan v. Turkey*, ECHR (2018), Applic. No. 13237/17, para. 207-208.

50 Additionally, the ECHR reiterates the chilling effect may be produced even when the detainee is subsequently acquitted *Mehmet Hasan Altan v. Turkey*, para. 212; *see also Ahmet Şık v. Turkey*, ECHR, (2014), Applic. No. 53413/11, para. 83.

51 For statistical data *see* K. Altıparmak & Y. Akdeniz, 'Turkey: Freedom of Expression in Jeopardy', *English Pen*, www.englishpen.org/wpcontent/uploads/2018/03/Turkey_Freedom_of_Expression_in_Jeopardy_ENG.pdf.

have been, in fact, an opportunity for the Court to deepen its own pro-libertarian interpretation on the freedom of expression. In its decision, the Court rejected the plea of unconstitutionality. It did not even provide the guidelines for the pro-libertarian constitutional interpretation of the relevant norm that could be insightful for the lower and apex courts.[52] Even though the Court recourses to such an interpretative canon in a similar fashion to *verfassungskonforme Auslegung* of German Federal Constitutional Court, it did not prefer to set standards of it despite the widespread use of insult legislation.[53] It did not either refer to its own principled approach adopted in the individual complaint case-law on freedom of expression as of 2012, which follows the case-law of the ECHR in a context-based analysis considering chilling effect.[54] According to the Court, criticism against public officers should not reach the defamatory level which would impair the honour and reputation of the individuals. The political criticism, its vital role in a constitutional democracy or the line between defamatory expressions and criticism are not matters of concern for the Court's assessment. Here, the Court reiterated its stance on criminal norms which esteems the discretionary power of the legislature to regulate the crimes and punishment. All in all, the Court's formalistic and isolated approach undermines the issue of tactical use and misinterpretation of criminal law by populist governments.

In the individual constitutional appeal proceedings regarding the insult, the Court declared the file as inadmissible by referring to the use of aggressive words targeting the personality of the state president.[55] The suspension of the punishment in the relevant case is interpreted as a proportional measure.

10.5 CONCLUSION

Turkish politics has long known a vast amount of populist strategies and preferences employed predominantly by right-wing governments. Confronted with these, the Constitutional Court has emerged as a decisive actor with three different roles: the game broker (till 2010), the populist (after 2010 constitutional amendments) and the popular actor

52 E. 2016/25, K. 2016/186, 14 December 2016.

53 For interpretation in conformity with the Constitution *see* E. 1984/8, K. 1984/10, 20 September 1984; E. 1984/9, K. 1985/4, 18 February 1985; E. 1988/63, K. 1989/47, 28 November 1989; E. 1990/36, K. 1991/8, 9 April 1991; E. 2002/108, K. 2004/55, 5 May 2004.

54 *Ergün Poyraz (2) Başvurusu*, Applic. No. 2013/8503, 27 October 2015, para. 79; *Erdem Gül ve Can Dündar Başvurusu*, para. 99; for the case-law of ECHR *see Goodwin v. United Kingdom*, ECHR (1996), Applic. No. 17488/90, para. 39; *Affaire Nedim Şener c. Turquie*, ECHR (2014), Applic. No. 38270/11, para. 122; *Ahmet Şık v. Turkey*, para. 111.

55 The offending words include 'the servants of fascist AK Party government', and 'thief and murder', *see Umut Kılıç Başvurusu*, Applic. No. 2015/16643, 4 April 2018; for refusal of the main opposition leader's violation claim as regards his offensive words against Erdoğan in a civil law case of compensation *see Kemal Kılıçdaroğlu Başvurusu*, Applic. No. 2014/1577, 25 October 2017.

alongside its populist stance (after the individual complaint mechanism was introduced in 2012). After the coup attempt in July 2016, the Court seems to have been more strategic and restrained in politically significant disputes in which it exercises a weak legislative review. In the individual constitutional appeal proceedings, it has exercised a stronger review, possible to correct its weak approach in the politically sensitive cases. This stance of the Court resulted in a limited model of horizontal accountability. The individual complaint procedure serves, however, as an incidental remedy responding to the lack of horizontal accountability.

Considering the approval of the recent constitutional amendment in Turkey that introduces a major shift from the parliamentary system to a sort of presidentialism,[56] one may expect from the Court to play a pivotal role in the new balance of powers. The amendment provides extensive powers for the president with limited parliamentary control. Furthermore, the referendum process itself has consolidated the populist rule in Turkey in which an intense polarization prevails. The amendment was adopted by a very narrow margin (Yes votes 51.41% and No votes 48.59%). The snap elections in June 2018 confirmed the deeply divided tendencies of voters: the electoral alliance of AK Party and nationalist party MHP von 53.70%, and President Erdoğan 52.5% of votes. The Court has to operate in this divided political environment with consolidated majoritarianism of the electoral alliance and the new presidentialism.

Under this new balance of powers, it is unlikely that the Court will emerge as a strong game broker once again. Here, the Court's review regarding the presidential decrees is to be examined carefully in the near future to assess the executive-judiciary relations. The presidential decrees provided by the new system can be enacted without statutory authorization. Their validity against the statutory legislation, however, is open to challenge before the Court by parliamentary minority due to vague provisions of the Constitution.

The Court's recent case-law mentioned above signals that it can sustain a strategic and decisionist approach in the context of the strong presidency and populist pressures. Accordingly, it may prefer not to clash with presidential preferences and the parliament in abstract or concrete review by sacrificing the horizontal accountability, but refrain at the same time from supporting these institutions to the same degree in the individual complaint procedure.

56 B. E. Oder, 'Turkey's ultimate shift to a presidential system: the most recent constitutional amendments in details', *ConstitutionNet*, 31 January 2017, www.constitutionnet.org/news/turkeys-ultimate-shift-presidential-system-most-recent-constitutional-amendments-details.

11 Romania: From Constitutional Democracy to Constitutional Decay?

Simina Tanasescu[*]

11.1 Introduction

Amid iterative failed attempts to revise the Constitution in order to set the balance of powers differently and under populist threats for its still consolidating democracy, Romania seems to follow an already existing pattern in fragile democracies and has recently reverted to a last resort instrument in order to defend democracy and rule of law, namely civil society. What sets Romania aside from other countries is the unusual attitude adopted by its Constitutional Court, which is the undisputed ultimate arbiter in constitutional matters but whose latest practice has succeeded to worry a recently awaken civil society. Can constitutional adjudication become an instrument of judicial populism? The answer seems to be affirmative in the case of Romania, where the gap between the civil society and the judicial system, which both display remarkable resilience towards populism and the Constitutional Court, which continuously enhances its compliance with populism, deepens day by day.

11.2 On Populism and Constitutional Democracy

Despite the chameleonic nature of the word, populism[1] has been increasingly studied as of lately, by political scientists[2] and constitutionalists[3] as well. A lot of empirical studies,

---

* Professor, University of Bucharest.

1 The etymology of the word populism is the Latin word *populus*, meaning people. Dictionaries define the term 'populism' as a belief in the power of regular people. A secondary meaning, specifically in political science, refers to a political discourse that opposes moral people to immoral elites and proclaims the superiority of the political will of that righteous people upon any other possible political will (dissident, marginal, plural *etc.*).

2 J. W. Muller, *What is Populism?*, University of Pennsylvania Press, Philadelphia, 2016; B. Moffit, *The Global Rise of Populism: Performance, Political Style, and Representation*, Stanford University, Stanford, 2016; Y. Mounk, *The People vs. Democracy – Why our Freedom is in Danger & How to Save It*, Harvard University Press, Cambridge/MA, 2018.

3 C. Pinelli, 'The Populist Challenge to Constitutional Democracy', *European Constitutional Law Review*, Vol. 7, No. 1, 2011, pp. 5-16; L. Corrias, 'Populism in a Constitutional Key: Constituent Power, Popular Sovereignty, and Constitutional Identity', *European Constitutional Law Review*, Vol. 12, No. 1, 2016, pp. 6-26.

particularly in political and social sciences, focused on the description of populist movements in specific countries, ultimately attempting to present a global theory on populism. Although different on many accounts, the main features that various authors identified as characteristic for populism, are an authoritarian exercise of power based on the claim of a genuine representation of the people; disdain towards elites and establishment; anti-pluralism in all societal and political debates; a tendency to colonize and capture all state institutions in order to get entrenched power and then openly oppose democracy and rational legal constraints imposed by constitutionalism.

Populism requires a *pars pro toto* argument and a claim to exclusive representation, with both understood in a moral, as opposed to empirical, sense. There can be no populism, in other words, without someone speaking in the name of the people as a whole.[4]

From this principled anti-pluralism derives authoritarianism and therefore disregard for norms and institutions. This last feature deserves keen consideration from the point of view of constitutional theorists, as one common denominator of all empirical analysis of the phenomenon of populism is the threat that it poses to democracy and constitutionalism.

For the purpose of this chapter, constitutionalism refers to the theory that explains why and how state authority derives from and is limited by a fundamental law called Constitution. Descriptive observations and prescriptive statements of numerous authors support the idea that constitutions are necessary elements in contemporary democracies due to the functions they perform, namely they create and frame state powers thus protecting fundamental rights. Associated with various other attributes, the word constitutionalism is most often related to the apparently antithetic concept of democracy, which refers to a system of government where citizens exercise power directly. The paradoxical antinomy between constitutionalism and democracy only enjoys a superficial plausibility: nothing in the contemporary definition of democracy allows the view that citizens should exercise power free of any constraints and particularly without any regard to rules that they have imposed on state authority. On the contrary, democracy needs Constitution because the fundamental law makes possible the predictability of democratic behaviours and, through its own permanence and stability, it allows for public consent to grow and consolidate, thus entrenching cohesion and solidarity within society and, ultimately, democracy itself. Constitutional democracy encapsulates the legal expression of the self-limitation of the will of the people performed in order to allow for freedom, equality and pluralism to flourish.

The threat posed by populism to constitutional democracy is easily noticeable but not easy to decorticate from a legal analytical point of view. One area where this tension is most obvious refers to the relation between populist claims against elites and legal norms

4 Muller, 2016, p. 20.

created by them and the role played in any constitutional democracy by courts as technocratic guardians of legality and protectors of fundamental rights. Thus, courts – and particularly constitutional courts which derive their legitimacy not from direct popular vote but from the Constitution – can easily be labelled as elitist institutions obstructing populist governments and opposing their policies. Scholars have already noticed that experiences of thc global South, particularly of Latin America, might become relevant for other countries facing conflicts between apex/constitutional courts and populist governments.[5] More generally, abusive constitutionalism[6] and sham constitutions[7] partly address the same issue, namely the way in which constitutional design of contemporary democracies is able to display resilience in the face of the rise of populism across the globe. Thus, by performing their role of upholding the basic principles and constitutional guarantees, courts are opposing unrestrained populist governments and may easily become their target. In fact, situations where apex/constitutional courts have been reshuffled or packed in order to be neutered have already been registered around the world and their survival strategies have been scrutinized by legal scholarship.[8]

It follows that the role of courts is and remains important in relation to populism, although the substance matter of this role may vary: courts can be an important element of resistance against populism or they can succumb to judicial populism and merely support the populists in power. These two alternatives are not simply opposite in practice as they tend to be in theory.

At a theoretical level, resistance of courts against populism can be framed by the now classic controversy between Hans Kelsen and Carl Schmitt,[9] or by the well-known counter-majoritarian argument[10] or, still, by the tension between political and technocratic approaches towards societal issues and public policies. Depending on the argument fol-

5 A. Arato, 'Populism and the Courts', *VerfBlog*, 25 April 2017, https://verfassungsblog.de/populism-and-the-courts/.

6 D. Landau, 'Abusive Constitutionalism', *UC Davis Law Review*, Vol. 47, 2013, pp. 189-261.

7 D. S. Law & M. Versteeg, 'Sham Constitutions', *California Law Review*, Vol. 101, No. 4, 2013, pp. 863-952.

8 B. Petkova, 'Populism and Judicial Backlash in the United States and Europe', *VerfBlog*, 30 April 2017, https://verfassungsblog.de/populism-and-judicial-backlash-in-the-united-states-and-europe/.

9 All through his writings Hans Kelsen strongly supported constitutional review as performed by a constitutional court, although he agreed that judges of constitutional courts will inevitably be confronted with political decisions, but he defended the view that even in such situations their decision will be based on rational legal arguments. According to Kelsen, there is no such thing as people's will. One can only know the result of elections and any organic conception of the unity or coherence of the people are mere 'metapolitical illusions'. *See* P. Pasquino, & H. Kelsen: Verfassungsgerichtbarkeit und demokratietheorie, *in* O. Beaud & P. Pasquino (Eds.), *La controverse sur "le gardien de la Constitution" et la justice constitutionnelle. Kelsen contre Schmitt*, Editions Panthéon Assas, Paris, 2007, p. 30. At the opposite, Carl Schmitt considered that constitutional courts can only transform justice into politics and not *vice versa* and maintained that popular will prevails on legal interpretation and even on the Constitution. *See* C. Schmitt, *Théorie de la Constitution*, Quadrige/PUF, Paris, 1993, p. 377 *et seq.*

10 A. Bickel, *The Least Dangerous Branch: The Supreme Court at the Bar of Politics*, The Bobbs-Merrill Company, New York, 1962.

lowed, courts, and particularly apex and/or constitutional courts, can be considered as a key factor in the response given by legally constituted expert institutions to populist threats on constitutional democracy. But recent research has it that courts, indeed, just like other independent institutions belonging to a state governed by the rule of law, are critical but no longer sufficient to protect constitutionalism from populism.[11] The role of courts in a constitutional democracy consists of protecting the fundamental rights mostly by balancing powers in accordance with the Constitution. If this general framework changes, courts can be severely impaired and their democratic role may be compromised. Legal and political culture, historical context and many other softer variables can impact greatly on the effectiveness of their resistance towards populism, potentially bringing courts to a point where they reach an altogether different attitude, namely judicial populism.

Judicial populism[12] does not necessarily equate with support for populists in power in a given state and is not always contradictory to constitutional democracy. Political scientists have shown that judicial review regularly translates deeply held popular convictions into positive constitutional law. And awareness of public choices or accountability of judges may be factors to weigh-in in a constitutional democracy. But external and cumulative pressures on an independent judiciary, or packing apex/constitutional courts with judges favourable to populists in power, may prove to be efficient tools meant to curb their resistance and limit their action against those very populists. Such practices are not unheard of recently, in several parts of the world, and they have an influence on the effectiveness with which courts perform their role in a constitutional democracy. Although it has been argued that "opposing popular regimes in the long run is not an option",[13] and even if in some particular instances judicial populism has been interpreted as tactics meant to protect courts from direct political influences, in order to allow them a margin of manoeuvre, intended to preserve their role as defenders of fundamental rights, at a more general view, such an attitude inevitably ends up by weakening court at large, as well as their role in a democratic society. In a constitutional democracy courts should protect the separation of power as enshrined by the Constitution, that is to say that courts have to make sure that nor the legislative neither the executive can assume and monopolize popular sovereignty and that both have to respect fundamental rights as legally preserved and not as subjectively interpreted by popular will incarnated by populists. If instituted powers – such as the legislative or the executive – get to impose their views on the popular sovereign and manage to overcome the democratic constituent power, irrespective of the fact whether this may have been accomplished with or without the blessing of the courts, the impact of the

11 K. L. Scheppele, 'Parliamentary Supplements (or Why Democracies Need More than Parliaments)', *Boston University Law Review*, Vol. 89, No. 2, 2009, pp. 795-826.

12 J. González-Jácome, 'In Defense of Judicial Populism: Lessons from Colombia', *I·CONnect*, www.iconnect-blog.com/2017/05/in-defense-of-judicial-populism-lessons-from-colombia/.

13 *Id.*

judiciary on democracy is void of meaning and the loss of confidence of citizens in the role, importance and even independence of judges may be in danger. Indeed, courts cannot simply ignore popular beliefs and public opinion. Their power resides as much in the rationality of the legal arguments which support a judicial decision as in the people's consent to obey the law. But judges cannot afford to ignore or disrespect law even more than public opinion and that confronts them with a choice which should not be considered difficult – between legality and populism. Although there may be a difference in ultimately reverting to the judicial respect of public opinion and simply supporting populist views through court decisions, in the end the role of courts in constitutional democracies can suffer from such strategies. And the danger looms large particularly in transitional or fragile democracies.[14]

11.3 Romania: A Still Fragile Democratic Transition

Romania can be considered a still consolidating democracy. Following the popular upraise in December 1989, an entirely new Constitution was adopted on 8 December 1991. This fundamental law designed a semi-presidential system of government, with a directly elected president and a government appointed by the president, based on a vote of confidence by a bicameral Parliament (Chamber of Deputies and Senate), political pluralism and a multiparty system generated by a proportional type of electoral formula, and an almost perfect parliamentary bicameralism. The revision of the Constitution in 2003 changed from 4 to 5 years the duration of the mandate of the president and introduced a functional differentiation between the two houses of Parliament, while maintaining an identical electoral system for deputies and senators.

Electoral legislation conserved the proportional representation for parliamentary elections held in 1992, 1996, 2000 and 2004 and reverted again to this electoral system from 2016 to the date. Elections organized in 2008 and 2012 were based on a so-called uninominal system, in fact a proportional representation disguised in circumscriptions divided into electoral colleges where several mandates were distributed. All elections resulted in several political parties represented in Parliament and determined coalition governments. Turnover in elections has constantly and consistently decreased since the beginning of the democratic transition. The following figures (figures 11.1 and 11.2) illustrate this general tendency, with results publicly presented by the Central Electoral Bureau[15] at the end of each electoral process.

14 *See* S. Issacharoff, *Fragile Democracies – Contested Power in the Era of Constitutional Courts*, Cambridge University Press, Cambridge, 2015.

15 www.2016bec.ro/index.html and www.roaep.ro/istoric/.

Figure 11.1 Turnover in parliamentary elections (%)

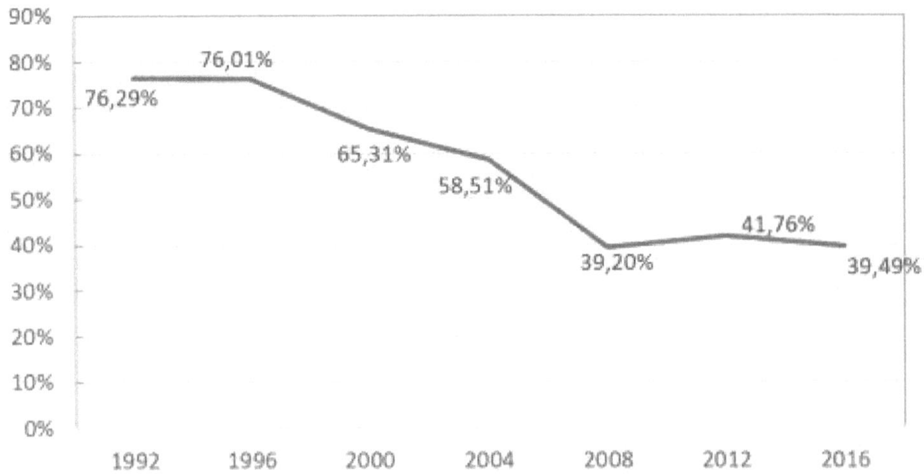

The turnover at the last round of national and local elections illustrates the lack of interest of citizens in traditional tools of political representation, with the noticeable exception of presidential elections and even there, only in the second round.

Figure 11.2 Turnover in last national and local elections (%)

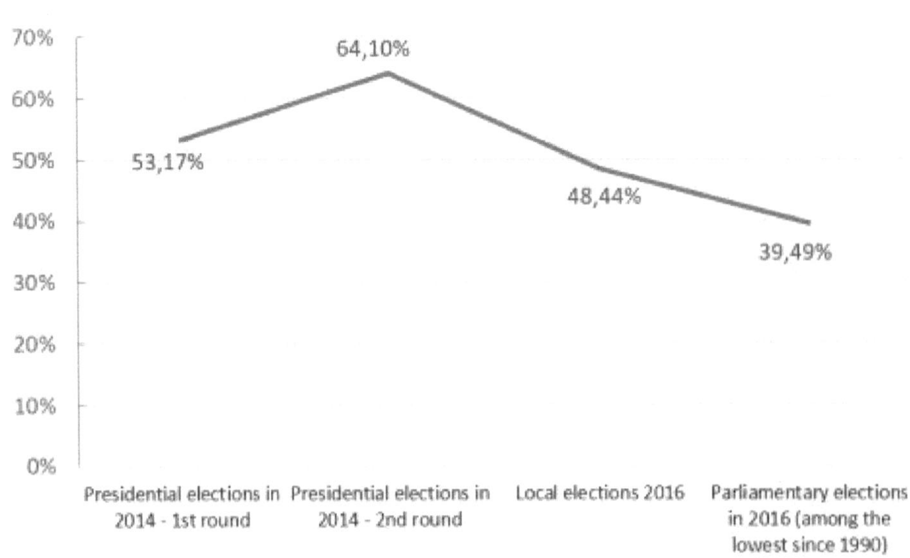

Two recent attempts to revise the political regime introduced by the 1991 Constitution have failed. As an expression of the crisis of political representation, both efforts intended to replace the semi-presidential system either with a presidential or with a parliamentary one.[16] Neither of them has reached the stage of parliamentary debates and each time presidential elections have taken centre stage before the electorate could have a chance of understanding their scope and signifying its preference.

The disillusion of citizens with classical constitutional democracy did not pass unnoticed. An NGO,[17] created initially in order to defend community interests in urban planning within the capital Bucharest, transformed itself into a political party in 2015 and managed to get almost 9% of seats in Parliament in 2016.

Following the parliamentary elections in December 2016, a coalition formed of a political party considered to be on the left of the political spectrum (Social-Democratic Party, won 46% of seats in Parliament) and the another one declared liberal (Alliance of Liberals and Democrats, won 6% of seats in Parliament), supported an executive that started to implement a populist agenda. Confirming patterns[18] noticed elsewhere as well, populist actions concerned first the redistribution of the national wealth through economic measures of apparent empowerment of the poor, who were only to discover later that inflation eroded their purchasing power and continued with systemic reforms of the judiciary and other strategic areas, while maintaining a public discourse in praise of majoritarian (as opposed to consensual) democracy and morally nationalistic values and identifying enemies particularly in independent and/or cosmopolitan institutions.

Thus, among the measures implemented in 2017 and 2018 are increases of salaries in the public sector and of some pensions coupled with the reduction of taxes on revenues, of some social contributions and the elimination of some taxes (*e.g.*, taxes pertaining to urban planning). A popular initiative for the revision of the Constitution in order to explicitly eliminate the possibility of marriage between same sex persons has been adopted with a comfortable majority in one of the houses of Parliament and is currently awaiting

16 E. S. Tanasescu, 'Conflicting Revisions to Romanian Constitution Give Rise to Questions about Semi-Presidentialism', *in* D. Liao, Y. Shen, & Y. Wu (Eds.), *Semi-Presidentialism Across Continents: A Dialogue Between Asia and Europe*, Wunan Books, Taipei, 2015, pp. 57-87.

17 Building upon the popular support gained for its activities against the City Hall of Bucharest, which finally managed to demolish old private and public buildings in order to draw a new boulevard, the NGO *Uniunea Salvati Bucurestiul* (Save Bucharest Union) transformed itself into a political party towards the end of 2015 and participated in local elections in June 2016. After a new metamorphosis into a political party of national relevance and a consequent change of its official denomination, *Uniunea Salvati România* (Save Romania Union) got spectacular results in parliamentary elections of 2016.

18 Yascha Mounk offers a good description of how a democracy can be dismantled by populists, starting with a genuine popular grievance against the economic situation, which may prove difficult for some layers of the population, continuing with populists identifying enemies (preferable non-nationals) for angry voters to blame, gaining popular support and (sometimes frail) majorities in elections in order to allow populists to grab power and from then on the capture of the state is ensured via systemic reforms of strategic areas that will allow them to remain in power indefinitely. *See* Mounk, 2018.

approval in the second house, despite a decision of the Constitutional Court declaring unconstitutional the parliamentary procedure followed in this specific case. A 'sovereign' discourse has been adopted with regard to the European Union. Last but not least, important reforms of the judicial system and in particular of the criminal legislation have been initiated and, partly, they already succeeded, despite fierce opposition from the judiciary itself, civil society and remaining independent authorities such as the Romanian President.

11.4 Can Constitutional Adjudication Become an Instrument of Judicial Populism?

These developments seem to follow a pattern that is not new in Eastern Europe or Latin America.[19] Nor is the concentrated attack on the judicial system a feature specific only to Romania. What is peculiar in the Romanian case is the ease and speed with which such transformations took place and the obedience displayed by the Constitutional Court in embracing judicial populism in a context that can be considered inducing but not obliging to this type of attitude. The compliance of the Constitutional Court with populist requirements did not start with parliamentary elections of 2016. Both, in litigation on fundamental rights and in litigation on the separation of powers, the Court started to display signs of judicial populism years before, but it was packed in an activist attitude that could disguise its appetite for power grabbing under the shape of an in-fight with the rest of the judiciary.[20] Over time, its support for the populist policies of the government installed towards the end of 2016 became clearer. A few examples may help to understand this judicial transfiguration, which came without any packing, reshuffling or visible political pressure.

---

19 Andrew Arato has suggestively described the situation in the following terms: "The common neglect of populism in government reveals a very important feature of the phenomenon itself: even when in political power populist leaders (and their supporters) imagine themselves to be still outside and opposed to it, fighting what is now often called a deep state and its inherited institutions: the bureaucracy, the security services, plutocrats and yes, generally the courts as well. We have seen this peculiar self-understanding surface in all the cases mentioned, including recently in the United States. External political actors and institutions can also be cast in the same role as in the case of many European populists, even before they enter government, focusing their attacks on the EU Commission as well as the European Court of Justice." *See* Arato, 2017.

20 E. S. Tanasescu, 'The Romanian Constitutional Judge: Lost in Transition', *in* M. Jovanovic (Ed.), *Constitutional Review and Democracy*, Eleven International Publishing, The Hague, 2015, pp. 223-252.

11.4.1 *Deriding Fundamental Rights*

On the protection of fundamental rights, the Romanian Constitutional Court proved at best ambiguous. Confronted with a popular initiative, meant to revise the Constitution in order to alter the definition of marriage from 'freely consented marriage of the spouses' into 'freely consented marriage between a man and a woman' – as intended by the Coalition for the Family (a pan-European NGO) – the Court decided that such a revision is consistent with the eternity clause of the Romanian Constitution, which only forbids revisions that suppress fundamental rights or their safeguards. In its decision No. 580/2016, the Court noted that the popular initiative refers to the legal institution of marriage, as regulated by Article 48, and not to family life, protected by Article 26 of the Constitution. Therefore, it argued that the initiative does not suppress the right to marriage, while leaving intact the respect of the private, intimate and family life. The Court did not address separately and explicitly the suppression of a safeguard of the right to marriage as provided by the current version of Article 48 of the Constitution. Indeed, although the Civil Code does not provide for the possibility of persons of the same gender to get married, the Constitution allows for a gender-neutral interpretation of the concept of spouses, thus safeguarding potential same-sex marriages and leaving room of manoeuvre for a future change of the relevant legislation. Mixing biology with arguments extracted from an originalist interpretation of the Constitution that entrenches an *ad hoc* grounded constitutional identity of Romania based on moral and/or religious foundations, the Constitutional Court simply eluded the last part of the eternity clause enshrined in the fundamental law and made possible an unconstitutional revision of the Constitution.

The parliamentary procedure for this revision of the Constitution started in September 2016, when the popular initiative was registered with the Senate and should have been approved or rejected there. However, the Senate did not pursue and, through an *ad hoc* procedure with no precedent or pre-existing written norm, it sent the bill to the Chamber of Deputies on an administrative basis. A month later, the Senate also altered its standing order to make it compliant with the *ad hoc* procedure created in this specific case. Meanwhile, the Chamber of Deputies adopted the bill with the majority needed for a revision of the Constitution (two-thirds of its members) and sent the bill to the Senate. The irregularity of this entire situation was notified to the Constitutional Court, which – in its decision No. 431/2017 – found the alteration of the standing order of the Senate unconstitutional, but failed to specify the consequences this might have on the procedure so far undertaken and, indeed, on the overall process of the revision of the Constitution. All along the spring of 2018, the political majority in Parliament claimed it would organize a referendum in order to find out the choice of Romanians on same-sex marriage, and thus defeat the resistance of the opposition instead of simply pursuing the parliamentary procedure for the revision of the Constitution. Against this background the fact that the referendum organised on the 6th and 7th of October could not be validated due to the low turnover is telling for the contradiction between the vision of the Constitutional Court and the vision of the population with regard to the fundamental rights at stake.

Thus, the ambiguity of this specific revision of the Constitution persists, and, in the process, the Constitutional Court has not been instrumental neither for the protection of fundamental rights, nor for societal pluralism, not even in comforting majoritarian trends or social mores that could justify popular consent for its case law. Its ambivalence with regard to values and procedures, coupled with apparent self-restraint that did not allow it to articulate the very legal consequences of its own decisions, contributed to the public perception that the Constitutional Court was not acting as a guardian of the Constitution.

The possibility of judicial populism looms large and it displeases all social groups with vested interests in the matter. As it happens everywhere, when a Constitutional Court pronounces its view of the Constitution, it is equally possible that it triggers controversy just as it may put an end to it, but it is important to remember that court decisions are not necessarily a final word on a specific issue. The power of courts depends on the force of their arguments, and constitutional controversies are finally settled only when the citizens accept their wisdom and the solution offered, not simply when courts have spoken. From this perspective, both decisions of the Romanian Constitutional Court on the issue of same-sex marriage are neither innovative in rights adjudication, nor meant to end societal controversy around the issue at stake, while still failing to secure popular consent. If their intention was to comfort majoritarian trends within the Romanian society, at large their success remains mitigated.

11.4.2 Disdaining Checks and Balances

On the separation of powers, a restrictive selection of recent decisions of the Constitutional Court, with impact on the judicial system, may explain the public questioning of its institutional legitimacy and systemic integrity. The political context is not void of interest. Within a fortnight after it was installed, in January 2017, the executive adopted an emergency ordinance decriminalizing some deeds related to corruption. The justification put forward was referring to an imminent conviction of Romania by the European Court of Human Rights due to the dramatic conditions of its prisons. Emergency ordinances are acts of delegated legislation[21] that the executive can adopt without explicit delegation from

21 Art. 115 of the Romanian Constitution provides: "(1) Parliament may pass a special law enabling the Government to issue ordinances in fields outside the scope of organic laws. (2) The enabling law shall compulsorily establish the field and the date up to which ordinances may be issued. (3) If the enabling law so requests, ordinances shall be submitted to Parliament for approval, according to the legislative procedure, until the expiry of the enabling time limit. Non-compliance with the term entails discontinuation of the effects of the ordinance. (4) The Government can only adopt emergency ordinances in exceptional cases,

Parliament, but only in exceptional cases, the regulation of which cannot be postponed. Emergency ordinances come into force immediately, although later they must be debated upon and approved or rejected by Parliament through a law.

Faced with an explicit opposition from the President of Romania, strong resistance from the judicial system and confronted with mass protests of citizens against what has been perceived as a blow against the fight against corruption, the government abrogated the respective emergency ordinance days after its approval.

However, the Superior Council of Magistracy and the President of Romania lodged institutional complaints with the Constitutional Court, asking it to sanction the executive for abuse of power, as it intruded an area (criminal law) where, according to the Romanian Constitution, even the legislator can regulate only with the absolute majority of MPs and after appropriate consideration and full respect of several procedural requirements. The Constitutional Court rejected all complaints and declared that government did not infringe the legislative powers of Parliament when adopting the respective emergency ordinance. Decisions No. 63/2017 and No. 64/2017 did not address the substantive matter of the emergency ordinance, which could have given the Court the opportunity to reach this type of conclusion. Instead, they were mere nominal interpretations of the constitutional requirements provided by Article 115 for legislative delegation and of the powers of the Constitutional Court.

This formalistic approach was probably meant to present the solution under a technocratic cover and underline the self-restraint of the Court. Public opinion perceived a lack of democratic debate on important issues for the public community and continued mass demonstrations. Prosecutors started to investigate potential misdeeds related to the adoption of that emergency ordinance. The follow-up was decision No. 68/2017, in which the Constitutional Court found that prosecutors could not investigate the way in which normative acts were adopted; it also ruled that, when adopting (delegated) legislation, ministers enjoyed the same immunity as MPs. This time the Constitutional Court proceeded

the regulation of which cannot be postponed, and have the obligation to give the reasons for the emergency status within their contents. (5) An emergency ordinance shall only come into force after it has been submitted for debate in an emergency procedure to the Chamber having the competence to be notified, and after it has been published in the Official Gazette of Romania. If not in session, the Chambers shall be convened by all means within 5 days after submittal, or, as the case may be, after forwarding. If, within 30 days at the latest of the submitting date, the notified Chamber does not pronounce on the ordinance, the latter shall be deemed adopted and shall be sent to the other Chamber, which shall also make a decision in an emergency procedure. An emergency ordinance containing norms of the same kind as the organic law must be approved by a majority stipulated under article 76 (1). (6) Emergency ordinances cannot be adopted in the field of constitutional laws, or affect the status of fundamental institutions of the State, the rights, freedoms and duties stipulated in the Constitution, the electoral rights, and cannot establish steps for transferring assets to public property forcibly. (7) The ordinances the Parliament has been notified about shall be approved or rejected in a law which must also contain the ordinance that ceased to be effective according to paragraph (3). (8) The law approving or rejecting an ordinance shall regulate, if such is the case, the necessary steps concerning the legal effects caused while the ordinance was in force."

with a substantive interpretation of constitutional requirements for legislative delegation and found that only Parliament can appreciate the opportunity of delegated legislation, while prosecutors and courts have to comply with the legal framework as adopted by the legislative and/or the executive. This explicit support of the discretionary powers of the legislator, be it Parliament or government, and contempt for the express provisions of the Constitution, which encloses procedural and substantive limits for the legislative action, has contributed to the public perception that the Constitutional Court became instrumental for the political majority in Parliament. Within approximately one month from the official instalment of a populist government and without any packing, reshuffling, change of internal procedures of visible political pressures, the guardian of the Constitution started to dither in performing its functions and to rubber-stamp populist policies instead. This could have been a short-lived tactic in order to achieve greater goals, but further evolutions proved this premise to be false.

In June 2017, the Constitutional Court adopted an internal regulation in order to draw "the limits in which a constitutional judge may exercise his/her legal right to write a dissenting or concurring opinion", forbidding separate opinions that are not explicitly approved by the President of the Constitutional Court. Being an administrative act, this internal regulation has been challenged in administrative review and invalidated by regular courts in June 2018. However, *de facto* separate opinions have almost disappeared from the case law of the Constitutional Court.

Last but not the least, decision No. 358/2018 is practically an injunction to the President of Romania, who is summoned to dismiss the head of the chief-prosecutor on anticorruption because a member of the executive (the minister of justice) asked him to do so. Practically, despite the fact that the procedure for appointment and dismissal of chief prosecutors is provided by law and not by the Constitution thus making the Constitutional Court non-competent to deal with the substance matter at stake, and against the plain letter of the law ascribing a procedure where the minister of justice is empowered to make proposals, the Superior Council of Magistracy has to deliver an expert opinion on the initiative of the minister, and the President of Romania has to reach a decision based on all these elements, the Constitutional Court found that the proposal of the minister of justice is binding for all other public authorities involved in the process.

To reach this conclusion, the Court delved into a remarkable number of important questions of constitutional law, stretching concepts specific to a state governed by the rule of law to extremes that remind of abusive constitutionalism performed by the guardian of the Constitution through unconstitutional interpretations of the Fundamental Law. For instance, it declared that the content of the presidential decree of dismissal cannot be reviewed by administrative courts, as an entire legal theory has it since the adoption of the Constitution in 1991, and judicial practice has validated on numerous occasions, but it can only be subject to parliamentary control. However, the Court failed to mention the precise procedure or instrument that Parliament would have to use in order to ensure this original type of checks and balances. It also declared that, despite his direct legitimacy, the President of Romania enjoys no discretionary powers in issuing such a decree, whereas the minister of justice relishes a larger marge of manoeuvre in making this type of proposal because his powers derive directly from the Constitution. Nevertheless, the Court also failed to indicate the legal basis or, indeed, legal argument which allows a minister, member in a collective cabinet vested through a vote of confidence by Parliament, to display a larger decision-making power than a head of the state voted directly by citizens. The Court offered an interpretation of the constitutional provision which places the activity of prosecutors under the principle of legality, impartiality and hierarchical control, under the authority of the minister of justice,[22] according to which prosecutors are subordinated to the minister of justice, thus denying their functional autonomy. Scholars have glossed a while on this decision[23] but, eventually, they have been submerged by later evolutions of the constitutional case law, which proves that the distinction between constitutional review and the power to revise the fundamental law, including through unconstitutional interpretation, is no longer clear.

Indeed, all along 2018 an impressive number of decisions of the Constitutional Court have constantly validated the manner, substance and goals of the all-encompassing reform of the judicial system initiated by the populist government in place, irrespective of the legal or constitutional arguments against this reform put forward by the opposition in Parliament, by the judicial system itself or by the President of Romania.[24] In 2018, it became clear that the judicial populism displayed by the Constitutional Court over the previous two years was not an elusive tactic.

This attitude of the Constitutional Court contradicts the global approach taken by the judicial system, *i.e.* regular courts, the Supreme Court of the land and Superior Council of Magistracy, and remains difficult to understand, particularly when contrasted with the defiance displayed by the civil society over the same period of time. Early in 2017, in reaction to the now infamous emergency ordinance, more than 500,000 citizens have demonstrated in front of the government during a harsh winter, with temperatures reaching -20°C and continued to do so even long after the delegated legislation had been repelled by its author. The judicial invalidation of the internal regulation of the Constitutional Court forbidding separate opinions is the result of a case initiated by an individual lawyer on the basis of the law guaranteeing public access to information of public interest.

22 Art. 132 provides: "(1) Public prosecutors shall carry out their activity in accordance with the principle of legality, impartiality and hierarchical control, under the authority of the Minister of Justice. (2) The office of public prosecutor is incompatible with any other public or private office, except academic activities."

23 B. S. Gutan, 'The Taming of the Court – When Politics Overcome Law in the Romanian Constitutional Court', *VerfBlog*, 6 June 2018, https://verfassungsblog.de/author/bianca-selejan-gutan/.

24 *See* decisions No. 33/2018, No. 45/2018, No. 61/2018, No. 65/2018, No. 66/2018, No. 67/2018, No. 250/2018, No. 252/2018, No. 251/2018, No. 357/2018, No. 385/2018, No. 417/2018.

And the reform of the judicial system has kept citizens in the street for more than one year. Not just regular citizens became active, but a whole plethora of intermediate bodies (NGOs, forums, networks) have been created or stirred up by the idea of the need to resist attacks such as those described above on constitutional democracy.

11.5 Concluding Remarks

The remarkable resilience of the Romanian civil society, constantly supporting the independence of justice, stands in stark contrast to the compliance of the Constitutional Court to populist decisions. What could have been a path towards anarchy became a method to cure populism as one of the "pathologies of modern popular sovereignty".[25] In spite of claims of the current Romanian government that it enjoys large popular support and that its policies are meant to service the majority of citizens, who oppose elites, experts, deep state or any other designated enemy, the reality on the ground showed a different picture. While the discourse of those in power often resorts to a sort of plebiscitary legitimacy, interpreted in a radical majoritarian fashion, constantly reverting to the results of the last national elections as they could have granted government a wild card to perform anything in an arbitrary manner, lots of mediating institutions within the state proved active in holding government accountable between elections and independently of their results. Organized civil society regularly makes use of transparency and mass demonstrations, while regular courts still perform their function of balancing powers in order to protect individual rights.

Against this background, the expansion of populist strategies at the level of the Romanian Constitutional Court, without the usual pressures that have been observed elsewhere, casts doubts about its independence and systemic integrity, while questioning its role in relation to constitutional democracy. Through the constant validation of a systematic weakening of checks and balances, the Constitutional Court is contributing to the constitutional capture[26] or constitutional decay[27] of constitutional democracy in Romania. Although this damaging process has not yet reached the stage of irreversibility, judicial populism, selective as it may appear to be, is likely to accelerate the phenomenon.

The presentation of the evolution of populism in Romania has to take into account what has become a pattern for populist governments all across the world. While the role of courts in relation to populism remains important everywhere, their mere functioning

25 P. Ronsanvalon, *Counter-Democracy*, Cambridge University Press, Cambridge, 2008, pp. 265-729.

26 J.-W. Müller, 'Rising to the Challenge of Constitutional Capture – Protecting the Rule of Law Within EU Member States', *Eurozine*, 21 March 2014.

27 T. G. Daly, 'Enough Complacency: Fighting Democratic Decay', *I·CONnect*, www.iconnect-blog.com/2017/01/enough-complacency-fighting-democratic-decay-in-2017-i-connect-column/.

is no longer sufficient for the survival of constitutional democracy as they become one of the main targets of populist threats. The awakening of civil society in support of judiciary's independence becomes vital and this trend has been noticed in Romania as well amid criticism of potential counter-democratic manifestations. What is peculiar in the Romanian case, is the speed with which populism managed to corrupt the state, in spite of a vivid civil society and the gap created within the judiciary between a Constitutional Court overtly and, at times, even proactively prone to judicial populism and the rest of the judicial system, which is still resilient in front of constitutional decay.

12 If Schmitt Were Alive ... Adjusting Constitutional Review to Populist Rule in Serbia

*Violeta Beširević**

12.1 Introduction

It has already been some time that populism has returned to political arena worldwide. Although populism means different things for different people, there are no doubts that populist politics reveals the growing vulnerability of constitutionalism. Thus, it is generally agreed that populists have been persistently (and successfully) eroding what Rosalyn Dixon and David Landau call "substantive 'minimum core' of democracy": commitments to free and fair elections, the separation of powers, fundamental rights and governmental accountability.[1] However, the aim of this chapter is not to join an open discussion on what populism stands for. Instead, the focus will be on the issue of whether courts can confront populism.

In conventional democracies, constitutional review is the logical companion of a constitution and competitive political system. It is established with an aspiration to secure the basic goals to which democracy is streaming: the supremacy of the constitution, human rights consciousness and alleviation of parliamentary tyranny.[2] However, the relationship between the courts and the political institutions of the representative government is always tense, due to the ever-present allegation that constitutional review deprives the constitution of its legitimization by the constituent power.[3]

This constant tension particularly escalates during the emergency crisis (whether a real or fabricated), when the populist executive tends to exclude the emergencies measures from a judicial check, claiming that the rule of law cannot govern the state of crisis. Having

---

* Professor of Law, Union University Law School, Belgrade. This chapter is written within the project 'Advancing Serbia's Competitiveness in the Process of EU Accession', No. 47028, financed by the Serbian Ministry of Education, Science and Technological Development.

1 *See* R. Dixon, *'Populist Constitutionalism and the Democratic Minimum Core'*, *VerfBlog*, 26 April 2017, pp. 1-2, https://verfassungsblog.de/populist-constitutionalism-and-the-democratic-minimum-core/.

2 V. Beširević, 'Constitutional Review in a Democratic Deficit Setting: The Case of the European Union', *in* M. Jovanović (Ed.), *Constitutional Review and Democracy*, Eleven Publishing International, The Hague, 2015, pp. 83-107.

3 A. Sajó, *Limiting Government: An Introduction to Constitutionalism*, CEU Press, Budapest, 1999, p. 240.

in mind that in the emergency first to suffer are civil liberties, many, like David Cole, warn that if "extraconstitutional measures are appropriate during emergencies, and that the only real check is political, much would be lost and little gained in the protection of civil liberties".[4]

In mapping the actors available to challenge populism, some find the courts, in particular, constitutional courts, to be among the most relevant resources to oppose the populist rule.[5] The courts responded differently to this kind of a new threat, however.[6]

On one hand, constitutional courts, in cooperation with populist forces, have proven effective in undermining democratic order.[7] Some courts themselves, like the Venezuelan Supreme Tribunal or Israeli High Court of Justice, have embraced populism.[8] The US Supreme Court joined this group recently. Whether because it is currently ill-equipped to resist populism,[9] or because travel ban policy fits into security issues on which courts are generally prone to defer to the political institutions, or for other reasons, but its green light to Trump's controversial travel ban seriously questions the ability of the courts to limit the manoeuvring room for the populists.[10] On the other hand, some courts, like the US lower courts that blocked Trump's travel ban[11] or the UK Supreme Court, which made UK politicians go back to Parliament to implement the Brexit vote,[12] managed to resist the populism and defend constitutional values.

This chapter aims to advance a general question of whether the courts, in particular constitutional courts, can confront the politics of populism, by assessing the approach of the Serbian Constitutional Court to the populist politics in Serbia. Based on the Serbian example, I will show that the courts, which have never served as 'counter-majoritarian difficulty', can hardly confront the populist regime and be an alternative to resist populism. To prove that the Constitutional Court in Serbia has collaborated with the ruling populists

4 D. Cole, '*Judging the Next Emergency: Judicial Review and Individual Rights in Times of Crisis*', *Michigan Law Review*, Vol. 101, No. 8, 2003, p. 2587.

5 *See, e.g.*, C. R. Kaltwasser, 'Populism and the Question How to Respond It', *in* C. R. Kaltwasser *et al.* (Eds.).

6 M. Hailbronner & D. Landau, *'Introduction: Constitutional Courts and Populism'*, *VerfBlog*, 22 April 2017, pp. 3-5, https://verfassungsblog.de/introduction-constitutional-courts-and-populism.

7 D. Landau, 'Term Limits Manipulation across Latin America – and What Constitutional Design Could Do About it', *Constitutionnet*, 21 July 2015, www.constitutionnet.org/news/term-limits-manipulation-across-latin-america-and-whatconstitutional- design-could-do-about-it.

8 *Id. See also* A. Harel, *'Courts in a Populist World'*, *VerfBlog*, 27 April 2017, p. 1, https://verfassungsblog.de/courts-in-a-populist-world.

9 Long before the Supreme Court upheld Trump's travel ban policy, Or Bassok argued that "[t]he American Supreme Court is currently ill-equipped to confront populism". *See* O. Bassok, *'Trapped in the Age of Trump: the American Supreme Court and 21st Century Populism Or'*, *VerfBlog*, 28 April 2017, p. 1, https://verfassungsblog.de/trapped-in-the-age-of-trump-the-american-supreme-court-and-21st-centurypopulism or.

10 *See Trump, President of The United States, et al. v. Hawaii et al.*, No. 17-965, 585 *U.S.* (2018).

11 Several U.S. lower courts blocked Trump's travel ban policy. *See, e.g.*, *State v. Trump*, 265 F. Supp. 3d 1140 (2017); *International Refugee Assistance Project v. Donald Trump*, No. 17-1351 (2017); *Aziz et al v. Trump et al.*, No. 1:2017cv00116 – Document 111 (E.D. Va. 2017).

12 *R (Miller) v. Secretary of State for Exiting the European Union*, [2017] UKSC 5.

rather than confronted them, I will assess the Court's rulings regarding Brussels Agreement, aimed at normalization of relations between Belgrade and Pristina, the government's austerity measures and the rulings concerning pre-trial detention ordered against persons accused of corruption in privatization cases.

To enter into the perspective of my view, it makes sense first to highlight the following two preliminary points: one regards the nature of post-Milošević Serbia's polity and the other relates to the position of the Serbian Constitutional Court in the constitutional framework and its role in democracy consolidation in Serbia.

12.2 A Note on Transition in Serbia[13]

Starting from the fact that the politics of populism is hostile to constitutional democracy (usually equated with liberal democracy), the first point I want to emphasize is that before a present populist administration took power in 2012, Serbia had been a state that had a constitution, but it had not practiced liberal constitutionalism. Several facts confirm this point.

The fall of the Berlin Wall in 1989 did not signal a substantial political rupture in Serbia, in the sense of liberalization from sham constitutionalism, as it did in the countries governed by the Soviet-style communism at the time. Approximately at the same time when the Central and Eastern European countries began to build their functional or semi-functional democracies, Yugoslav-style communism in Serbia was replaced by another type of authoritarian rule, installed by the adoption of the 1990 Constitution, at the peak of Milošević's rule. Besides, long delays in the transformation from communism to constitutional democracy were caused by the tragic war in the Balkans; several pressing needs to rethink the state, the territory and the people;[14] as well as an extended period of frustration with the international pressure to deal with the war legacy.

---

13 This part of the chapter relies on my previous works: V. Beširević, 'Transitional Constitutionalism in Serbia: Is the Glass Half-Full or Half-Empty?', *in* V. Beširević (Ed.), *Public Law in Serbia: Twenty Years After*, European Public Law Organization & Esperia Publications Ltd, London, 2012; V. Beširević, '"Governing *Without* Judges": The Politics of the Constitutional Court in Serbia', *International Journal of Constitutional Law*, Vol. 12, No. 4, 2014, pp. 954-979.

14 Before regaining the status of an independent state in 2006, the country went through several wars and territorial remodeling. At the beginning of the Balkans conflicts in 1991, Serbia was a constitutive part of a large ex-Yugoslav federation. Following the dissolution of this original federation, Serbia emerged as a part of the Federal Republic of Yugoslavia formed by Serbia and Montenegro in 1992. To mitigate growing Montenegrin secessionist claims, and with a significant push from the EU, Serbia's political leaders compromised on the formation of the State Union of Serbia and Montenegro in 2003. This turned out to be a wrong strategy, and the short-lived Union collapsed when Montenegro declared its independence in 2006. Nor did the formation of an independent Serbian state bring political stability, since another wave of secessionist claims, this time coming from Kosovo, also proved to be successful and, in 2008, resulted in

When in the year of 2000 the Milošević regime finally collapsed, Serbia underwent what Sorensen termed a process of 'illiberal social transformation'.[15] Although some transitory arrangements pushed forward political reforms,[16] the adoption of the new Constitution in 2006 did not represent a clear departure from the authoritarian past. Thus, the Constitution reflected the tendency of the legislature, executive and judiciary to blend and overlap, instituted the mandate imperative, severely curtailing the freedom of members of parliament, and spoke incoherently on the vertical division of powers, which produced additional polarization in the Serbian society.[17]

Apart from constitutional imperfections, a lack of accountability, corruption, a weak position of courts, ombudsmen and other independent institutions, as well as naïve public support to unrestricted majoritarian democracy also posed challenges to the establishment of deeper constitutionalism in the country. Besides being patently illiberal, transitional constitutionalism in Serbia was also highly communitarian. From the very beginning of the transition, highly prioritized collective interests – retaining sovereignty over Kosovo and bolstering national loyalty – have become co-equal to, if not dominant over, rights-based liberalism. Additionally, in the aftermath of Kosovo's independence, the Constitution has been brandished as a tool of control aimed at furthering another proclaimed collective, but arguably rival, interest: the country's accession to the EU, which favours rather than constrains political liberalization.

The elections in 2012 confirmed the old thesis that 'authoritarianism is an inherent tendency of democratic regimes'.[18] The general elections held in spring 2012 brought a full-scale return of Milošević's former allies to power, for the first time since the democratic change in 2000. Thus, the leader of the Serbian Progressive Party (SNS), won in the presidential election, end ever since, the SNS, a Serbian version of a populist party, has run the country either on presidential or the governmental level or on both.[19]

Kosovo's unilateral declaration of independence and the amputation of a significant part of the country's territory. *See* Beširević, 2014, p. 958.

15 For more *see* J. S. Sorensen, 'War as Social Transformation: Wealth, Class, Power and an Illiberal Economy in Serbia', *Civil Wars*, Vol. 6, No. 4, 2003, pp. 55-82.

16 The abolition of capital punishment, the closure of military courts and the adoption of a modern Criminal Procedure Act with fair trial guarantees and defendant's rights are cases in point. In addition, the adoption of national minority rights legislation, religious communities' legislation (although not a masterpiece), and amendments to the Criminal Code, which eliminated the discriminatory approach in conceptualizing certain crimes related to sexual assaults, showed that these substantial changes were meant to protect from both totalitarianism and unfettered majoritarianism. *See* Beširević, 2014, p. 960.

17 I have explained this polarization in V. Beširević, 'Muke po Statutu: Da li će jezička dogmatizacja Ustava ukinuti političku autonomiju Vojvodine?' [Passion According to the Statute: Will the Textual Dogmatization of the Constitution Abolish the Political Autonomy of Vojvodina?], *Pravni zapisi*, No. 2, 2013, pp. 476-510.

18 For more *see* R. Pildes, 'The Inherent Authoritarianism in Democratic Regimes', *in* A. Sajó (Ed.), *Out of and into Authoritarian Law*, Kluwer Law International, The Hague, London, New York, 2003, pp. 125-149.

19 For a detailed analysis of the populist rule in Serbia, *see* the contribution of D. Spasojević in this volume.

On the whole, although there were some manifestations of emerging constitutional democracy before the ruling populist took power in 2012, Serbia closely resembled those political systems that were commonly classified as democratic but non-liberal.

12.3 A Silent Feature of the Constitutional Court

The valid Constitution (2006) clearly emphasizes the political dimension of the constitutional review. The Court, as an independent state authority, is empowered to exercise both a priori and subsequent judicial review and thus to declare invalid legislative acts adopted by the National Assembly. Besides, it is authorized to resolve conflicts of jurisdiction between horizontal and vertical branches of government, participate in the proceedings concerning impeachment of the president, resolve electoral disputes in the absence of other judicial proceedings, ban political parties, trade unions and civic organizations.[20] The Constitutional Court also serves as a last resort for an individual to file a petition claiming violation of rights by different state authorities.[21]

The Constitution stipulates the split-appointment mechanism, which minimizes, at least theoretically, the chance that any political institution makes influence over the politics of the Court. Thus, the President of the Republic appoints five judges from among 10 nominated by the Parliament; another five are elected by the Parliament, among 10 proposed by the President of the Republic; the last five judges are appointed at the general session of the Supreme Court of Cassation, among 10 candidates proposed by (arguably) independent bodies bestowed with judicial appointment powers – the High Judicial Council and the State Prosecutor Council.[22]

To impact democratic consolidation, the broad jurisdictional authority and safeguards regarding judicial independence do not suffice: the presence of the judges' willingness to

20 Art. 167 of the Serbian 2006 Constitution, which speaks on the Court's jurisdiction, reads: "The Constitutional Court shall decide on: 1. compliance of laws and other general acts with the Constitution, generally accepted rules of the international law and ratified international treaties, 2. compliance of ratified international treaties with the Constitution, 3. compliance of other general acts with the Law, 4. compliance of the Statute and general acts of autonomous provinces and local self-government units with the Constitution and the Law, 5. compliance of general acts of organizations with delegated public powers, political parties, trade unions, civic associations and collective agreements with the Constitution and the Law. The Constitutional Court shall: 1. decide on the conflict of jurisdictions between courts and state bodies, 2. decide on the conflict of jurisdictions between republic and provincial bodies or bodies of local self-government units, 3. decide on the conflict of jurisdictions between provincial bodies and bodies of local self-government units, 4. decide on electoral disputes for which the court jurisdiction has not been specified by the Law, 5. perform other duties stipulated by the Constitution and the Law. The Constitutional Court shall decide on the banning of a political party, trade union organization or civic association. The Constitutional Court shall perform other duties stipulated by the Constitution."

21 *See* Art. 170 of the Constitution.

22 *See* Art. 172 of the Constitution.

interfere and produce transformative jurisprudence is equally essential. This turned to be the Achilles' heel of the Serbian Constitution Court. Thus, despite the presence of highly divided politics in Serbia, which is continuously nudging the Court to intervene, the Court has not turned into 'a dog that barks and bites'. Simply put, before the present populist regime took power in 2012, the Serbian Constitutional Court had not been the relevant institution of governance. The Court had not managed to escape the communist-era legacy of dependency and distance itself from the strategy of strict deference to the ruling power, established and brought to the maximum level in the communist time.

In my previous work on the Serbian Constitutional Court, the scrutiny of the most controversial political cases capable to make changes in the public policy, including the cases concerning constitution-making, the state of emergency, judicial reform and political decentralization, confirmed the Court's proclivity to rule only when either its decisions became politically irrelevant or when the preference of the ruling majority became manifestly clear.[23]

The Court's inherent incapacity to contribute to democratic consolidation in Serbia also stemmed from its failure to build transformative 'jurisprudence' due to subjective legal-cultural perceptions of the judge-made law.[24] The production of highly technical and inconsistent rulings, the judges' subscription to a narrowly conceived positive jurisprudence, the absence of precedential authority and poor legal reasoning, substantiated the claim that constitutional review in Serbia has not amounted to an effective mechanism of governance.

In sum, the Serbian Constitutional Court never served as 'counter-majoritarian difficulty'. On the contrary, although rhetorically it has been considered as 'the guardian of the Constitution', in practice, it has rarely confronted political institutions, and instead of limiting the executive power, it adjusted constitutional review to its preferences. Its politics of strict deference to the ruling majority is all too present in the present populist rule in Serbia. Consider the following.

12.4 Constitutional Court in Populist Politics

Under the present populist rule slowly emerging constitutional democracy in Serbia has been gradually changed for Schmitt's identitarian and plebiscitary conception of democracy and populist constitutionalism. An appeal to 'the general will of the people', is used to a significant extent to erode the emerging institutions of constitutional democracy in Serbia, including separation of powers, governmental accountability and human rights protection. A shift towards 'the political guardian of the constitution' is justified by the claim that the

23 *See* Beširević, 2014, pp. 966-974.
24 *Id.*, pp. 974-978.

consent of the majority is the crucial ground of legitimation in politics. The state of emergency, reflected mostly in Kosovo's unilateral declaration of independence, the financial crisis which brought Serbia to the edge of bankruptcy, and the portrayal of the whole previous government as criminal and corrupt, gave then-prime minister and now the president, to paraphrase Schmitt:

> the opportunity to connect itself immediately with this unified political will of the Serbian people and to act, on that basis, as the guardian and the preserver of the constitutional unity and wholeness of the Serbian people.[25]

The fact that Serbia is in the 5th year of the Europeanization process, which is supposed to have a democratizing effect on candidate states during the accession period,[26] has not much changed the state of affairs. Moved predominantly by strategic reasons, instead of making the building of constitutional democracy the basis of the conditionality process of EU accession, the EU has made the stability of the Western Balkan region, including 'normalization of relations with Kosovo', a precondition of all conditions for Serbia's accession to the EU.[27]

As a result, unlike in the case of the EU accession of the Central and Eastern European countries, the very accession process has not influenced a consolidation of constitutional democracy in Serbia. On the contrary, the current ruling forces proved to be successful in cementing their authoritarian tendencies. Manipulation with the election process,[28] affirmation of draft constitutional amendments that increase rather than decrease politicization of the judiciary,[29] and progressive deterioration of media freedom well illustrate this point.

---

25 Schmitt wrote: "The constitution, in particular, seeks to give to the guardian of the constitution authority of the president of the Reich the opportunity to connect itself immediately with this unified political will of the German people and to act, on that basis, as the guardian and the preserver of the constitutional unity and wholeness of the German people." *See* L. Vinx, *The Guardian of the Constitution: Hans Kelsen and Carl Schmitt on the Limits of Constitutional Law*, Cambridge University Press, Cambridge, 2015, pp. 172-173.

26 For more, *see* W. Sadurski, *Constitutionalism and the Enlargement of Europe*, Oxford University Press, Oxford, 2012.

27 *See* accession document, European Union Common Position: Chapter 35: Other Issues. Item 1: Normalization of Relations between Serbia and Kosovo, Brussels, 30 November 2015, AD 12/15, http://mei.gov.rs/upload/documents/pristupni_pregovori/pregovaracke_pozicije/ch35_common_position_eu.pdf.

28 Since 2012, in addition to regular elections on presidential level, parliamentary elections were three times held although ruling populists have qualified majority in the parliament.

29 In the EU accession process, the EU made it clear that no membership was possible without a thorough reform of the judiciary, including the necessary constitutional revision. The amendments to the Constitution are drafted to satisfy this obligation. Yet despite some envisaged improvements, draft constitutional amendments do not eliminate but rather reallocate the sources of political influence on the judiciary. For more see V. Beširević, '*The Draft Amendments to the Serbian Constitution: Populism before Judicial Independence*', *VerfBlog*, 24 April 2018, https://verfassungsblog.de/the-draft-amendments-to-the-serbian-constitution-populism-before-judicial-independence/.

In sum, the present populist rule in Serbia satisfies all three vital elements of populist constitutionalism defined by Jan Werner Muller.[30] First, there is a claim that the ruling populists speak for the will of ordinary citizens, and there is no need for mediation between the administration and the people by traditional democratic institutions, including political parties, parliament, media and courts. Second, a discourse that is critical of existing political and institutional arraignments is present. Third, the presence of anti-pluralist politics is evident.

The Serbian Constitutional Court has done nothing to prevent this undermining process. To confirm this claim, I will now turn to the Court's rulings regarding Brussels Agreement, aimed at normalization of relations between Belgrade and Pristina, the government's austerity measures and constitutionality of detention orders issued against persons accused of corruption in privatization cases.

12.4.1 Constitutional Review of Kosovo's Knot: If Schmitt Were Alive...

In Serbia, the most popular tool to mobilize public support has become a claim to retain sovereignty over Kosovo. At the time when they took power, the chances to open accession negotiations with the EU, proved a powerful enough incentive for the populists, often portrayed as hard nationalists, to refresh the process of political negotiations with Kosovo, this time as pre-accession rationality.

In 2013, after often exhausting talks pushed and supervised by the EU, Belgrade and Pristina signed in Brussels the "First Agreement on Principles Governing the Normalization of Relations".[31] The key provisions of the Agreement concern the governance of the northern part of Kosovo inhabited almost exclusively by Serbs, who rejected Kosovo's independence and have since lived in separation from the rest of Kosovo. Under the First Brussels Agreement, Belgrade and Pristina agreed that the northern part of Kosovo should come under the control of Kosovo's authorities as well, but should receive certain special self-determination prerogatives. Therefore, the agreement envisaged formation of the Association of Serb Municipalities in Kosovo.

The ink was barely dry on the First Agreement when in Belgrade, it was attacked as an evidence that Serbia recognized Kosovo. The Agreement was challenged before the Constitutional Court in Serbia by 25 MPs of the Serbian Parliament belonging to the opposition party which fanatically opposed both any negotiations with Pristina and candidacy of Serbia for EU membership.

30 For more *see* J. W. Müller, *'Populist Constitutions – A Contradiction in Terms?'*, *VerfBlog*, 23 April 2017, https://verfassungsblog.de/populist-constitutions-a-contradiction-in-terms.

31 The Agreement was signed on 19 April 2013.

Now, there are not many situations that breach the logic of Kelsen's resistance to pure politics in the constitutional order than the situation which emerged in the aftermath of Kosovo's unilateral declaration of independence. In my view, the Brussels Agreement was not reached to allow the re-functioning of the state power on the territory of Kosovo but to protect the Serbian minority living in Kosovo and general state interests to the extent possible in the given political situation. The Constitutional Court was not equipped nor it was in a position to decide whether the establishment of the Association of Serb Municipalities as well as the organization of judicial power and police units, could have protected Serbs and general state interests in Kosovo, because this was a political question which was unjusticiable and could not be resolved by legal standards.[32] However, the Constitutional Court's ruling on the Brussels Agreement does not follow the logic of political question doctrine and its articulation by Bickel, but the Schmittian idea of legally unbounded politics. Consider the following.

From the view of the populist administration in Serbia, the amputation of a significant part of the country's territory and the trapped position of the Serbian minority in Kosovo represented the state of emergency that ultimately demanded the management through a 'primacy of the Political' in the sense of Schmitt. Therefore, the populist government first tried to postpone the Court's ruling suggesting to the Court to stay of proceedings until the adoption of the constitutional law on Kosovo's substantial autonomy.[33] I hasten here to say that the law has not yet been adopted, though it was envisaged in 2006 when the Constitution came into force.

The Court did not officially stay of proceedings, but like in other high-profile political cases, it played its well-known safe strategy, rejected to rule in a timely manner and after a two-year delay, it dismissed the challenge on jurisdictional grounds.[34] The Court found that the Brussels Agreement was neither international agreement nor any other kind of general act that could be reviewed by the Court.[35] For the purpose of this discussion, it should be stressed that the majority of the judges insisted that the engagement of the prime minister in reaching the Brussels Agreement represented his political activity within the negotiations with Kosovo's provisional institutions.[36] The fact that the government accepted the Brussels Agreement could not be understood as an approval of competent institutional authority of a particular legal act, but as a political approval of prime minister's political

---

32 I have developed this thesis in V. Beširević, 'A jedan razlog menja sve: kontrola ustavnosti Briselskog sporazuma u svetlu doktrine političkog pitanja' [The Reason That Changes Everything: A Judicial Review of the Brussels Agreement Under the Political Question Doctrine], *Hereticus*, Vol. 14, No. 1&2, 2016, pp. 127-151.

33 *See* the Constitutional Court's ruling from 14 December 2014, No. 247/2013, p. 3.

34 *Id.*, p. 1.

35 *Id.*, p. 29.

36 *Id.*, p. 24.

activities.[37] The Court particularly emphasized that in the approval procedure, the government was bound *neither by law nor by legal acts,* but only by political guidelines included in the Resolution of Serbian Parliament from January 2013 to serve as key principles for political negotiations with Kosovo's provisional institutions.[38]

Moreover, a significant part of the majority opinion, and in particular the part of the opinion that insisted on the idea of legally unbounded politics, was based on the *amicus curie* opinions delivered by the Legal Adviser to the Serbian Ministry of Foreign Affairs and the Serbian representative in the Venice Commission, appointed by the populist government.[39] It is yet another evidence of judicial submissiveness in politically sensitive cases even when judicial restraint should be clearly exercised.

12.4.2 Judicial Endorsement of 'Discriminatory Legalism'

As Jan-Werner Müller observes in his book *What Is Populism?,* populism goes hand in hand with unequal protection.[40] It is a usual business of populists to identify groups whether political, class-based, ethnic or racial as the enemy. What follows, according to Müller, is a form of 'discriminatory legalism' in which a group tailored as the enemy receive harsher treatment.[41] In other words, "for my friends everything; for my enemies, the law".[42]

Transposed to the Serbian context, 'discriminatory legalism' was manifested by populist administration in confronting the economic and financial crisis, when the government made differentiation in taxation policy to protect 'ordinary folk' and, at the same time, to attack middle class in Serbia, from which an 'elite' opposing the populist government usually recruited.

Facts first. In 2013, Serbia came at the edge of bankruptcy, with a public debt of 59.6%, budget deficit of 5.5% and unemployment rate of 22.1%.[43] To avoid bankruptcy, the austerity package was introduced in 2014. The measures included the so-called 'solidarity taxation', ranging from 10% to 25% on salaries and social benefits in the public sector that were approximately above 60,000 RSD (525 EURO) a month.[44] According to the populist

37 *Id.*
38 *Id.*
39 This fact was expressly mentioned in the majority opinion. *Id.*, p. 24.
40 J. W. Müller, *What is Populism?*, University of Pennsylvania Press, Philadelphia, 2016, pp. 82-83.
41 *Id.*, p. 83.
42 *Id.*
43 M. Prokopijević, 'Some Sensitive Issues of Serbia's Economy', 19 October 2015, https://rs.boell.org/en/2015/10/19/some-sensitive-issues-serbias-economy.
44 The law introducing solidarity taxation did not refer to taxation but to public sector pay cuts. Yet, unofficially, the Act was immediately termed 'Solidarity Tax' Act.

administration, solidarity taxation was the way to eliminate unequal pay and make possible for low-skill workers who worked in hard conditions to have decent salaries.[45]

More than 20 initiatives challenging the constitutionality of the 'Solidarity Tax' Act were logged before the Constitutional Court. Like in other high-profile cases, the Constitutional Court stuck to its play-it-safe strategy and delivered the verdict after the challenged Act became manifestly irrelevant, with an eye on the preference of the ruling populists.[46] Although in November 2014 it formally opened a review procedure, the Court ignored the case for almost 4 years. When, at the end of 2014, after 9 months of its application, the populist administration replaced the 'Solidarity Tax' Act, with the law lowering all salaries over 210 EURO in public sector by 10%,[47] the constitutional review of the 'Solidarity Tax' Act seemed losing its meaning.

However, long after public discussion of the Act died, the Constitutional Court woke up from its deep slumber, delivered the decision and validated the Act. In other words, it rejected the request to declare it unconstitutional.[48] The Court argued that the Act was 'a budgetary consolidation measure' and that its adoption was justified by the legitimate interest of the legislator to secure normal functioning of the state in 'time of crisis'.[49] To support its stance, the Court turned to constitutional decisions delivered by the constitutional courts in Greece, Croatia and Lithuania on austerity measures introduced by the governments of these countries during the recent economic crisis.[50]

Now, it is not disputable that it is a job of the government to secure economic and financial stability and propose the implementation of different austerity measures in the time of crisis. What worries here is the Constitutional Court's avoidance to examine whether the 'Solidarity Tax' Act was, in fact, a taxation measure and whether as such it was introduced on discriminatory grounds and in violation of the general Income Tax Act which in Article 1 envisaged that "income taxes shall be regulated exclusively by this Act". Instead, in the laconic matter the Court only noted that the challenged Act was a budgetary consolidation measure, and "*argumentum a contrario* [...] it was not a special income tax measure[...]".[51] Therefore, it found no reason to examine whether the Act was contrary to the general income tax law and whether it was discriminatory in its nature.

To sum up: for the Serbian Constitutional Court, even in the case which involves the constitutional review of the *prima facie* discriminatory law, drafted on two pages and no

45 This is how then Deputy Prime Minister and the current President of the Republic explained the reason behind 'solidarity taxation'. *See* www.rtv.rs/sr_lat/politika/vucic-solidarni-porez-ostaje_461565.html.

46 *See* the decision of the Constitutional Court from 26 April 2018, IУз-138/2016.

47 The Constitutional Court has not yet ruled about the law on reducing salaries, although many initiatives challenging its constitutionality were logged.

48 The decision IУз-138/2016, p. 1.

49 *Id.*, p. 5.

50 *Id.*, pp. 5-6.

51 *Id.*, p. 6. However, Justice Tamás Korhecz in his separate opinion strongly disagreed.

longer in force, opposing a populist administration was not an option. The Court again missed an opportunity to enhance its reputation and legitimacy by delivering decisions that would make sense of constitutional values, in a way the Hungarian Constitutional Court did when, in the middle of 1990s, it exercised a robust constitutional review and invalidated key elements of austerity package introduced to ensure financial stability of the country.[52]

The 'solidarity taxation case' testifies that the Serbian Constitutional Court has not distanced itself from its deferential ideology. This conclusion is further confirmed by the similar Court's approach in other cases regarding austerity package from 2014. At the same time when the populist administration replaced the 'Solidarity Tax' Act, with the law lowering all salaries, the legislation regarding cutting pensions above 210 EURO progressively was also introduced. After receiving 133 initiatives challenging the constitutionality of the law reducing pensions, the Court dismissed all initiatives in a procedural ruling and upheld the austerity measure of the populist government,[53] which despite savage cuts maintained its popularity, and won again in the next elections, proving thus the thesis that populism is hardly a matter of policy preferences.

12.4.3 Rights Adjudication: What Stands behind the Court's Assertiveness

The following example speaks more about the Court's resistance to the populist pressure than about its collaboration with the executive. However, the Court's approach does not reflect its institutional politics but rather its calculation strategy in cases embedded in international law.

The populist programme usually includes pressure on the fight against organized crime and corruption – in fact, due to the persistent public demand for action, especially in societies in transition, this is one of the leading populists' strategies to distance themselves from their political rivals. In countries of young democracies, the pressure to develop an effective state policy also comes from external factors, like in case of Romania and Bulgaria, where the EU Commission has persistently insisted on a decisive action in this area.[54] The same is valid for Serbia. In words of EU Commission, although Serbia has some level of preparation in the fight against corruption and the fight against organized crime,

52 For more *see* A. Sajó, 'How the Rule of Law Killed Welfare Reform', *Eastern European Constitutional Review*, Vol. 5, No. 1, 1996, pp. 44-49.

53 For more *see* J. Jerinić, 'The Easy Way Out: How the Serbian Constitutional Court Delivered its First Ruling on the Constitutionality of the Government's Austerity Measures', *European Review of Public Law*, Vol. 27, No. 4, 2015, pp. 1711-1726.

54 For more *see* D. Smilov, *Populism, Courts and the Rule of Law: Eastern European Perspectives*, The Foundation for Law, Justice and Society, Oxford, 2007.

> [...] Corruption remains prevalent in many areas and continues to be a serious problem [...] Serbia has yet to establish an initial track record of effective financial investigations, as well as of investigations, prosecutions and final convictions in money laundering cases. The number of convictions for the organized crime remains low.[55]

The Serbian ruling populists quickly recognized that prioritizing criminal policy in this area might be an excellent choice to mobilize public support. One of the first moves of the present populist administration was an arrest of several persons connected with 24 cases of privatization, earlier flagged by the EU as problematic.[56] Then deputy prime minister in charge of the fight against corruption and organized crime, and now the president of the Republic, in a Schmittian manner claimed: "Two things have been proven in Serbia – that nobody is protected and untouchable and that the state is stronger than any individual."[57] On several occasions, he called the first accused in privatization trials 'the enemy of the state'.[58] From that time, it became a habit for the media to announce many of the arrests before they happened and the suspects were declared guilty in the media even before they were indicted. Interestingly, none of the court cases has resulted in guilty verdicts in force. On the contrary, the first accused in privatization cases was recently declared non-guilty by the final instance court.

For the purpose of this discussion, it is important to note that many from those arrested in privatization cases challenged the constitutionality of their pre-trial detention orders before the Constitutional Court. In sharp contrast to the previously mentioned cases, the Court reacted promptly and issued several rulings finding the violation of defendants' constitutional rights.[59] The populist administration publicly labelled its rulings 'problematic' and 'unjust'.[60]

When assessing the Court's approach in these cases, one should have in mind that the Court based its decisions on the relevant jurisprudence of the European Court of Human Rights.[61] Thus, it particularly emphasized that the reasons for keeping the accused persons in pre-trial detention stand contrary to the Strasburg Court' case law.[62] The Court's approach in detention cases confirms my thesis that after the regime change in 2000, the constitutional judges have started (but have not fully managed) to enhance their legitimacy

---

55 European Commission, Serbia 2018 Report, Strasbourg, 17 April 2018, SWD (2018), pp. 3-4.
56 www.b92.net/info/vesti/index.php?yyyy=2012&mm=12&dd=12&nav_category=16&nav_id=668314.
57 *Id.*
58 www.slobodnaevropa.org/a/priveden-miroslav-miskovic/24796051.html.
59 *See, e.g.*, the decisions of the Constitutional Court No.УЖ-3231/2013 from 3 October 2013 and No. УЖ-3391/2013 from 18 July 2013.
60 www.vreme.com/cms/view.php?id=1143163.
61 *See, e.g.*, the decision of the Constitutional Court No.УЖ-3231/2013, pp. 13-14.
62 *Id.*

through rights adjudication, while in resolving the separation of powers disputes they have stayed strikingly inactive.[63]

For the Court to voice its opinion in rights adjudication required that it makes minimal strategic calculations since, on one hand, this action coincided with the priority of the country's political élites to promote Serbia's integration into the European Union, while, on the other, it was backed by the authority of European human rights law.[64] This approach made attacks from the political majority less severe, and the Court grew more assertive. However, as a rule, the Court has displayed a consistent tendency to deliver decisions with an eye on the political majority.

12.5 CONCLUSION

Ever since Marbury proclaimed that judges are authorized to adjudicate constitutional issues as part of their mandate,[65] the tensions in the relationship between political institutions and the courts have been vivid across states and ideologies. Yet, some authors have already noticed that populist administration usually more directly confronts the courts when not under their control, by instituting the impeachment of judges, limitations of their jurisdiction and packing of the courts with loyal judges.[66] The responses of the courts to populist politics could generally be schematized in the following way: they may resist populist regime, may embrace populism themselves or may turn to passivism.

This chapter attempted to theorize the approach of the Serbian Constitutional Court to the populist regime in Serbia. It started with a general reflection that in transitional Serbia, a constitutional review had been discouragingly irrelevant to the struggle for democracy consolidation. By focusing attention on the Court's decisions delivered within the mandate of the ruling populists, it showed that a constitutional review in Serbia is not an available strategy to confront the populist regime, either. On the contrary, so far the Court has endorsed most of the populists' measures aimed at undermining an already fragile democracy in Serbia.

There is little hope that the Serbian Constitutional Court would sooner rather than later start to challenge robustly populist administration. The ruling populists used the first opportunity to safeguard the Constitutional Court's deference. When in 2016 the terms in office of nine judges expired (out of 15 judges in total), the Court was quickly packed mostly by those loyal to the regime and by its followers, through a non-transparent election

63 Beširević, 2014, p. 966.

64 *Id.*

65 *Marbury v. Madison*, 5 U.S. 137 (1803).

66 J. F. G. Bertomeu, 'Working Well Is the Best Strategy: Judges under Populism', *VerfBlog*, 3 May 2017, pp. 1-2, https://verfassungsblog.de/working-well-is-the-best-strategy-judges-under-populism.

procedure. The populists left no chance for the Court to become more than a rubber stamp of its programme.

Democracy and the Rule of Law (Series editor: Miodrag A. Jovanović)

Volume 1: Miodrag A. Jovanović and Đorđe Pavićević (eds.), Crisis and Quality of Democracy in Eastern Europe, ISBN 978-94-9094-767-5
Volume 2: Miodrag A. Jovanović and Dragica Vujadinović (Eds.), Identity, Political and Human Rights Culture as Prerequisites of Constitutional Democracy, ISBN 978-94-6236-077-8
Volume 3: Miodrag A. Jovanović and Kenneth Einar Himma (eds.), Courts, Interpretation, the Rule of Law, ISBN 978-94-6236-096-9
Volume 4: Lidija R. Basta Fleiner and Tanasije Marinković (eds.), Key Developments in Constitutionalism and Constitutional Law, ISBN 978-94-6236-396-0
Volume 5: Miodrag A. Jovanović (ed.), Constitutional Review and Democracy, ISBN 978-94-6236-512-4
Volume 6: Kenneth Einar Himma and Bojan Spaić (eds.), Fundamental Rights: Justification and Interpretation, ISBN 978-94-6236-656-5
Volume 7: Hauke Brunkhorst, Dragica Vujadinović, and Tanasije Marinković (eds.), European Democracy in Crisis: Polities under Challenge and Social Movements, ISBN 978-94-6236-799-9
Volume 8: Violeta Beširević (ed.), New Politics of Decisionism, ISBN 978-94-6236-897-2

Printed by Libri Plureos GmbH in Hamburg,
Germany

9 789462 368972